£4-50

COMPETITIVE FLY-FISHING

COMPETITIVE FLY-FISHING

Tony Pawson

PELHAM BOOKS

First published in Great Britain by
Pelham Books Ltd
44 Bedford Square
London WC1B 3DU
1982

Copyright © Tony Pawson 1982

All rights reserved. No part of this publication may be reproduced, stored in a retrieval system, or transmitted, in any form or by any means, electronic, mechanical, photocopying, recording or otherwise, without the prior permission of the Copyright owner.

ISBN 0 7207 1414 1

Phototypeset in Linotron 202 by
Graphicraft Typesetters Hong Kong

Printed and bound in Great Britain by Billings & Sons, Guildford and Worcester

To Hilarie, whose dapping expertise and love of waterside nature has saved her from being a fishing widow; to Anthony whose cancer research work has sited him in Vancouver, Canada's best fishing centre; to John who has twice qualified for English nationals; and to Sarah who spins with skill, but still toils a bit when it comes to casting a fly; to all my family indeed my thanks for their support and their interest in my favourite sport.

ACKNOWLEDGMENTS

My grateful thanks to the many international fly-fishermen and other expert anglers who have co-operated so readily in providing the anecdotes and practical advice which are a feature of this book.

My special thanks to Alan Pearson for his major contributions; to Bill Milne for his help on the early years and to B.C. Hall for his information and for permitting the use of extracts from his autobiography *Round the World in Ninety Years*. I am also very appreciative of David Biggart's assistance in checking past records and allowing me to use extracts from his book *The First Hundred Years*, and to Alastair Nicoll for loaning me a rare copy of *The Loch Leven Angler*. Other books which have been of value to me are P.D. Malloch's *Salmon, Sea-trout, Trout and other Freshwater Fish* and *The Field Bedside Book* in which most details are given of Georgina Ballantyne's record salmon.

I am grateful also to *The Observer* for allowing me to use extracts from articles I have written for the paper; to John Wilshaw and Steve Windsor of *Trout Fisherman* for their contributions and for permission to use extracts from the magazine; to *The Flyfishers' Journal* for permission to use extracts from the letters of C. Ross-Munro and M.A. King-Webster.

My especial thanks to the kind and helpful people who have allowed me to use their photographs or have searched out pictures for me.

CONTENTS

Acknowledgments	6
Foreword	9
1 Hooked on competition	12
2 Qualifying for England	21
3 The oldest national	34
4 The early internationals	49
5 The captain's views	64
6 Winning ways	74
7 The double internationals	94
8 Ireland's individual internationals	117
9 The spread of competition	132
10 Going for a record	150
11 The big trout man	159
12 Internationals for the Disabled	172
13 Competition lakes and lochs — and how to fish them	184
14 The lough and llyn of Ireland and Wales	217
15 Of codes, coaching and competition	233
16 Equipped for competition	242
17 Final reflections	255
Appendices	262
1 International Fly Fishing Association: match rules	262
2 Rules for English national competition (*sample*)	264
3 International Results 1928–81	265
4 International Records	268
5 Teams in first international 1928	269
6 International Associations and addresses	270
7 Qualifying method for internationals	271
8 Loughs Mask, Melvin and Conn competition rules and entry arrangements	272
9 (World Cup) Preliminary Notice 1982	276
10 Claims procedure for record fish	277
11 Disabled Anglers	278
12 Useful addresses	279
13 Avoiding weight loss	282
14 Insurance and discounts	283
15 Other significant competitions	284
Index	285

FOREWORD

International Bob Johnson concluded the account he sent me of catching the largest trout taken in over a century of major competitions in Scotland with the comment: 'I feel that you are publicizing an area of angling which appears to have been neglected by writers, but which forms the basis of the Scottish angling scene, and has done for many years past.'

He is not a man given to fanciful exaggeration. The capture of his monster rainbow was described in just ten lines full of relevant fact at the end of which he added, 'I am sure you will be able to cut this down to proper perspective.' Most of us would have written several pages about it if we had been the captor! His summary of Scottish angling is equally to the point, and equally accurate. It applies, though perhaps in lesser degree, to areas of England such as the Midlands, and to Wales and Southern Ireland as well.

Certainly it has been a surprise to me to find how widespread is competitive fly-fishing in Britain and how many thousands of devotees it has. Yet in all the vast range of angling books none has ever covered this significant aspect in any detail. Inevitably then, some chapters have to outline the development of this type of fly-fishing, and particularly of the national and international competitions which provide its climax. The main aims, however, are twofold: to pass on practical advice to those who already compete, and to let those who haven't yet tried it savour the taste of competition and give them guidance on how to become successfully involved should they wish to do so. You don't have to be an expert to enjoy competition. Even the average angler has the chance of achievement, the certainty of learning and of extending his friendship with fellow fishermen.

Traditionally, fly-fishermen are regarded as reserved individuals jealously guarding their own secrets of success. That would be especially understandable in competitive fishing, since helping your rival beat you is not normal practice in other sports. But in fact the goodwill and fellowship it generates is reflected in that more than sixty internationals have willingly passed on in this book advice and anecdote about their winning ways.

National and international fishing had its origins in Scotland and its format has remained loch-style fishing from drifting boats. In such matches there will be up to thirty boats required and such contests can only be staged on waters with the facilities to arrange the simultaneous launch of such an armada. There are only a limited number of these competition lakes and guidance is given here on fishing all the main ones.

When I went to put in a day's practice on my own on my first visit to Trawsfynydd, it was some time before I could find where to purchase a ticket and no advice about the fishing was available in the newsagent's where these tickets are dispensed. So time was wasted and my early fishing was without any confidence on this very unusual lake. Anyone who reads this book and its appendices can at least make a prompt start on any of nine main competition waters and fish with hope from the first drift, fortified by the advice of local experts on flies, methods or areas which can bring success.

That should help even internationals. For as Bob Draper, England's most effective fly-fisherman of recent years, explains, adjusting to different waters is their main problem. They may qualify on an English reservoir with well-defined catching areas and trout that are better struck slow, then have to represent their country on some vast Irish lough, where the trout are lightning fast in rejecting the fly and are attracted by quite different patterns.

Those not interested in competitive fishing may still find here useful information which will help them enjoy all the more their pleasure fishing. Those thinking of having a try should be better able to choose a competition which suits them from the wide range which varies from great contests on loughs Mask, Melvin or Conn, to sea-trout competitions on a Welsh river or an Irish lough, to a Charity competition on the Thames Water reservoirs, to inter-club competitions which are so popular in Scotland.

As the paraplegic Olympics have shown, the disabled enjoy competition and in fishing they may well be as successful as the fully fit. Tom Mackenzie, Moc Morgan and Lynn Francis

FOREWORD

outline the developments which have led to the disabled receiving such encouragement in the sport and to their staging their own internationals.

A specialized form of competitive fly-fishing is the catching of record fish, whether by accident or design. These are only accepted as records if the proper procedure is followed to establish that you have caught a larger fish than anyone else. And certainly there is no accident about the only two British record fish taken on fly, the largest rainbow and the largest brook trout. Both were caught by the same Alan Pearson to beat his own earlier record fish. Alan has made a major contribution to this book, particularly in advising on the methods of catching such record trout, as he too passes on the secrets of his specialist art, and the thrill of his captures.

Practical guidance is one main purpose of this book. Another is to share the enjoyment and the experiences — amusing, unusual or entertaining — which make all fishing such a pleasure.

CHAPTER 1
HOOKED ON COMPETITION

Where every prospect pleases,
And only man is vile.

Two Lakes near Romsey is one of the most successful fisheries in Hampshire because it caters for the solitary and anti-social instincts of most fly-fishermen in pursuit of their prey. That at least is what its designer claims was the purpose of turning a round lake into one crinkled with little bays and inlets, where each individual can concentrate on catching trout undisturbed by other intrusive humans. The Garboesque desire to be alone is a part of many fishermen's nature. It is this which sends them on happy expeditions to distant hill lochs in pursuit of small, dour brownies.

Relaxation from the pressures of the modern world is a main part of the sport's charm as they fish on with only the wind and the wild scenery for companions. So it is understandable that for many the idea of competitive fly-fishing is anathema, a denial of its essential attraction. But, however masked, the competitive urge is latent in all of us. One magnetic aspect of catching trout or salmon is its trial of skill between fish and fisherman, the primaeval hunter's contest. Even the solitary fisherman is only too keen to display his large catch as the plethora of fishing registers testify, and as those hotels know well that arrange for the catches to be publicly displayed each evening. It is evident, too, in the tone of the disgruntled salmon fisherman, with a blank behind him, who dismisses another's two twenty-pounders with a contemptuous 'Oh, caught on a *spinner*', as if he, of course, could have been just as successful had he only sunk to using *that* legal lure.

Just how easily the normal angler allows himself to be hooked by the competitive urge is neatly summed up in this account from *The Loch Leven Angler* of a fisherman in 1929:

One does not go to 'the' loch for a holiday. There is no place where the urge to get results is greater. There are three reasons for this. The first is that from the moment you leave the pier you are in the hands of the boatmen. These fellows are all good anglers themselves so urge number one is to give a good account of yourself to them.

The second is that the loch costs a lot of money to fish and you can't spend that amount happily without something to show for it. Eight hours costs 32 shillings plus 3/- for the boatmen's lunch and 5/- for tips. The customary two rods halves the cost and you can reduce it further by fishing three to the boat. But that means a sacrifice of comfort.

The third reason is that having come thirty miles to fish and paid so much you feel it horribly irritating to see the hours slipping away unrewarded. You know the loch is full of fish. You know the occasion so keenly anticipated is turning fruitless and you do your darnedest to catch something. No! you don't go to the loch for a holiday. You go to fish hard because you don't want to see your name in *The Scotsman* next morning with only one fish to your credit. For then you can imagine the humorous telephone calls you would receive all day.

Wrenching the mind back from contemplating the time when a day's fishing with two boatmen was *expensive* at less than one pound all in, it is easy to appreciate the insidious stirrings of the competitive instinct. The hunger for respect of the knowledgeable watchers, the desire to get value for money, the compulsion to catch fish because they were there to be caught, and the fear of ridicule, all kept him trying his hardest to the end. No doubt, too, that urge was sharpened when his partner caught fish and he did not. For all such reasons most anglers become natural competitors whether or not they enter competitions. If you do compete for the first time, there is no need to be nervous. The experience generates only the same kind of pressures, as the day described by this visitor to Leven.

So it is no surprise that a growing number find enjoyment in testing their skill in equal competition. It was Scotland's fly-fishermen who took the lead in organizing such events. The oldest major competition anywhere in the world was started at Leven more than a hundred years ago. Informal challenge matches had been staged on the loch further back still, long before the Scottish national began in 1880.

That competition is now more popular than ever and set the pattern for other countries to follow. A place in the Loch Leven national is a focal point of ambition for upwards of ten thousand competitive anglers every year. For those who win through to it there is the further aim of qualifying for the national team to fish against England, Ireland and Wales in the four-country internationals which have been fished for the past fifty years. Leven, the birthplace of such competition, is no longer the sole centre. The two internationals fished each year rotate round the four countries and in the Jubilee Year of 1982 the arranged venues were Lake Trawsfynydd and Lough Conn.

The surge of interest in competitive fly-fishing is such that those taking part are now counted in hundreds of thousands. Europe is belatedly following Britain's lead with an international competition staged for the first time in 1981 on Lake Echternach with Luxembourg as host country. Scotland's interclub championship has reached saturation point with 196 clubs entering teams of three. That competition was in its tenth year when Benson and Hedges launched in 1982 their national club team championship with seven regional heats involving teams of six from clubs in all parts of the United Kingdom.

Ireland stages some of the largest individual contests with upwards of 200 fishermen taking part in the Conn 'intercontinental' or the Mask 'world cup', and with similar competitions started both sides of Lough Melvin, which straddles the border. In England and Wales those qualifying for the national team have increasing competition in their series of eliminating matches with the Welsh anglers having to prove themselves expert in both bank and boat fishing.

The very variety of the competitions is startling to the uninitiated. In Scotland it ranges from inter-city matches to champion of champions contests on Leven or Menteith, to that oldest competition of them all, the river-fishing contest on the Whiteadder, organized as it has been since 1831 by the Ellem club. In Wales there are sewin contests on rivers at night; in Ireland there are sea-trout competitions on loughs; in England the range is from disabled internationals, to inter-services competitions, to inter-reservoir charity matches within the Thames Water Authority, to Pro-Am competitions on Rutland Water or at Patshull Park. Add to these all those challenge matches, serious or humorous, arranged in their hundreds by clubs and pubs and the scale is as wide as the enthusiasm.

Many are just for the fun, some to raise money for charity, some with prizes from a bottle of whisky to a place in the national team. An individual may win £1000 at Lough Conn, a club £1000 in the Benson and Hedges championship. In addition, Benson and Hedges run a popular fly-dressing competition which was attracting 300 entrants by its second year, and there are a variety of casting competitions. But this book is concerned only with 'live' fly-fishing competition decided by the weight of fish caught. Included under that head is the catching by design, or accident, of record fish on fly as the angler has to establish that his catch beats all others. The new coaching scheme, with its bronze, silver, and gold performance awards in game fishing is in effect another type of competition with set standards to beat, and an examination to pass.

The pressures of competition, no matter how intense, never destroy the natural love of fishing. The TV Fishing Race programme was designed by the BBC partly to explore human reaction under the unrelenting challenge of three days of continuous competitive fishing. In its two series, millions watched Ian Wooldridge interview competitors at their most stressful moments as the three teams of two battled to catch more species and better specimens than their rivals. So how did Gareth Edwards, no stranger to competitive pressure in his rugby days, react to this when he took part in the second 'Race'? This is his view:

> There is always an element of competition in fishing, unconscious though it usually is. You take pleasure in using your skill to defeat the fish, and to overcome any problems posed by wind, weather, water conditions, or natural obstacles. Yet I never *feel* competitive when out fishing, and I didn't at any time in this TV Race, despite the constant presence of the cameras.
>
> The sport absorbed me, and yet I was not unaware of a subtle form of competitive drive. Deep down I wanted Clive Gammon and myself to win, and was disappointed when we didn't. That aspect never surfaced in my mind until the race was over. It had been a latent instinct, just like the urge to catch fish on any normal day, but in retrospect it had been stronger than I realized.
>
> The *pressure* wasn't in trying to beat the others, however. It was the sheer physical and mental fatigue of

fishing eighteen hours a day, when coupled with having to travel great distances in uncomfortable conditions all over Sweden. When I started I was as fit as ever I was for a rugby international. When we finished I was absolutely drained, and some of the older contestants really suffered. People tend to underrate the concentration and mental effort required in fishing, which wears you down if you have no real rest.

Our programme gives some idea of the strain. We had a 24-hour journey as we crossed Gothenburg by boat. There was only a brief respite that night, as we were out fishing by 2.0 a.m. on until late evening. Then it was a 700-kilometres drive to Stockholm for the same sort of day in that area. What was meant to be a rest day was taken up in a tiring and perilous flight to Lulea, and on up north to fish a river full of grayling, trout, and char.

That was probably put in specially for me to have some fly-fishing, which is my main interest. I fish a lot for salmon and sea-trout, mostly with fly, but spinning or worming if that is what the conditions demand. So the all-round expertise required in the TV Race was not foreign to me. But the northern river was the one chance I had to relax and really enjoy myself.

We arrived at the riverside about five o'clock in the afternoon. Tired as we were we couldn't resist a practice fish even though we were meant to be resting. In most places the river was very deep, as well as freezing cold. We would have needed to use worms there to get down to the grayling, let alone the trout or char. But we wanted to fly-fish so we looked for rapids with shallow areas beside the main stream. Even in the practice we caught as many grayling as we liked. Clive had one he barely bothered to play. Only when it got off at the net did he regret not taking trouble to land and weigh it as he estimated it to be $5\frac{1}{2}$ lb. Compared to the British record of 2 lb 13 oz that was some grayling!

We started competition fishing again at 3.0 a.m. using traditional wet flies, and by breakfast had caught about fifty grayling up to 4 lb. It was exciting fishing in that lonely river with its clear running water, and the prospect of trout up to 10 lb. There were large char there too, but we only caught grayling, fishing on intent despite the bitter cold before the early dawn. For me this was the one invigorating experience of the whole trip, and fate seemed determined to prolong it. The helicopter coming to fly us out was forced to turn back, nearly leaving us stranded. The pilot however arranged for a small sea-plane to pick us up. It came gliding in at dusk to set down on the river with a remarkable display of skill and courage.

Each team was encouraged to play practical jokes on the others to add to the pressure, or else it would be Ian Wooldridge, our organizer, arranging for something unexpected to hit us for the amusement of viewers. Clive had the best coup. He flew to Stockholm earlier having discovered where Gibbinson and Gillespie were going to fish there. Over the local radio he made a broadcast, tongue in cheek, saying two world-famous English international fishermen would be on the bank of the river in front of the Royal Palace in a week's time to give expert fishing instruction. Any schoolchildren would be warmly welcomed by them, and shown how best to fish. Poor Gibbinson and Gillespie were so mobbed by youngsters they could hardly fish. We thought that very amusing, but they were mad. So were we later when a similar prank was played on us at our weariest.

This was the second instalment of the 'Fishing Race' with those involved knowing just how demanding it would be. Yet the fishing instinct was merely stirred and heightened by a challenge such as this, which none could refuse. It was typical, too, that the urge to fish a new and mysterious river, with unknown monsters in its depth, instantly banished weariness, and competitive good sense, which demanded that a rest be taken.

No doubt as a cricketer and footballer my competitive nature is as highly developed as most. Certainly it was there when as a seven-year-old I first went holidaying in Ireland at Leenane in Connemara, a fisherman's paradise. That was in the thirties, but memory still sharply recalls the enchantment of the hotel with its oil lamps, its smell of peat fires, and its trays of fish displayed each evening on the hall table. Our first night my elder brother and I watched in awe as the resident fishermen displayed their catches of sea-trout from Kylemore's loughs, of salmon from the Erriff river, and of the large Corrib trout. These last might come from nearby Joyce's river in time of flood, but when we attacked it with our worms the following morning it was low and clear. Our aim was already decided. We were going to catch more that day than anyone else, and display the biggest tray of fish in the hotel.

While the Irish gillie, assigned to look after us, slumbered peacefully in the heather we crept along the banks whipping out the small trout. And not trout only, since we had not then learnt to distinguish salmon parr with their distinctive thumb-print markings, or realized that killing them was as heinous a crime as shooting a fox. So in late afternoon we were back at the hotel eagerly piling vast numbers of small fish on a large tray. Reaction was not however as favourable as we had hoped, and my father's face a study of embarrassment when he saw it.

That damped my competitive urge for many a year, but at least it ensured we had another gillie in future, a delightful character and marvellous teacher. Despite his one arm, James Meehan was still an expert fisherman and could tie on our flies for us as we progressed to that more skilful art. There was a distinctive Irish flavour, too, to his advice. 'Will we catch anything today, James?' we used to ask eagerly as we reached the water. James would contemplate the ripple on the lough, moisten his finger and hold it to the wind, look wise, and then deliver always the same verdict. 'Catch anything? Sure, you might — and then again you mightn't.' He was never wrong, unlike most fishing forecasts.

We varied the question once when we were at the riverside one stormy morning, looking at a river we had never fished before:

'Where will we catch them today, James?'

'Sure they will be under the bridge, sheltering from the rain.'

They were too, though we thought it a piece of Irish whimsy that aquatic fish might have to take cover from the rain. James also introduced us to the idea of quality being even more important than quantity — to the lure of catching big fish. Each night we used to gaze at a showcase in the dining-room with four brown trout mounted in it ranging from nine pounds to three. They had been caught by James in the Finney river. By day we used to get him to recount how he had cycled over, caught them all in the morning, stopping when he felt he could not manage to carry any more fish, and cycle home with his one arm making balance difficult.

Trying to catch record fish is another natural expression of the fisherman's competitive drive. None have ever come my way though some of the sea-trout caught in Norway's Laerdal river would have enabled me to put in a claim had they been in Britain, where, as I write, there is no established record and any sea-trout of 15 lb or over would qualify if properly claimed.

That Laerdal fishing was as exciting as any I have experienced. The lower reaches cut through mountains so sheer that for months on end the winter sun never lights the valley bottom. My fishing was in August when the great sea-trout would come gliding up through the crystal clear water to take a small black dry-fly by day. In this land of the midnight sun you could fish round the clock without ever being in complete darkness. The real thrill was in the warm luminous night hours, fishing with large streamer flies, as the double-figure trout suddenly sent the reel singing as they ripped off a hundred yards of line and backing in their head-long rushes.

It was there I saw my host's son, Einar Wahlstrom, catch a record sea-trout of 25 lb on a small No. 10 Butcher fly. Sadly, he wasn't very interested in fishing then, and even catching a monster fish like that when in his teens did nothing to convert him. So many live in hope of a record fish, but for most of us it is a matter of chance with fortune not always favouring the most deserving.

Not until I was in my fifties did the idea occur to me of entering a fly-fishing competition. One day while fishing on Sundridge Lake near Sevenoaks, which Geoffrey Bucknall has developed into an entertaining and productive water, a number of us were asked if we would enter for the southern qualifier for the national final. At once the competitive instinct was awakened, and through it a new world of fishing enjoyment and interest. As an occasional change I was to find competition adds a new edge to your fishing. The trout lost at the net is as bitter a disappointment as any of those first fish lost in boyhood. The one landed brings the same swelling sense of triumph as the earliest captures in the keeness of youth. In a fishing sense you see again with the clear eyes of childhood, rather than the jaded world weariness of the too experienced angler.

If the odd competition brought a new sharpness to my fishing, a more vivid enjoyment both of the pressures of contest and of the contrast of relaxed fishing, it also opened new horizons in meeting and mixing with the more expert. From them there was much to learn. Those who don't compete sometimes dismiss it as a matter of luck. I have found that there is indeed enough luck involved that an ordinary fisherman, like myself, may find himself representing his country. No one of average ability should be hesitant to have a go. But real skill has its reward, too. There are some of exceptional talent who show it by qualifying over and over again, their margin of ability eliminating the luck factor. They are the ones who can set you new standards.

England's 1981 captain, Bob Draper, qualifies through the highly competitive Midlands. Yet he had battled his way into eleven of the last twelve internationals. No luck involved there.

Any level of fisherman can relish competitions, and have some success, but skill will out. There is an analogy with bridge. Over a couple of rubbers a pair of novices might beat Terence Reese and Rixi Marcus *if* they have a lucky deal from the cards. Over 100 rubbers they will be beaten out of sight. In competitive fishing the matches are the equivalent of just a few rubbers. So while the odds are on the expert, the less expert may still have his days of triumph when he is in the right place at the right time. Certainly in nationals and internationals places have been shared around enough that many have had a chance to participate. What follows may stimulate more to try, and perhaps help them to become internationals, and enjoy the experience.

Some, reading of the pressures of competition, may prefer not to expose themselves to it and sensibly continue to opt for the relaxation of uncompetitive sport. At least this book may help them make the choice after considering the experience of others, and there may be tips here to help them improve their own fishing and their enjoyment of it.

CHAPTER 2
QUALIFYING FOR AN INTERNATIONAL

> *Sometimes ower early*
> *Sometimes ower late*
> *Sometimes nae water*
> *Sometimes a spate*
> *Sometimes ower calm*
> *Sometimes ower clear.*
> *There's aye something wrang*
> *When I'm fishing here.*
>
> The Fly-Fisherman's Lament

How well many of us fly-fishermen know that feeling!
  One of the pleasantest aspects of the competitions, however, is that no matter what the conditions it is the same for everyone. That is certainly true of nationals, and internationals. It has not always applied, though, in all parts of England in all stages of qualifying, through eliminators, for the national final.
  From 1975, it has only been possible to get into England's national team by performance in the eliminating matches which start with those arranged in the five regions — North-West, South, South-West, and the two Midland Regions. While most of these were already well organized for competition, the South, where I fished, took a year or two to adjust fully to this new concept. Before the present, very fair rules had been evolved, there was a major element of chance outside the normal luck inherent in angling of any kind. The sixty or so who entered the qualifying competition had the choice of fishing on the Saturday or the Sunday. The twelve who went forward to the national final were those who had the heaviest weight, regardless of which day they fished. So, though we all fished under identical rules and on the same Chew Valley Lake, much depended on the weather conditions on the two different days.

My luck was in on my first nervous attempt at competition after fifty years of pleasure fishing. The Sunday was mild and cloudy with only ten of us fishing. All the rest had been caught in such impossibly stormy weather the day before that hardly any had caught anything. 'Catch one, and you are sure to qualify' was the cheerful greeting.

The next intelligence was not so reassuring. I was paired with Colin Harms, the Chairman of the Southern Federation, as my boat partner. Here clearly was a man of vast skill, experience, and authority. As a green novice what rule might I inadvertently break under his magisterial eye?

So I began to run over it all in my mind, as I put up my tackle. Entry had been easy enough. I had paid the very modest fee to join the Federation, filled in the entry form, and sent my cheque to cover the fee and expenses of a day on Chew. The Secretary, Tom Carter, had been patient in outlining the details and sending me the instructions. The main points of the rules I had mastered well enough. The maximum size of fly was $\frac{5}{8}$ in hook-length with the overall dressing not to exceed $\frac{15}{16}$ in. Only three flies were permitted, and each must be tied at least twenty inches apart from the next. They could only be fished in front of the boat, and when drifting, and must not be drawn so fast they resembled a minnow (not a very easy rule to administer in these vague terms!).

The competition hours were 10.0 a.m. to 6.0 p.m., and anyone arriving or finishing late was liable to instant disqualification. Once launched there was to be no landing until the finish. Only one rod might be assembled at any time, although a spare could be taken. So far, so clear. But now the queries began to flood into my mind, and the unfortunate Colin Harms was bombarded with questions long before we launched.

Could we use a drogue to slow the boat's drift? Yes, if we both agreed, or if the man in charge at the time wanted it. Did we have to keep a strict rotation of changing ends, and command of the boat every two hours? Yes, unless we mutually agreed otherwise. In any case it was best to agree in general on the main fishing area, rather than waste time dashing to far distant parts every two hours as command changed.

Would he want me to net his fish for him? No. It was best to net our own, then no one wasted fishing time, and there was no ill-feeling if a fish was lost through careless netting.

The one thing it didn't occur to me to ask was whether the competition rules overrode any local rules, as regards size or numbers of fish which might be kept. That naturally became the one practical issue to arise on the very first drift. Keyed up in the knowledge that a single fish might qualify me, there was a feeling of elation as the sunk line suddenly tightened. Chew has a reputation for big fish, and it was with a start of surprise I realized that this was a relative tiddler. The official limit was 12 inches, and Colin confirmed we had to abide by it. But was this keepable? I had no marker, and my only 'ruler' in such circumstance was my spread hand, which I know to be 8 inches from tip of thumb to tip of little finger (mine is a small hand). The trout was 'roughly' one and a half such hands, which meant it might be half an inch over, or under, limit. 'Shall I keep it?' I asked Colin. He stared at his own flies, and said it was up to me. Preferring disaster to dishonour, I finally tipped the little rainbow back in. Four hours later, when I still hadn't had another offer, I was querying the wisdom of that gesture!

Virtue was rewarded at last with several fair-sized browns. I owed these in part to Colin's perception. Part of the shore of Herons Green Bay was then lined with massive tree-stumps, the sawn-off trunks straddling the edge of the water with their roots spreading far out into it. On several of them bank anglers were perched like storks, long-hauling their casts far into the deep water. Colin guessed that in fact the browns might well be grubbing round the roots, so we drifted in on any untenanted stump, catching several lively trout, and missing many more. The bank anglers continued to hurl their flies vainly into the distance, while ignoring the fish at their feet. That was a useful lesson that there is more to fishing than winning casting competitions.

In the first informal years of Southern qualifiers there was another easy-going arrangement from which I benefited. Two years later they still had not introduced the present rule of drawing for boat partners, and not fishing with any close relative. So I was able to introduce my son, John, to competition as my boat partner. As an eighteen-year-old he was saved from those worrying uncertainties which had plagued me before my first competitive contest. We drove the hundred miles to Chew in the early dawn, arriving in the Woodford Lodge car park with time to spare for preparation. The hour before our final briefing on the rules was spent ensuring that he had carried out the necessary drill, testing his cast, trying each individual dropper knot, sharpening the hook points, tying up a couple of spare casts, eliminating all oversize flies from his box, testing that his reels ran smoothly, greasing the tip of his floater though we were both starting with a slow sink line. Anxious to check he did it right, I forgot to carry out the drill myself.

Our first drift was down to Denny Island, and soon we saw a patch of rising fish. As we eased into it, there was a vicious take of my dropper. In the same instant the fish was gone, and so was my fly. The untested knot had pulled out. Searching for a replacement I found I had left my made-up casts, and my glasses, in the car.

Without spectacles it was a time-consuming job to tie the dropper knots, and thread the new flies. Progress was further restricted by two welcome interruptions, as I netted a couple of nice rainbows for my son. By the time I was in action again, the fish weren't. So my son qualified, and I didn't, through failing to practise what I had preached. Ever after in any major competition I have made out a check list. Twenty minutes before the start I go through it to ensure each item is in the boat, each task done. For an absent-minded person like myself that is doubly important in internationals, when the tense atmosphere, the distractions of team photographs, and last-minute instructions from team managers make it all too easy to forget something vital.

There was only one other qualifier I fished in the same boat as my son. On that occasion he again outscored me heavily and by the final hour I had given up hope of qualifying. The standard Chew method of floating line had failed me, as had perming the usual patterns. As a last desperate throw I changed to something as different as possible, a fast-sink line and flies such as Black and Peacock Spider, and Muddler. With only half-an-hour left there was suddenly that happiest of sensations, a firm take, and the powerful surge of a large rainbow. The fish was played with such care that my son was soon enquiring if I had three on at once. Into the net it came at last, a fine trout of $3\frac{1}{2}$ lb to underline the first rule of competition fishing — never give up until the last cast is completed. For this on its own was enough to qualify me for my third national, and the first in which I was to come high enough to make the England team.

That qualified as an 'average' performance in the national. Once you have hurdled over the obstacle of the regional qualifiers, you are one of sixty who fish in the English national each September. Of them, twenty can win a team or reserve place in one of the two internationals fished the following season, so you have a one-in-three chance. Of the top sixteen in the national, the first eight fish in the May or June international, the second eight in the August or September one. The next four stand by as reserves, with England having for each match two reserves, who also fish in the competition, though their bag is not included in the team's total. The top four Englishmen in each international, reserves included, go forward to the next.

So the team of twelve always has a nucleus of four experienced internationals, with a sizable influx of new blood. Each country competing internationally is required to have some similar qualifying process, but the exact method, and the composition of the team, is for each to decide for itself. How the other countries organize it is set out in Appendix 7 on page 271.

In my experience, a national is as different from a regional qualifier as a first-round Cup match from playing in the final at Wembley. The atmosphere builds up in the car park as those sixty busy men, fifty-nine of them looking supremely confident and competent, set up their rods. Glancing at them, they all look dauntingly expert with their coloured lines, their fly-festooned hats, their large nets, and bigger bags. It reminded me of sneaking a look at Cup-Final rivals kicking in before a Wembley start. They all seemed ten-foot tall, broad as barn doors, and with the kick of a mule as their practice shots homed effortlessly to the corner of the net. To add to my anxiety at the start of my first national in 1976, I found my boatman was none other than the then England captain, the formidable bearded Don Fulcher, who for once had failed to qualify for the final.

It was awesome enough to think he would be scrutinizing my every cast for eight hours. To make it worse, I had just written facetiously in *The Observer* about a minuted comment of his at a Confederation Meeting to the effect that he would resign should a lady ever fish for England. Hoping he hadn't seen this I was disconcerted to be greeted with the enigmatic 'Ah, the *Observer* writer, I see.'

Don proved, however, to be the most helpful and interesting of boat companions. With the water shrouded in thick mist at the start, he successfully tracked the best-known Grafham expert, ensuring that, as we started where he did, we must be in a good spot. He advised on flies, spotted rising fish, manoeuvred the boat so that we could cover them, and generally gave us the best possible chance. My boat partner from the Midlands responded well-enough to qualify, but not even Don Fulcher's expertise could help me through. It was one of those dour days when few fish are caught. In my anxiety to do well, I broke the cardinal rule of keeping your flies in the water, and fishing with a steady purpose and rhythm. I was forever out of action changing lines, changing flies, changing method. Without giving nymphs on a floater a fair trial, I was fishing a fast sinker with the largest flies allowed. So the aimless changes became ever more rapid as the day went on to its inevitable disappointment.

Next season I qualified again, and again Grafham failed to respond to me, though my fishing now was better planned and executed. Final practice day was particularly encouraging, as I caught four good fish, while my Southern colleague and current international, Eddie Weight, caught nothing, as we fished together. Eddie was delighted. 'Anyone who catches them in practice, usually fails on match day' was his cheerful comment. How right he was! As I drifted past his boat only an hour after the start he held up two fingers — no gesture of disrespect, but indication of two fish already netted. He qualified. I didn't.

It was third time lucky in the 1978 national at Chew. Even here the start was not encouraging. Nothing came into our boat for the first hour. But drifting from the Lodge pier to Denny Island we seemed surrounded by bending rods. My anxious partner finally called across to a boat nearby to ask the fly on which they had just caught one. Back came the answer: 'Ace of Spades.' Now that black fly, shaped like an ace, is an effective catcher of rainbows, but at the time neither of us had heard of it. My partner thought he was having his leg pulled. At once, however, he was into a fish, and netted it. It was the other boat's turn to enquire the fly. 'Bloody Jack of Diamonds' was the exultant reply — or tit-for-tat as he imagined it, perhaps unfairly.

By late afternoon he had three fish, I had two. The drift, which we had hammered as long as the trout moved there, had been 'dead' for the last hour. At five o'clock we saw fish being taken on a parallel drift the other side of the pier. At once we motored over to join the throng. Immediately my partner had a good rainbow. Then it was my turn as three large rainbows hit the Dunkeld dropper, with barely a cast between landing each of them. Two more I should have had in that hectic half-hour, but their smash takes removed the fly. The trout seemed to soar up from the bottom and hit the Dunkeld with such violence they leapt half out of the water as they took. That thrilling and explosive finish gave me seventh place, and qualification to come back to fish for England at Chew in the first international of 1979.

That's the excitement of competition fishing. However bad the start, you never know when your luck will change if you continue to fish with unrelenting concentration and purpose. In his first competitive eliminator at Ravensthorpe Bob Draper, England's most successful fly-fisher of recent years, caught two fish, but nineteen had to be returned as below the limit. He was almost in despair before he caught the two sizable trout which qualified him. In another Midland eliminator in 1981 he lost two fish early on, and had the frustration of watching trout being hauled out all round him, while he caught nothing. By one o'clock he had seen one angler take seven, another eight, but still had nothing. In the next hour he netted eight good trout himself, and, with another five later, ended overall winner. You never know when luck will change.

Keep fishing and smiling and you may recover from any misfortune as Victor Byrne found in a Leicester Fly-fishers' eliminator at Rutland. Fishing with a friend, who was fortunate to retain his friendship throughout, their early drifts brought not a rise. When they headed for the dam, racing yachts occupied the area. Still fishless after three hours, they diverted into a bay along Hamilton Bank.

First drift there Byrne hooked two good fish at once. His partner responded to the request for netting help, but knocked off the top fish, and made an equal mess of landing the other to lose that as well. Next drift Victor again hooked two at once. This time his friend expertly netted the top fish, cutting it off the dropper. He then took this trout out of the net, and threw it back into the water rather than the boat. After scooping out the tail fish he commented: 'Two nice fish landed.' – 'It would have been,' said Victor, 'if you hadn't thrown one back.' His friend stared at him in bewilderment, and as Victor told me later:

'He didn't believe me until he had searched the bottom of the boat thinking I was joking. Then he looked at me, I looked at him, and we both burst out laughing.' Fortunately it remained a laughing matter as Victor qualified with eight fish, his partner with five.

If you let your partner, or the boatman, net your fish most times you have to grin and bear it if the result is disaster. What is not easily forgiveable, however, is when he causes a crisis by ignoring a specific request.

In the 1976 national at Grafham Brian Furzer was provoked in just that way. The day was calm, and only when he switched to an aqua-sink line did Brian hook into a good rainbow. Soon the fish headed straight towards him, swimming slowly near the surface and revealing itself as over 3 lb. On a hard fishing day that trout alone might have qualified Brian for the England team, as he instantly realized. The boatman, however, already had the net out over the water. '*Don't* try it,' said Brian, 'it's not ready yet.'

Undeterred the boatman plunged in the net, startling the fish into explosive action. As the rainbow powered away the dropper caught in the rim of the net and was only released when the heavy cast was strained to breaking point. So were Brian's feelings towards his boatman. When the trout was netted at last the culprit looked at the lacerated hold, from which the hook had so nearly been torn, and commented on Brian's good fortune in landing it. 'With you on the net it was a ruddy miracle,' was Brian's response, but that fish, with two others, made him an easy qualifier, third on the day.

Such moments can be very fraught when fishing with a stranger. In the 1979 national at Grafham Bob Draper watched the boatman go to net his partner's large fish of some $2\frac{1}{2}$ lb, only to knock it off with an ill-judged lunge. 'Funny,' said the boatman, 'I've never lost a fish like that before.'

There was a long pause...a pregnant silence...and Bob kept his head down and concentrated on his fishing. There is indeed nothing to say at these moments with silence the best policy.

I had not qualified for that national, but had arranged for *The Observer* to sponsor it. So I was invited to fish alongside the competitors, which enabled me to catch an occasional glimpse of my son, John, who had qualified by right. Since my bag didn't count in the competition it was, of course, one of those days when every fish in the lake seemed intent on grabbing my flies. I ended with nine fish weighing 3 lb more than the winner's total! My hope was to see John doing the same, and in early afternoon I noted him into a large fish. This was his first national at the youngest permitted age of eighteen, and this is how he writes of the experience:

> I had prided myself on possessing the one essential quality for successful fishing — being lucky. That was until this national of 1979. The initial pre-match nerves had eased as I took a 2 lb rainbow on the first drift. My luck was holding, and I settled down to concentrated fishing, with dawning hope of an England place. A couple of hours later we saw rods bending by the dam wall, and motored

over to join the flotilla of boats. On the second drift there my line and nerves went suddenly taut as a large fish seized the tail fly. Away it raced at speed, stripping line effortlessly from the reel, then leaping high to confirm that it was indeed a rainbow of 4 lb or more.

The natural excitement of playing a good fish was immeasurably heightened by the knowledge that here was my ticket to the international, if only I could land him. The rainbow had other ideas, changing tactics from energy-sapping runs to boring steadily down to the depths, conserving his great power. My nerves were aquiver again as he headed straight for the drogue, a dangerous hazard as it trailed behind the boat. Carefully I steered him clear, and as the trout began to weaken I was confident that now he must be mine.

Soon he was in view close below the surface, looking almost as tired as I felt. This surely was the end. He was wallowing quietly now on the top as the boatman slid the net towards him. The great prize was inches away, when the rod snapped straight, the fly flew free, the huge fish sank slowly from sight. I stared in disbelief at the cast flapping in the breeze. Exultant anticipation had turned in an instant to total misery. My despair was utter and unbearable. I sat there drained, shaken, and inconsolable. My boat partner, unusually quiet during the fight, now began to babble about what a marvellous fish it had looked. That merely heightened my despondency, and tinged it with annoyance. No doubt he meant to cheer me, instead it gave the distorted impression that he was relieved at a rival's misfortune. Not even a tot of whisky, or two more fish caught later, could lift my gloom, which intensified when I failed by half a pound to qualify.

Writing about it three years later, memory is just as sharp, the moment just as bitter as on that September afternoon. Sadly, the one that got away is the one I shall never forget.

Watching that struggle I had managed to ground the boat, with President Adrian Ashness aboard, just as the fish was ready for the net. When I looked again instead of the expected triumphant gesture my son was sitting head in hands, and my own day, so full of pleasure and fish, was suddenly shadowed and soured.

In much the same spot the year before I had watched a similar tragedy. My expert boat partner, Clive Greenaway, had just landed a good rainbow, taken on his own tying of a Jack-Frost-type fly. It was the sort of day when one good fish was enough, and we prepared to motor in at 5.30 p.m. with much distance to cover back to Grafham's pier. At that moment in the boat in front Tom Carter was suddenly into a large fish. Into the weeds it took him, and he worked it free; under the boat it went, and he brought it back. It jumped, and plunged, and fought with fierce insistence. At last it was mastered, only to come off, like John's, on the very lip of the net.

These are moments when the fisherman is best left to his own private thoughts, with no cheery conversation from uninvolved partners. But the general spirit of these nationals is one of pleasurable excitement, with more joy than grief. This is how two internationals experienced it for the first time — Douglas Young in the original 1975 Grafham competition, Chris Ogborne in the 1981 final at Rutland.

This was Douglas Young's impression:

> The morning dawned cold and bright. An odd band of people assembled on the car park, all wearing funny hats decorated with flies. Some were clad in huge rubber boots, some in oilskins, some in breeches. Some carried cushions, and everyone was festooned with bags, baskets, nets, and at least two rods. In all, we added up to three score of walking christmas trees.
>
> Thirty boats were lined up at the jetty. My mouth dropped open at the sight of our boatman: he wore a polished black sombrero with little bobs dangling and dancing all around the brim. He scored an immediate success. As we clambered aboard he handed out boxes of flies, a box of five churchillian cigars, and an invitation to a reception to be held in the fishing lodge that evening.
>
> Zero hour: 10.0 a.m. Down the jetty walked an elderly gentleman with side whiskers, wearing plus-fours, and carrying a formidable looking double-barrelled shotgun. A rather feeble bang followed as the gun was fired, and soon it was like the battle of Trafalgar. Motors roared, everyone tried to reverse, turn round, race off for their part of Grafham Water. What a melee! What banging, bumping, and boring! The wonder was that none of the boats was sunk.

Like a flock of mallard taking flight, we skimmed over the surface, fanning out in all directions, each intent on reaching the spot where he could catch more fish than the rest. We were there. It became quiet. Tranquillity cloaked the lake as anglers fished. Almost immediately I boated a fish. Great optimism as I offered copies of the successful fly to my fellow contestant. For a while, things became quiet. A boat nearby played three fish in quick succession, and we began to feel gloomy of our chances. There was no need to worry. We learned later that all were lost at the net.

It developed into a glorious day. The fishing was difficult, and catches were not great, but we managed to get sunburned. As the contest ended, everyone wanted to fish to the last minute. So it was the morning in reverse as thirty vessels, gunned to full throttle, converged on the jetty. Any boat not in by the time Davy Crockett blasted his second barrel was disqualified.

The lucky ones queued up to weigh their catch, which would decide England's champion fly-fisherman of the year and dictate the team to represent England in the two international competitions in 1976. It was a long drive home — but a car full of happier, more contented people would have been hard to find.

Your first national is indeed a very special experience. It becomes a memorable one when you win it in your first season of competition. This is how Christopher Ogborne enjoyed it as he became English national champion at his first attempt:

> The atmosphere around any fishing lodge and car park before a day's fishing is normally one of pleasant anticipation, tinged perhaps with a little apprehension about the weather. A chat about flies, a studious look at the water, and then a leisurely (well, reasonably leisurely) stroll to the boats.
>
> At 9.0 a.m. on a September Saturday at Rutland it was none of these things. True, there was the initial appearance of calm with smiles all round and casual greetings to friends, but beneath that the excitement was tangible indeed. Knots being checked three times instead of the usual once; niceties such as the careful application of fuller's earth to the leader, instead of the usual haphazard

pinch — all these things made a lie of the carefully contrived smiles. Anticipation was all. The atmosphere continued to build until thirty-one boats with sixty-two fishermen milling around the landing stage were released by the starter's gun. Tension broken, thirty of them headed for the South Arm in a formidable Armada. The 1981 national final was on.

This was my first season of competitive fly-fishing, and I had registered for the eliminators back in January with more than a little trepidation. I had to balance this new dimension to my fly-fishing against the feeling that the competitive element cut right across my basic concept of peace and relaxation. However, the appetite was well and truly whetted at the South-West eliminator in June, and I decided then that my basic yardstick was simply this: as long as I genuinely enjoyed this departure from my normal fishing routines, then I would carry on. In any event, the traditional loch style is the way I always fish from a boat, so the only real departure from the norm was less time spent eating and drinking!

The weather on final day was very much suited to the style of those of us from the West Country: warm, fairly gentle breezes, with intermittent cloud cover. At times during the afternoon we were becalmed, but at others there was a soft ripple, and it was here that we took fish. Personally, I very rarely use a sinking line, and only then as a last resort. This is not through any sense of purism — rather that I get far more pleasure from using a floater and casting to fish in the surface layer. On the day the fish were rising sporadically through the morning, and I had three small rainbows by lunchtime, all to very small surface fished flies.

Under the expert guidance of our boatman, Peter Hawes, we gradually moved away from other boats into one of the bays in the South Arm, and here we found fish in the early afternoon. With only the slightest of ripple, I scaled down to very small flies, and finally settled on a team of Soldier Palmer, Mallard and Claret and Red Buzzer, all on size 14 hooks, and fished on light (4 lb) line. The Buzzer accounted for two good rainbows on consecutive casts, and as one of them weighed just over $2\frac{1}{2}$ lb, against an average weight for the day of barely 1 lb, I began to have tenuous thoughts: was there, perhaps, a chance of qualifying? Two more fish in quick succession brought my tally up to eight, and at that stage I had to admit (only to myself of course...) that the adrenalin was running.

By now I was becoming a little embarassed for my boat partner. Unfortunately he had only taken two fish so far, and as any fisherman knows you can't get too enthusiastic about your own catch when your partner is having little or no success. Similarly, if you are the one that's failing you begin that awful process of self-doubt, to which the only antidote is a fish. Against this, Peter Hawes was really excellent company, and kept up an effective mix of humour and encouragement which made the whole day so much more enjoyable.

During the mid-afternoon I took six fish, and all of them had been cast to — loch-style fishing at its best. The final that made up my total of ten also came to the Buzzer, and then came the longest half-hour boat ride I can ever remember — back to the lodge. Optimism, however cautious, was upon me.

I weighed in at 12 lb 11 oz, and then followed a pleasant hour which, I am afraid to admit, is full of confused memories. Incredibly — to me — I had won, but there was more to come: the first five places had been taken by West Country fishermen, from our own Bristol Reservoirs Fly Fishers' Association. A sixth angler, in fact my regular fishing partner, qualified in sixteenth position, having taken the best brown of the day.

It was all heady stuff, and inevitably it put the seal on my verdict on competitive fishing. But in the final analysis, was it really so different from a normal day's fishing? The weather had been pleasant, fish had been moving, and the company had been excellent. Surely that's the blueprint for the perfect day — competition or no competition. There were even added bonus factors: anyone who has experienced the social side of such events will know that this plays a big part, as you cannot help but make new friends.

In the depths of winter as I write this, immersed in fly-tying and rod-building, my thoughts stray to the honour of fishing for England next year. Yet another dimension to this wonderful sport called fly-fishing.

CHAPTER 3

THE OLDEST NATIONAL

Now, happy fisherman, now twitch the line!
Now thy rod bends, behold the prize is thine!

John Gay

The start of it all was at Loch Leven and those lines of Gay are appropriate enough to the prospects of the first fishing competition in 1880. Leven remains *the* great centre of competitive fly-fishing, but sadly its catches and its reputation have declined of late. This was, however, the ideal starting place in the days of its plenty, when big baskets of trout were commonplace.

That is important for fair competition. The more fish caught, the more likely it is that skill will be the decisive factor rather than luck. If a single fish may qualify you for a prize, or a team place, too much depends on chance. In competitions meant to be a pleasure as well as a contest, it is also desirable that most of those taking part have some cheering taste of success, rather than creeping back 'clean' after eight hours of concentrated endeavour. The elements of enjoyment and friendship have always been important in national and international fishing competition, and both are better fostered if all have some reward for effort.

The lucky thirty-two who took part in that first organized fishing contest of any kind on Loch Leven certainly had plenty to catch. They averaged more than four fish each on that productive day. The start of it all has been described in David Biggart's admirably researched booklet *The First Hundred Years*, which he produced for the Centenary of the Scottish National Angling Clubs' Association:

> Thanks to a few members of seven angling clubs, the oldest national Trout Fly Fishing Competition in the world was held for the first time on 1 July 1880. The lead

was given by the West of Scotland Angling Club, many of whose members were shareholders of the now defunct Loch Leven Angling Association Ltd., which then had the lease of the fishings on Loch Leven.

The printed notice, setting out the conditions for the event, invited intending competitors to remit their entry money of One Pound to Mr David B. McGregor, on or before 10 June next. The entry money was to provide a fund for prizes. This ranged from a first prize of £15 for the heaviest basket to £2 for the fifth heaviest. It was hoped that as many as forty competitors would take part.

A further printed notice, dated 10 June, stated that as a result of only sixteen boats being available, only thirty-two could take part in the competition. On 25 June, a further printed circular was sent out to inform the competitors that Francis Francis, Esq., Editor of *The Field*, had requested the secretary, Mr McGregor, to inform the competitors that he would give a sixth prize, namely a copy of his book *Sporting Sketches in Pen and Pencil*.

The 'Conditions' read as follows: 'Such of the competitors whom it may suit will meet together in Kirklands Hotel, Kinross, on the evening preceding the competition, at eight o'clock, when a Meeting shall be constituted and the boats balloted for; but it is imperative that all the competitors shall be ready to start at 9.0 a.m. from the pier under pain of being thrown out of the competition, with forfeiture of the entrance-money paid.'

The competitors were required to measure their rods under Messrs Clark and Steedman's scrutiny, with 15 ft the permitted length. Mr Church was appointed umpire, but does not appear to have had any disputes to settle.

Newspaper reports gave very lengthy accounts of the new 'tournament', with these extracts typical of the descriptions:

> The competition is the most important that has taken place in Scotland. It has been alleged against anglers that they are a selfish set of sportsmen, and treasure the lessons Dame Experience teaches them, in the same profitless fashion the miser does his gold. As to that it is no doubt true our crack anglers have no disposition to hang their knowledge on their sleeves for budding Waltonians to peck at. Heretofore — in Scotland at least — there has been no

such commingling of the members of Scotch angling clubs, and inter-club matches have been as rare as angels' visits are said to be. The men of rod and reel have preferred enjoying themselves 'on their own hooks'.

The report them noted that the response from all over the country had 'exceeded the most sanguine expectations, the entry list being soon filled to overflowing'. Leven was said to be fishing so well that the Loch Leven Angling Association 'will for the first time be paid a dividend'. Drought had produced poor baskets for a week or two as the rare atmosphere, the hard wind, the want of rain, and the clearness of the water had all made hard fishing. The drought had also dried up the burns in places, killing off a number of small trout. The supply of them in the loch was, however, large and 'the more gratifying since it has not been replenished from Sir James Maitland's breeding ponds at Sauchie for a couple of years', and since the new breeding ponds, long promised, had not materialized.

Fortunately a storm preceded the event, improving conditions. The favourite, to be hailed as 'Conquering Hero', was Malloch: 'Malloch is a tackle-maker in Perth — a professional we heard him dubbed — and a well-known prize taker, who in a recent river competition made an extraordinary big basket of 50 lb.'

Peter Malloch certainly made an impressive start. His boat began its drift only 150 yards out from the pier, and first cast a good trout seized his yellow-bodied and woodcock-winged imitation mayfly: 'Mr Malloch knew how to deal with such gentry and the finny one was soon captured. A regular beauty he was, and the biggest got during the day.'

That 2 lb $5\frac{1}{2}$ oz trout won Malloch the largest fish prize, but it was McGregor's fourteen, which finally outweighed his ten: 'McGregor fished mainly at the north-east end of the loch and his trout, one of which weighed 2 lb 3 oz, were principally got on the shallows near Grahamston Avenue. The fly he used was one with green body and teal wing.'

McGregor was partnered by Alex Dickson in the boat named 'Clutha', Malloch by Robert Knox in the 'Mary Courcell'. Each partner managed to net only three fish, but no doubt enjoyed seeing the experts at work beside them. Only Messrs Farrer, and Moir of the Perthshire Anglers Club, and John Ritchie of Walton were unlucky enough to catch nothing. Of the thirty-two entrants, seven came from the Stirling Fishing Club, six each from the West of Scotland Angling Club and the Perthshire Anglers Club, five from Kinross-shire Fishing Club, four from Edinburgh Walton, three from Waverly, and one from the Dundee Angling Club.

No women were entered for that first 'national'. But for the first half century of the competition there was nothing in the rules to prevent a lady qualifying. Indeed in 1933 one entered, as was recorded in the Dunroad Club's annual report: 'Mrs Richard Blanche qualified to represent the club in the Loch Leven championship, but in her absence Miss Grace G. Blanche, as next in the list of aggregates in the June competitions on Loch Leven, deputized for her. This brought to the club the distinction of being the first to be represented by a lady angler. In addition Miss Blanche was the first lady to compete in this championship, which fact was given prominence in the sporting press.'

Perhaps there was too much prominence, or some were fearful of the Blanches' prowess, for Dunroad's pride found little echo elsewhere. Next year it was proposed that a new rule II be added to the constitution to read: 'Clubs who are members of the National Angling Clubs Association must be represented at any competition only by a male representative.' This was passed with only former chairman, Andrew Buchanan, dissenting.

More than forty years elapsed before the changed outlook fostered by the Sex Discrimination Act affected the national. From 1977 the rule has read simply 'Members may be represented at any meeting or competition by a person over eighteen years of age.'

The first lady to fish in the national was Miss Freda Macrorie of Helensburgh Club in the first preliminary competition of 1979. The trout, however, were in obdurate mood that day proving as unresponsive to the woman's touch as to the blandishments of the men. Along with sixty males Miss Macrorie reported in fishless. That was more comment on her luck than her skill for only eighteen trout were caught by the seventy-six competitors. That average of 0.2 fish apiece was repeated in the second preliminary to emphasize how poorly the loch was fishing at the time.

How different it all was in that inaugural contest in 1880.

Loch Leven has had a special attraction for Scottish anglers, and anyone interested in trout fishing the world over. It is rich in history with its muddy bottom still concealing the key flung there by Mary Queen of Scots as she fled from imprisonment on Castle Isle. It is rich in scenery with tree-girt islands, with a shoreline now wild, now touched by well-cultivated fields, and with the humped Benarty hill catching the wandering eye. The colourful setting is echoed in the landmarks of the loch — the Green Isle, the Black Wood, the Yellow Sands.

Especially is Leven rich in the quality, if not now in the quantity, of its trout. They are of splendid colour and shape, with a two-pound 'yellow-belly' a prize to delight the eye, and for a gourmet to savour.

Peter Malloch himself was remarkably knowledgeable on trout and most of the large ones caught anywhere in Scotland were sent to him to mount. So he was a good judge of quality, and there must be respect for his views. For him the Leven strain was supreme. In his view 'Leven trout are admitted by all to be the finest trout in Great Britain, if not the world, and nowhere can they be seen to such perfection as in Loch Leven itself.'

We know exactly what Leven was like at the start of these competitions for Malloch has described it in terms which, in the main, still apply. Writing of Leven in 1908 in his book *The Life History of Salmon, Sea-trout, and other Freshwater Fish*, he has this to say:

> Loch Leven is almost round and covers an area of 3,400 acres, in which are several islands, the largest being St Serf's occupying about 80 acres. The loch is 350 ft above sea-level. No less than 85 per cent of the bottom is covered by less than 20 ft of water. This large extent of shallow water is the means of producing a large amount of food.
>
> The chief food of the trout is the larvae and flies of the blood-worm, which begin to appear in early April, and are usually more numerous about the 20th of the month. The larva of the blood-worm, which lives in the mud, is about an inch long, blood-red in colour, and about the thickness of a stocking needle. In April the perfect insect often retains the blood colour of the larva.
>
> The larvae of this fly have the power of rising to the surface and falling to the bottom again, and while in this state the trout devour great numbers of them. In my opinion the most important food for trout in Great Britain, though little known to anglers, is the fly and larvae of the blood-worm. One who has not seen them can have little idea of the immense swarms which appear on Loch Leven.

As the season advances more appear in the evening, and on warm nights the surface of the water is almost covered with them, and the trout suck them down everywhere.

For subsidiary diet Malloch listed the olive dun as next in importance, followed by 'stone-flies, caddis-flies, also a small fly, Cain, the lesser Ephemerae'. They fed also on shell-fish and from August, on perch fry. Malloch pointed to the height above sea-level, and consequent cold, as inhibiting growth, so that few exceeded 3 lb. He records the occasional specimen of 4 or 5 lb, and 'one I know of was 10 lb'. The great majority, however, died before reaching 3 lb, at age 7–8 years. Many that reached 3 lb then decreased in weight, 'becoming long and lank' before dying.

On the unusual colour of Leven trout he wrote: 'Those in the streams have red spots, but after they have been a short time in the loch the spots disappear. This is peculiar to Loch Leven. They then become quite silvery, and retain their silvery coat until the spawning season arrives. As they grow older there is more yellow in their colour.'

Of that important aspect, the fishing, he comments:

> At one time Leven was netted and the fish sent to market, where they fetched a high price. For the last thirty-five years, however, the loch has been reserved for angling, and during that time has had many ups and downs, success or failure depending on the number of pike in the loch.
>
> Fortunately these pests have now been destroyed, and during this year — 1908 — the number of trout caught has far exceeded the catch of any previous year, since 34,000 trout were caught on the rod. With care this famous loch is capable of yielding even a much larger annual catch than this.

In the pierhead bar is a photograph from a time when it did yield more, only four years later. In just two days the fishermen of Leven caught 2,200 trout between them in June 1912. In this fabulous year it is no surprise to find Malloch winning the national with an all-time record for the number of trout caught — thirty-seven — with the runner-up, John Ritchie of Rowbank Club, catching thirty-five. Malloch's weight of 21 lb 11 oz has, however, been exceeded on a number of occasions with the heaviest catch for national winners shared between F.A. Rottenberg of Kelvinside Academicals in 1909, and Dr James

Cuthbert, of Bothwell and Blantyre, as late 1966, each winning with 27 lb 11 oz.

In one way at least Loch Leven hasn't changed. It continues to have its ups and downs, and is currently in the middle of a lengthy down. The records of the competition log the change in the fish and fishing over the years with reasonable accuracy. In that inaugural contest thirty-two anglers caught 132 trout weighing 121 lb 2 oz. So the average catch was 4.1 trout per rod, the average weight 14.7 oz. In the seventies the Leven nationals involved two preliminary rounds on the loch as well as the final. In that decade 1442 fishermen, taking part in those contests, caught 1240 trout — less than a fish apiece on average.

But these trout weighed 1538 lb to average around $1\frac{1}{4}$ lb per fish. The most disastrous day was one of sun and calm in the second preliminary of 1971, when fifty-three anglers managed just one trout between them. That complicated qualification for the final! The most successful of these were those of 1977 and 1978 in both of which the thirty competitors averaged 3.1 trout each.

The old maps of Leven marked an area as Vain Fishing. Sadly, that can now apply to most of the loch on its bad days.

The decline of Leven is most clearly shown by looking at the lowest catches in the 121 finals and preliminary matches fished on Leven since the start of competition. Fish per rod is the only reasonable measure of comparison as numbers of anglers involved have varied so widely. *All* the thirteen occasions on which the average catch has been less than 0.3 per rod have been in the sixties and seventies, and nine of them in this last decade.

Overall the decline is not quite as bad as that indicates. At first glance, comparisons of the annual catches do not reflect too badly. In 1903 for instance only 2,002 trout were caught all season, with the 3,725 fat pike netted out as the obvious cause of decline. The fairest comparison, however, is to take three normal years 1899 to 1901, with their average catch of 20,933 trout against the three 1976 to 1978 with their average of 17,241.

That doesn't seem very different — until you add that in that early period there were only half the number of boats, fishing was only for six days rather than seven, and there were never more than two anglers in boats, which now often have three. Those early anglers were also handicapped by gut casts, old-fashioned techniques, and a more limited range of fly patterns. Or was that in fact an advantage? An heretical thought the tackle-makers at least would wish dismissed from the mind!

In the sixties concern was already such that the Freshwater Fisheries Laboratory at Faskally organized research on the loch over a period of years. In essence the scientific conclusions were confirmation of commonsense observation. Chemicals draining into the loch from effluent or cultivated fields had damaged fly-life, and overpromoted underwater plant growth; stocking was only through trout from the burns and growth rate there is much slower than in the loch (as Malloch had already exactly plotted). The report recommended the control of the inflow of chemicals to improve conditions, and opined that good fishing was subject to the severity of the algae concentration. It was confident, however, that good sport could still be expected, and that good trout in quantity were available to be caught.

Ten years later that optimism was fading. Andrew McKenzie of Dunfermline Artisan Angling Club had a motion carried without dissent at the 1979 AGM of the Scottish National Angling Clubs' Association which commented on the deterioration of fishing and demanded representations to the Loch Leven Fisheries to 'warn them in the strongest possible terms that urgent practical measures such as stocking, and netting of pike, must be adopted if the fishery is to retain its reputation as one of the foremost in the country, fit for national and international competition.'

What has caused the fall-off in catches? The loch's best period embraced the years 1909 to 1921, when not only was it owned by Tayside Salmon Fisheries Ltd., but their manager was Peter Malloch himself. So it is particularly relevant to recall Malloch's classical definition of how such declines occur in any loch: 'Sometimes you will hear a complaint that thirty years ago a loch contained plenty of trout, and yielded fine baskets of free risers, each fish averaging a pound, but now the loch contains nothing but large trout of a sulky nature. Thirty years ago sixty trout weighing 60 lb were often caught in a day, but now it is most difficult to capture more than three trout in a day weighing 6 lb. The reason of this is not too much spawning ground, but want of it; and if 200 yearlings are put in to the acre, the 'fine baskets' of the old days will return.'

In Leven's case 200 to the acre is too much to expect as it adds up to nearly three-quarters of a million trout. It is, however, surprising that the old fish ponds and hatcheries have not been restored to full production, or the spawning grounds of the burns improved where they have been damaged by gravel workings. Stirling University has experimented with hatching some trout, but the first batch failed, and the second was not accepted back into the loch. Yet the clear problem is too few trout to the acre. Back in 1903 only 2000 were caught all season, but the average weight had shot up to 21.9 oz, compared to the previous six years' average of 12.2 oz. Now, as in the past, a high average weight seems to go with few and sulky fish.

The stocks come into the loch only through the burns. These were hard hit by the abnormal drought a few years ago, and have been more consistently affected by the gravel workings. This no doubt has damaged spawning, and meant fewer numbers returning to the loch. As a visitor I have been surprised to find that the limit is as low as nine inches at a time when it seems necessary to conserve stocks of small trout to grow on. It used indeed to be eight inches in old competitions, but that was in the days of plenty.

Another surprise and disappointment was the first fish I caught in both the two competitions I have fished on Leven.

As an invited guest to the Centenary competition I thought I had done England proud when my rod bent early on, and it became apparent that I had two on at once. Both turned out to be perch! In the 1981 international my Welsh boat partner and I had had few rises, and no captures, on a morning of bright sun. When I changed to a fast sinker as we started to drift round the tiny Green Isle, the adrenalin flowed in response to a heavy pull and welcome strain. This time it was *three* large perch! And they succeeded in tangling the four-fly cast beyond redemption to waste more fishing time. The perch stocks are clearly too high for my comfort, and probably for the good of the trout in the loch. Perch are voracious feeders, and predators as well, and in leading Irish lakes, such as Mask and Melvin, too large shoals of them have lead to deterioration of trout stocks. In Mask that happened when the pike were eliminated to the point that the perch flourished unchecked. The balance needs careful watching as the pike 'pest' is attacked.

Compared to the lack of a proper head of fish per acre, the destruction of much fly-life is a secondary menace. But that, too, is evident enough. To back Malloch's description of the immense clouds of flies on warm evenings, experienced boatmen there will tell of it being part of their duties at some seasons of the year to sweep off the pier the inch-thick litter of dead flies which carpeted it. That work has become as redundant as most of the boatmen, needed two to a boat before motors, so heavy are they to row.

If the day is sunny at Leven you are not likely to catch much now in competition hours. Those that are taken will probably be caught fishing deep. With wind and cloud, however, floating and slow sink lines are still effective, as is the dropper worked close to the boat. Indeed my competition boatman related how he often took out a pair of expert fishermen, one of whom cast long, the other very short, working his dropper on the surface. The short-caster caught the most on nearly every occasion. That has not been the recent experience of the English team which won the last three Leven internationals by fishing long in the traditional reservoir, rather than loch, method.

On good days the Leven trout still behave much as Malloch noted:

> In April when feeding on flies, Loch Leven trout travel at about two miles an hour, their speed gradually increasing until July, when it reaches about three miles an hour. They travel from six to eight inches under the surface, sucking down one fly after another and usually heading upwind. In streams these trout remain in one spot and the dry-fly fisherman casts his fly almost over the rings its rise made. Should he do this on the loch the trout would be yards away by the time his fly alighted.

The sight of a rising trout has been a rarity in my own competition experience at Leven. A pity because it is always more intriguing to be able to cast with direction. On the last occasion my fixed concentration on the unyielding water was relieved by listening to the boatman's tales.

Jimmy Abel junior had many more years experience than his name implied. His knowledge, and expert recall of the vast bags made on days in the past at the places we were fishing without an offer, left unanswered whether it was the skill or the fish which were in decline. But of his many amusing tales one in particular took my fancy. A doctor coming up often from the South to fish Leven had never caught a really large specimen there. Finally he hooked into one of 5 lb and fought it until it was close to exhaustion. Not so close, however, as to prevent a premature attempt at netting stirring it into explosive action. As it tore away the boatman's deerstalker hat fell off in the confusion, and was promptly hooked by the top dropper. The doctor was irate at having to play fish *and* sodden hat, but at last brought both quietly in, ready for the net.

'No mistake this time, Donald,' he ordered. Donald made none, sweeping his net expertly under the prize. But it was his own favourite hat he netted out, breaking the cast as he did so. The huge fish rolled over and sank from sight, and the doctor made off home in silent fury. Perhaps that was in the days of the thirties when the charge for a boat and *two* boatmen was £1.75 per day, with one pound for the boat and 75 pence the wages of the pair. How much more anglers must usually have got in the way of help and service than they had paid for!

In Scotland's national final no modern can compete with the legendary Peter Malloch, the great expert of his day, who fished in the first competition in 1880. In the next forty years, Malloch was in twenty-nine finals, was champion six times, runner-up thrice, and on occasion was both national champion and Leven champion in the same year. His brother Gilbert was in the final twenty-two times and was also a winner. In recent years qualification has been progressively harder as more have become involved in competition fishing. But there are many current Scottish fishermen whose skill clearly needs little support from luck. Gilbert McIver has fished in twenty-five finals, William Wallace and Peter Keay in twenty-two. Leaving out the few who qualify by office, other leading anglers are Eric Campbell, who has qualified for twenty, David Biggart for seventeen, and Dr James Cuthbert for sixteen entries into this oldest of all national finals.

1966 was a vintage competition year on Leven. In that same season in which Dr James Cuthbert equalled the Scottish national record with a winning basket of 27 lb 11 oz, an English international, R.W. Beaty, made the highest ever individual catch in any national or international match. Robert Beaty was a member of the English International Fly Fishers and that June he took forty-two trout weighing 36 lb 7 oz in the English national, which was always fished on Leven until the seventies. Nearly all his fish were caught on a size 16 double Greenwell's Glory with a pheasant tippit tail. They were taken drifting within fifty to a hundred yards of the north-east bank in a light south-west wind, with Tom Stark as his boatman and H. Hartley as partner. This qualified him to fish again in the preliminary round of the Scottish national next season when some fifty rods caught only about ten trout between them. He had one of 12 oz and failed to qualify by 2 oz — a rather different day's fishing!

In all my long fishing career there has been no greater pleasure than being invited as England's only representative to take part in the Centenary match of this great competition. This special contest was the largest ever staged on the loch, and a glittering group of talent it brought together. The fly boys of distinction assembled then included eight international presidents, twelve past Scottish presidents and captains, sixteen Scottish national winners and nine runners-up, together with fifteen who had fished five times or more for Scotland. There were also two invited representatives from Wales, and two from Ireland to complete the array of fishing talent. Sadly, the trout were unimpressed. Only seventy-three surrendered to this formidable armada, and seventy-six of the distinguished company had to return fishless.

Yet, for all who took part this was a riveting experience, a day to savour. For a newcomer like myself there was the additional excitement which goes with fishing any new loch, let alone one as famous as Leven. The feeling was heightened as we were piped away from the quayside. Then the boats were speeding off, each to its favoured spot, with engine roaring, and foaming wake. The urgency of those first few minutes was to fade for many as the trout stayed dour and unresponsive. But no one worried. For this was a day of stirred memory, of friendships renewed or newly forged, of involvement in a very special occasion, which no one present would live to see repeated.

Of the guests, the most successful was appropriately the Welshman, Trevor Hirons, International President of the year. His was the third heaviest catch of the day to remind us how successful his country has been in the past decade of internationals. My own good trout put me in the top dozen as an added bonus to my first experience of Leven. There is a story in *The Loch Leven Angler* of how in 1873, one of the most prominent Leven fishers of the day caught only a couple of small trout. Hovering miserably around the quay, he was comforted a little as angler after angler came in with equally poor baskets. Finally one arrived full of smiles and weighed down by fish. To the query as to how he had achieved it, he said he had listened to all the advice about how to fish Leven and done exactly the opposite. I was as perverse, and as fortunate as he in my choice of method, but had the advantage of being expertly guided by two past presidents in my boat, Angus Hutton and John Stirling. At the day's end, there was a perfect demonstration of the Leven traditional short-lining method as John Stirling took a trout working his dropper within inches of the boat. That was a happy end to a happy day's fishing.

Trevor Hirons did Wales proud that day and he gives this account of the day's most successful boat:

> My boat partners were Mike McKinnell with whom I'd fished in three Leven internationals, and Bill Small, another old friend from Dundee Anglers' Club. What a sight it was as the boats sped away for this colourful and memorable occasion. With Bill on the engine we headed for St Serf's and as we passed Castle Island some were already drifting the Thrapple Hole, some veering off towards the Deeps.
>
> We agreed to change positions every hour and I started in the centre, a good position in these large boats. A strong blustery wind was blowing with good cloud cover and, thank goodness, no sun. We checked the depth with our net handles and started to drift in approximately five feet of water. I was using a 10 ft 6 in carbon-fibre rod and a sinking number 8 line with four flies sizes 10 to 12, casting twenty-five yards and retrieving fast. Raising my rod as soon as the flies touched the water, I bobbed my top fly right to the boat. We had only drifted a hundred yards or so when I saw a swirl to my right and Bill shouted 'I'm in.' That was confirmed as a good trout jumped two feet into the air. Mike netted it after a good fight — a $2\frac{1}{2}$ lb brown, its beautiful golden colour matching the sandy bottom. It had taken a 12 Grouse and Claret and the first fish in the boat set our adrenalin flowing.
>
> I changed my bob fly to a Grouse and Claret. There was no talking now with all eyes watching our droppers. Five minutes passed then Bill again called 'I'm in', very quietly this time. The trout did not show for some time, keeping down and fighting more strongly as it took out line. It was my turn on the net this time lifting out a nice $1\frac{1}{2}$ lb trout taken on the same fly.
>
> Back we went over the same drift with Bill now in the middle. Half-way in I was removing some weed from my fly when a fish head-and-tailed close to the boat. That was a proper Loch Leven take and Bill was into another trout, a small one this time and quickly netted. It was not quite an hour from the start and he had three already. But that was the last movement for some time as we drifted the same

area, then moved to the Sluices with the few boats around us signalling blanks.

Back we went to our first area eating lunch on the way and starting about one mile out in deeper water, though on the same line. Second cast I turned over a good fish which didn't touch the fly. Moments later, as I lifted off, it took, and nearly jumped straight into the boat hitting the side with a bang. 'That's done it', I thought as the line went slack, but soon the welcome weight was there as I tightened and worked it round the back. I felt a lot better once it was in the boat, a relief after five hours without a rise. It had taken the second dropper, a size 12 Coch-y-Bondhu. So I made another change putting an Alder on as bob fly. This has the same body as a Coch-y-Bondhu and is a favourite fly of mine for this type of water.

Another drift into the bay with nothing doing until we were 100 yards from shore. Then a fish moved to my left, was immediately covered, and took first time in two feet of water. It ran straight into thick weed, but I gave it some stick, pulled it through, and Mike netted the 2 lb trout. At once the motor was on and we were away. The last drift started at 4.30 p.m. In the centre now, I moved two good fish very quickly, then had a lovely take just five feet from the boat.

The trout was soon netted by Bill, my third weighing $1\frac{3}{4}$ lb, and the second to take the Alder. Before I could restart Bill was into another and as I picked up the net Mike shouted that he was in, too. Both fish fought well before coming safely to the net and soon we were heading for the pier. How had other boats done? We had not seen many boats all day. Had others found the hot spots? We came in with five minutes to spare before the finishing gun. The weigh-in showed seventy fish weighing 107 lb 15 oz with 126 anglers taking part and only fifty catching fish. Bill Small came first with his four fish weighing almost 7 lb. My three for 4 lb 6 oz brought me fourth place, and the eight fish made our boat the top one of the day.

Bill won a watch from the sponsoring company, a most appropriate prize as he had smashed his own on the quay a few minutes before the start.
More than one hundred and fifty years before the first Scottish national John Gay wrote the lines which introduced

this chapter, his Scottish contemporary, James Thomson, must have the valedictory words with this optimistic wish for all future fishermen in this great competition on Leven:

> *There throw, nice-judging, the delusive fly:*
> *And, as you lead it round in artful curve,*
> *With eye attentive mark the springing game.*
> *Then fix, with gentle twitch, the barbed hook.*

CHAPTER 4
THE EARLY INTERNATIONALS

The aeroplane that roars across the world
And back again before the day is out
May still evoke less wonder than the curled
Low ripples that are started by a trout.

T.C. Yelland

The Scots, who had found such enjoyment in their own competitions, were also initiators of the internationals. Such was the popularity of Loch Leven that a number of Englishmen were regular visitors and easy to persuade to accept a challenge. The man who took the lead in organizing the match was John M. Johnstone, factor of the Kinross estate. When writing of it later he praised the work of William G. France of Glasgow, Secretary of the Scottish National Angling Clubs' Association for organizing the international as well as the national competitions. He had kind words also for R.H. Dodds for his enthusiasm and drive in getting together the first team to represent England. The early Secretaries of the other countries, T.W. Armstrong of England, D.S. Savours of Wales, and S. McLeod of Ireland were then commended for the hard work which had seen the competition so well established in the thirties. As Johnstone put it:

> The International Competition, which commenced between England and Scotland in 1928, but was extended to include Wales and Ireland in 1932, excites a great deal of interest in all four countries and is certainly the chief event in the angling world today. A team of sixteen rods representing each country compete and a silver cup is given by Lady Graham Montgomery of Kinross to the winning team in memory of her husand, the late Sir Basil T. Montgomery Bt.

Before that first competition in May 1928 the English International Fly-Fishers' Association was formed to select a team. Their minute book lists some distinguished angling names in the team, including J.J. Hardy. But what underlines the importance attached to the event is the nominated captain elect, H.R.H. The Duke of York. The teams for that first match were twenty strong, only reducing to sixteen when the entry of the Welsh and Irish put a strain on the available boats. Not sure of how many would be able to journey up to Leven, the English picked six to stand by in addition to their first-choice twenty. That was a wise precaution, as was naming a reserve captain in case affairs of State prevented the future King George VI taking part. There was indeed considerable change before the day, and it is clear from Press reports that W.H. McCreath did take over as captain, with the Duke unable to participate.

The English Minute Book in its fine copperplate handwriting makes no reference to this, nor to the background of events which launched the international. These, however, were described in the Berwick-upon-Tweed *Journal* as a prelude to its report of the 1938 match. This account had apparently been given them by a main participant, Mr R.H. Dodds, the 'well-known merchant'.

By Dodds' account, the idea germinated in a visit he and W.H. McCreath made to Leven in 1926 with two friends. They had challenged each other to see which pair could catch the most. When Dodds' partner failed to arrive the Leven boatman took over the spare rod to fish in his place. This Anglo-Scots combination of Dodds, and boatman John Todd, won the day. A further 'challenge' was then issued. For the following year Dodds and McCreath decided to fish together and to invite as many pairs as wished to fish against them. Facetiously they called it 'The trout fishing championship of the world', and proceeded to win it against considerable opposition with a bag of seventy-three trout weighing 56 lb.

The contest appears to have been something of a marathon on the lines of Gareth Edwards' 'Fishing Race'. According to Dodds the competitors were on the loch for fourteen hours, but had recognized periods 'off duty' for sleep and rest. The rules also laid it down that no individual should actually fish for more than twelve hours. 'Tactics' were apparently in use that day as several competitors went equipped with field glasses to spot if anyone else had found feeding fish. At one period when Dodds was resting, McCreath woke him roughly with the information that

Mr Short and Mr Chartress, whose record for a week on Leven was 244 lb of trout, were 'in amongst them', and that it was time to get busy.

Such interest was created by this haphazard contest that it led to the proposal in 1928 for an international match between England and Scotland. The *Fishing Gazette* gave publicity to the idea and Dodds, McCreath and Short were formed into a sub-committee to collect a side. They contacted all known English regulars at Leven and made a selection from those who might be available.

The contest had considerable advance publicity in the Press. The general tone varied between a marked reluctance to take the match seriously and the *Manchester Guardian*'s comment, in a Leader, that it was impudent and absurd to oppose a Scottish team on their own loch. The Leader concluded that for all the chance the English team had they might as well stay south of the border and fish in the streets of Manchester. Newspaper forecasting was as accurate then as now. England narrowly won the first contest. The result could hardly have been closer with both teams of twenty catching over 130 lb of fish and England victorious by just $15\frac{1}{2}$ oz.

As a further reminder of how well Leven used to fish the Berwick *Journal* went on to describe the international of 1938. The bright calm weather of the early morning was soon broken by a heavy shower with conditions of cloud and wind ideal for the rest of the day. Between them the sixty-four competitors caught no less than 642 trout for 475 lb $11\frac{1}{2}$ oz, an unbeatable record for the competition. Weighing in that lot gave the Scots a long wait before they could celebrate a handsome win, by the record margin of 59 lb 14 oz. The first woman to take part in these internationals, Mrs W. Wynne Kirkby, beat two other members of her Welsh team with a catch of six trout weighing 4 lb, though this did not prevent Wales coming last in this remarkable contest.

The international launched in 1928 was soon so popular it was extended to include Ireland and Wales. They 'tested the water' by sending a composite team to fish as guests alongside the international match proper in 1931. Satisfied with the experience, both sent a full team to compete in 1932, though with four countries taking part each put a side of sixteen on the water, since Leven could not cope with larger numbers.

Those contests have continued until the 'Jubilee' year of the four country internationals celebrated in 1982, with a break only for the years of the Second World War, which extended to 1950. In the last match before this rude interruption England was the winner with B.C. Hall catching their sixth heaviest basket of 8 lb 15 oz, while Lord Strabolgi had twelve trout weighing only one ounce less.

The *Manchester Guardian*'s belief that 'home' advantage would always give Scotland the edge ignored two facts. Most of the early English teams came from Berwick, or the North, and had been regular fishers at Leven. Then the team spent a whole week together at Leven, fitting in their own English 'national', and putting in some sustained practice.

In addition, selection solely through the English International Fly-Fishers allowed them to keep a settled team of anglers experienced in competition and in fishing Leven.

As David Biggart has recorded, Scotland had a very different approach. From 1932 their team was made up of President, Secretary, and the top fourteen from the previous national. This made for constant change. Not for forty years was more stability achieved by including the two with the heaviest catches in internationals in the following year's team. David Biggart had been pressing for some years for such an improvement, which was finally introduced when he was President.

The Scottish teams had had little preparation in the past. As he recorded: 'The approach to an international from the Scottish point of view had always been very casual. The team members arrived at the pier without any prior notification of whom they were to fish with and new team members were not even aware that there was a photograph before the match. In the 'sixties the moves to try and get the Scottish approach to internationals on a more businesslike footing began to gather momentum.'

Not before time it would seem, since there had been one unfortunate incident in the past when, once the competitor *did* discover who his boat partner was, he declined to fish with him, and the reserve had hastily to be drafted in his place. It was Biggart again who was first to press hard for an earlier get-together of the team more on the English pattern. But it was not until 1965 that the persuasions of President and team captain, Alastair Nicoll, succeeded in getting the pre-match meeting which paved the way for a Scottish victory to end a long winning run for England. All four teams now meet at least two days in advance of the match for practice outings, with some still spending up to a week to prepare.

The 'democratic' method of qualifying by performance which

Scotland had adopted from the start was slow to catch on elsewhere, except in Ireland. As the current Secretary of the Irish Trout Fly-Fishing Association, George Timmins, records:

> The Irish Trout Fly-Fishers' Competition Committee was founded in 1932, and from that date an international team took part in competition. The team of 12 anglers and 2 reserves was not picked on a competitive basis at first, but by invitation. The practice was for the Secretary to write to a number of anglers inviting them to take part. From the replies received the team was selected.
> This method continued until 1937 when the team was selected from the two major Irish competitions — the seven best rods from the national championship, and the seven best from the interprovincial championship. The following year the six best rods from the 1937 international were allowed to hold their team places. They were then joined by the four best rods from each of these two major competitions.

The Welsh and English took much longer to depart from the central selection method.

David Fleming-Jones, so well-known as a former Secretary of the Welsh International Association, and latterly as the kindly and effective Manager of Grafham Water before his recent retirement, has this recall of the early Welsh teams:

> I believe that only I and Colonel H. Hastings Clay (Harry Clay, cousin of the Glamorgan and England cricketer) now survive from the first post-war Welsh team. This included Lionel Sweet, Dr Robert Prytherch, Dr Alec Lindsay (captor on a trout fly of the record Towy salmon weighing over 50 lb), Dr Arthur Smith and, briefly, Dr Lees. Quite a plethora of medical men in fact, which at least ensured a high standard of social behaviour, whatever our fishing ability might have been. It was said that Lord Glanusk (who had captained the Welsh team before the War) had insisted that members must know how to handle their knives and forks properly, even if not too expert with their fishing rods.
> This might possibly have been the reason those early Welsh teams did not do so well. Myth however ascribes Wales' failure to win a match until 1967 to the fact that a

Welsh captain, W. Wynne Kirkby, had included his wife in the team. The chauvinism, which made her the 'Jonah' responsible for disaster, was disproved later by the Irish who have won at least once with a lady in the team.

The early days, particularly as regards the Welsh and English teams, were very much social occasions when one enjoyed a good fishing holiday for a week at Loch Leven in company of people who were in the team on reputation — and to hell with democracy! Wales were before England in joining the Scots and Irish in adopting a wider process of qualifying. I wondered what Lord Glanusk would have thought, however, when one new member of the team was reputed not to have removed his wellington boots, in which he had arrived, for the whole of the time he was in Scotland. He did not attend the dinner, departing in his caravan immediately after the match.

For my part, I regretted the effect this sometimes had on team spirit, through introducing competition between members each anxious to preserve his place in the side. The relaxed mood of early times changed to a more competitive outlook even among ourselves. On one occasion I saw another Welsh boat net a fish and called across to ask, 'What did you take that on, Ned?' Came back the shouted answer, 'Ham.'

Even if we didn't have great team successes there were a lot of good individual fishermen among the early Welsh stalwarts. After my time Moc Morgan has been an anchor man and others like Victor Williams of Aberystwyth (twice winner of the Brown Bowl), and Gwynfor Evans of Tregaron, a most consistent angler, have distinguished themselves. But it is not for me, or anyone, to pick and choose between the many excellent fishermen who have brought Wales so much success in more recent years.

England was the last to keep up the 'selection on reputation' system only recently abandoned. Personally I admire them for their adherence for so long to the original ideal. But I realize mine is very much a minority view in commending the old tradition.

Among the best-known names of that first post-war team Lionel Sweet stands out in another competitive connection. He was a master caster, the chief personality of the great Usk casting competitions. His party piece was to use both hands and feet to keep six rods casting at the same time without tangling. Most of us have trouble enough doing that with one. Purchasing tackle in his shop at Usk was as entertaining as fishing the river there. When I went in to buy a few flies shortly before his untimely death, I asked what was the favoured pattern of the season. Instead of the usual brief answer the ones he mentioned were all graphically illustrated, as he mimed the trout's likely response to each. Indeed he made himself *look* like a trout hovering inquisitively and deciding whether to take, as his widespread fingers fluttered like the fish's pectoral fins, and his eyes peered up at an imaginary Olive.

Dr Prytherch, for many years the Welsh captain, is another of them, like David Fleming-Jones himself, to make a deep impression on rival teams. B.C. Hall indeed wonders whether he was more dedicated fisherman or doctor. He tells of a friend, who had been invited to fish the doctor's stretch of the Glaslyn, going to meet Dr Prytherch at his surgery. The waiting room was full of women all knitting away. 'If you want the doctor,' they told him, 'You should be ready for a long wait like us. He usually forgets all about time when he's fishing, look you.'

The current Welsh Secretary, Moc Morgan, has this to add about the further developments in his country's approach to competition:

> Game-angling competition in the Principality grew apace with the growth of interest in reservoir fishing. With improved management of these waters bringing wider opportunity, there came a new breed of angler more geared to competitive fishing. The road he now has to take to get a place in the national team is a long one, rewarding for some, frustrating for others.
> The starting point is within his own club which must be a member of the Welsh Salmon and Trout Angling Association, the governing body responsible also for managing the national team. Each such club can send four representatives to the Welsh National Fly-Fishing Championship match which is fished from the bank of a reservoir with the venues changed annually. To represent his club the angler will have to fish one or more elimination matches as arranged within that club. For many it is really difficult to get into the 'frame' to fish in the national.
> For the national match, around 150 anglers fish it out for a place in the final trial. Again the contest is bank

angling with the top forty-eight, or the top sixty if enough boats are available, going forward to the final trial on Llyn Trawsfynydd. Only at this last stage is the fishing from boats with the top eight rods going into the team the following year. The twelve members and two reserves in each national team are completed by retaining a nucleus of six from the previous year. Wales also differs from other countries in having two nationals each year and two different teams, one for the spring international and another for the autumn. Many criticize the system for its mixture of bank and boat angling when the two techniques are so different. But boat fishing is not widely practised in Wales and the situation is worsening as boats have already been taken off a number of Welsh reservoirs.

National competition can attract clubs unused to reservoir fishing with surprising results. In the sixties a man even fished at Usk reservoir who had never caught a fish in his life. He was fishing between two very experienced anglers casting out thirty yards or more, while his own flies splashed in just by his rod tip. Suddenly a fish took hold and his only reaction was to shout 'Help'! But no help is allowed, so he finally put himself into reverse and towed out a two-pound trout. Even then he had no idea how to kill it, but was allowed assistance to do that. Out of 140 anglers he was one of only seven to catch a fish!

On another occasion, I was fishing in a national on the Cefni reservoir on a windless day of blazing sun. With conditions so hopeless, my mates were taking an extended lunch break on the bank behind me and passing comment as I flogged on. I decided on a 'working lunch' myself keeping the rod in my right hand and a porkpie in the left. No sooner was my mouth full than a trout seized the fly. The confusion which followed defied description. But when I finally netted the fish my line was wound twice round my legs and one of my trailing flies was caught in the reeds. No wonder a nearby angler commented to my convulsed friends, 'These beginners have all the luck!'

One aspect of competition everyone takes for granted is the administration. Having organized many matches over the past decade I understand the deep disappointment when anything goes wrong, and the worry when the inevitable problems arise. So often there are two sides to the problem and it really hurts the organizer to have to enforce the rules. That was the case for me in an incident in a Welsh national some years ago. Every angler catching a fish then had to have his card countersigned by a neighbouring fisherman. When I was checking totals, one came in with six fish — easily the best bag of the day. On being asked by me for his card and witnessing signatures he was shocked to realise he had forgotten all about it. All his trout had come in the last half-hour and in his excitement it had slipped his mind. I knew he was a genuine angler, but he still had to be disqualified, though it left me feeling guilty at his bitter disappointment. Sometime later to my delight he won the Welsh championship and we both shared his celebration that night. But it had been a harsh reminder that competitive anglers must take special care to master all the rules and ensure they keep them.

Right up to the seventies the English selection method limited choice, but ensured continuity and experience in their teams. The general policy was to keep a large nucleus of known successful international anglers in the side. But the method of keeping the six best rods from the previous international and adding the six best rods from the English national on Loch Leven, meant a number of new faces in the side.

Even with such a stable selection method it is remarkable that one man should have been good enough to fish for England over a period of forty years. B.C. Hall has that genuinely unique record, unrivalled by anyone else.

B.C. was looking forward to another active fishing season when I went to see him in his favourite Lindum Club at Lincoln in November 1981 on the eve of his 98th birthday. Apart from reminiscence of the internationals, his selections from his 6000 colour transparencies showed him catching fabulous rainbows in New Zealand and Australia. Phoning to wish him a happy birthday on 3 December, shortly after my visit, I asked the hotel manager if I'd left it too late as it was nearly 10.0 p.m. 'Too early you mean. He's out celebrating and unlikely to be back before midnight.'

I could believe it; for when I first saw him two years earlier he was about to take part in a competition against Bob Church's 'professionals' at Rutland. In his peaked cap and immaculate kit Brian Hall (known appropriately as B.C., his initials) was the smartest of all the anglers.

Before his eight hour stint in the boat on a hot day I asked him if he had specially prepared for the event. 'Of course not. I fish this long two or three times a week. And I'll be speaking at the dinner afterwards as usual. It's a good speech too — if you haven't heard it before.'

I asked if age affected his fishing? 'I gave up river fishing abroad when I passed ninety. Clumping round in waders became a bit tiresome and tiring.'

What changes had he seen in his ninety years fishing? 'Lighter rods have made it easier and there has been a great development of nymph fishing for trout. But the main change is in the ecology. Insecticides are killing off the fly life, particularly in intensively farmed counties like my own Lincolnshire. The flies and the fishing decline every year now.'

What are his favoured wet flies? 'I always have an Invicta and I wouldn't be without a Dunkeld and a Greenwell.' On his trips abroad from Canada to Chile he has caught many specimen fish including a 25 lb trout in British Columbia.

B.C. has recorded his memoirs in a privately printed publication entitled *Round the World in Ninety Years*. In that book Hall includes many interesting fishing stories from his world wide experience. An amusing one concerned the early internationals, and a fisherman called Harris, who was a two-bottle man. Until he had consumed enough each day he was all a-tremble. During the morning he could catch trout with more success than any man on the loch. By noon he had finished his first bottle, and thereafter he caught no more. His hands were steady as a rock. The 'Harris Shake' had vanished.

B.C. Hall was first asked to fish in an international by his Lincolnshire friend George Nicholls:

> I was astounded to be asked to represent England. But George got me to fill in the application form to the English International Fly Fishers, and in 1932 I was asked to go as reserve, but couldn't get away from work. Usually you had to fish one match as reserve so that they could have a look at you. Luckily I was included in the team in 1933. My partner was Sir Wilfred Air, and on a sunny day of hard fishing we each caught a brace. That wasn't bad in the conditions, but Ireland won the match for the first time. Next season I was reserve, fishing with a man from Carlisle. We caught eleven trout each, and won the competition for the heaviest boat weight. From then until 1972 I was chosen to fish in all internationals. In the early days

those annual gatherings at the Green Hotel were extremely friendly and enjoyable. The accommodation was all that could be wished, and they were very lively affairs.

Another to make a major contribution to English success was Bill Milne, who still efficiently organizes the English Fly-Fishers as their Secretary. The best winning run in the competition has been England's nine wins in ten years with seven successive victories between 1959 and 1965. For six of those years Bill was their President and captained the team on numerous occasions:

> We were fortunate to have a nucleus of very good fishermen like B.C. Hall, Sidney Taylor, Colonel Ruddy from Penrith, Radley Searle, and Henry Mossop. The first time I fished in an international I was paired with B.C. It was practice then to put a newcomer with an old hand, not just to give him guidance but so that his fishing could be reported on later. You knew you were being scrutinized and that could be upsetting. When one outstanding fly-fishermen, and later a successful captain, was paired with me for his first match he was so nervous he kept changing method or flies every few minutes. His flies were hardly in the water at all. We also had an old boatman with a most disconcerting habit of turning round and sitting facing away from the drift. That was unnerving, too, for a newcomer, and when my partner made a bad cast and flicked off his cap it completed an unhappy day for him. But I had seen enough to know he was really a first-class angler, and once he got his confidence he was an outstanding member of the team. The selection is said to have been narrow, but we had a lot of very good fishermen. Cyril Inwood was one of the most noted anglers of his time, but he could never perform well for us, had trouble holding his place, and was in and out of the side.

Bill recalls the difference in tackle and method when he first fished the Leven matches: 'In those pre-plastic-line days we either used a Hardy Corona Silk Line No 2 or 3, or a similarly numbered Kingfisher line, to which we applied a floatant such as "Mucilin", if we wanted to fish on the top. If we then wanted to go sunk we cleaned off the floatant with detergent and applied a mixture of Fullers Earth and Glycerine.'

Among his many happy memories of matches past were enjoyable days with Arthur Moores, one of the brothers of the successful business family. On one occasion in Ireland the team were taken to see an illicit 'potcheen' still in action and given samples. The rest determined to smuggle theirs through customs, but Arthur got cold feet in mid-crossing and paced the deck at midnight until it was deserted enough for him to pour it overboard. To his annoyance the customs man turned out to be a keen angler who asked about the match, then waved them through without inspection.

Henry Mossop was another who was very much at home fishing in Ireland. His uncle had started cuttings books of his own fishing there as far back as 1890. Henry comments: 'I found things little changed when I was over there. I was even gillied by Tom Malloy, whose grandfather used to take my uncle out on Corrib from Oughterard.' At Lough Conn Henry was able to check a remarkable capture by this uncle. Having confirmed the record in the Pontoon Bridge hotel register, he had a plaque inserted in the side of a large rock at the waterside. Mossop's rock is still a feature of Conn. The inscription reads: 'Near this rock on 23 May 1898 S.S. Mossop Esq hooked and landed a pike weighing 35 lb on trout tackle in $3\frac{1}{2}$ hours assisted by boatmen Michael Clarke and Edward Kenny. Erected 1967 by H.R. Mossop.'

Mossop's rock was the scene of many a party and remains a feature of the lough.

The Irish pike grow to great size and are often attracted to flies. But it is unusual to land so splendid a specimen on such light tackle, even when spinning. But was one double this size really caught on fly in Scotland? The Kenmure pike of 72 lb was at least reliably reported in the *Sporting Magazine* of July 1798 in these terms: 'It was caught in Loch Ken, near the small burg of New Galloway, with nothing more than a common fly made with a peacock's feather.'

The famous quote of that time — 'Bliss was in that dawn to be alive' — referred to the French Revolution, but would have been as apt an expression of the catcher's feelings. But how *could* he land one that size on fly tackle? How many hours did it take him? A pity it is not as fully documented as Mossop's pike from Conn.

To represent international competition as all fun and good fellowship with fine fishing on gently rippled, sunlit waters could be as misleading as a house agent's description of a property he is trying to sell. At times it can call for qualities of endurance, of courage even. In his book *Round the Word in*

Ninety Years B.C. Hall writes of his most unpleasant day on Leven: 'A violent south-east wind was driving the persistent rain sideways, striking us like steel knitting needles. On a day of dead fingers, running noses, wet seats and throbbing ears, we kept fishing thinking only of the team and England. Once in a while one of us would catch a trout, and the boatman would remove the hook with blue fingers like swollen sausages.'

When I first sat on an Industrial Tribunal, my chairman told me that the essentials were to come in with a full pen and an empty bladder. In an eight-hour fishing competition the last is also very important to remember. Whether B.C. had forgotten, or the miserable conditions of cold and wet were too much for the system, the moment came when he had to use the bailer. The layers of sodden clothing were unbuttoned with numb fingers, then done up again. But when he tried to get back in action the flies would not cast out: 'The boatman grasped the line, following it round my back, under my arm, then disappearing through the two middle buttons of my slicker. He pulled and I cried out in pain. So he cut the end of the cast. Now to find a fresh one in my sodden bag and tie the half-blood knot. The first three attempts just pulled out. Finally I managed it after three-quarters of an hour of distilled agony. More than three hours of this gruelling contest were left, and we slogged on. Six o'clock arrived and we crawled out of the boat onto the drenched land. Shivering, and with chattering teeth, we watched the weigh-in. Our efforts were rewarded. England had narrowly beaten Scotland to win the contest.' Stripping for a welcome bath at the Green Hotel, B.C. found his Peter Ross tail fly at last. It was stuck into him, well over the barb, two inches below his navel.

Then there was the day of the great storm at Conn, which left vivid memories for B.C., for Bill Milne, and for all who weathered it. It was 29 September 1962, at a friendly international. Conn then was less well organized for a major event with the volunteer boatmen sometimes difficult to round up. For some competitors the start was delayed with despairing calls over the loud hailer for missing gillies. One in particular was repeatedly summoned with shouts of 'Is Paddy Malone here for boat fourteen?' The final call for him was 'Paddy Malone, if you are not here will you please say so at once.'

Amid the confusion B.C. Hall was not launched until nearly midday. He therefore made the fortunate decision to fish the shallow Claughans bay close to the start point:

As we rowed up against the wind preparatory for the second drift I saw the other end of the lough shadowed by immense black clouds with white capped waves already visible below, and approaching rapidly. The boatman was instructed to row for the shore at once. Then the storm struck. The waves were up to ten-feet high, and when the boat climbed to the top you could look down on the bare rocky bottom of the lough drained of water in the trough between these mountainous waves. Down we would crash on these, nearly splintering the boat. Rowing was a waste of time with the boatman's oars always waving in the air. But finally we were washed ashore on the crest of a huge wave, pulled the boat up as high as we could, collected what tackle was left, and headed for the pub.

Two of us then set out in a car with the gillie as guide, driving down each lane as near as we could to the lough edge. By dark we had collected seventeen bedraggled fishermen. Fires could now be seen round the lough and on islands in its centre. Some were cut off by bogs and streams, some stranded on the islands for a wet, cold night. Robin Hilliard of the Irish team organized a rescue attempt to some islands, but was driven back. At 10.30 p.m. those who had escaped sat down to a miserable meal, with none of the high spirits of the usual international dinner. By morning the gale had blown itself out and the remainder were rounded up after their terrible night, fortunately with no real casualties. One of the English party, John Shaw, had spent the time in a widow's cottage, and some of the Scots in a nunnery. John Shaw later took out flowers and groceries to thank her, and had to endure ribald comment for years to come.

Bill Milne had launched earlier, and had no chance to seek shelter before the gale drove his boat onto an island. For a time he fished from the lee shore, and added a trout to England's total. But John Shaw was his partner, an elderly retired bank manager who was soon suffering badly from the cold. With the storm showing no sign of abating Bill Milne explored down the island. Through the heavy mist of driven spray off the wave tops he finally made out the mainland only some 200 yards distant. At first the boatman declined to try the crossing, but after several hours he, too, became desperate, and the dangerous row was safely made. John Shaw by now was blue with cold and had to be carried to a cottage they saw nearby, where a peat fire revived him. Bill then went in search of help. 'Through the curtain of driven rain, I thought I saw the top of a bus in the distance. I raced towards it and found it real. Henry Mossop had got hold of the bus and was driving round picking up the castaways.'

That must have been a day of equinoctial gales far and wide. For David Biggart recalls that on the very same day a freak storm hit Leven during a competition there and one boat was stranded all night on Castle Island. Even in fly-fishing, competition at the top can be tough in more ways than one.

International fishing remains a mystery to some as Trevor Hirons found on a trip to Ireland for the 1960 'friendly'. Travelling with Gillie Farr, one of the greatest of Welsh fishermen, he broke his journey in Dublin. As they entered the Royal Hibernian Hotel, encumbered with rods, a perceptive Englishman remarked: 'Ah! Anglers. What are you doing here?'

'We've come to fish for Wales,' replied Farr.

'What bait do you use?' was the next question. Gillie pointed to some trout flies in his lapel.

'Don't try to kid me!' rasped the Englishman. 'You can't catch bloody whales on those.'

Peter Keay is one of Scotland's outstanding anglers, who can look back in tranquillity on a lifetime's enjoyment of the sport. He has fished Leven for forty years:

> There is a great difference now with the evening your best chance of catching fish. Some nights you may only have a couple of rises whereas twenty years ago I've had from a dozen to sixty trout in an evening. Once, fishing four flies, I had six trout rise at once, hooking four and landing three.
>
> The internationals were a highlight for me, but my first love was river fishing. I have had to give it up now as the water is too cold, the hills too steep for me. Many of my trout there were taken on fly, but dare I say that clear water worming in bright sun was the most exciting method. When I was nearly six my first trout was taken on worm on a little side-stream of the Almond river. I was hooked too then and I still am 72 years later.

Internationals have a wealth of other fishing experience, but these matches provide many with their most colourful memories of their sporting lives.

CHAPTER 5
THE CAPTAIN'S VIEWS

And to my way o' thinkin'
There's naething for't but drinkin'
When a trout he lies winkin' and lauchin' at me.

W.C. Stewart

Acceptance of that philosophy on practice day was seen by Bob Draper as being vital to England's last win at Loch Leven in 1981. The correspondent for *Trout and Salmon* thought he was having his leg pulled when his earnest enquiry of our captain for his team's victory secret was answered with, 'It was our tactical drinking that won the match.'

The answer was only half in jest. This was England's third successive win both in internationals generally, and at Loch Leven. As captain, Bob always insisted his team came fresh to the match day ready to give concentrated effort for every second of the eight hours of the competition: 'So don't tire yourselves with a hard day's fishing on the eve of the match' was his firm instruction. For this Leven final practice the morning was cloudless and sunny, the wind, and the prospect of fish, both negligible. So his final words put it even more strongly: 'Fish your allotted areas carefully for a couple of hours. Then take it easy for the rest of the day, and come off the water early. All of us fishing anywhere near the pier will meet in the bar there for a *very* long lunch.'

So while others sweltered in the sun catching little, and learning less, the English took their ease, downed their pints, yarned about better days, or discussed the flies to use on the morrow. When conditions are against you, it is difficult to fish the long hours of the competition always with the same keen expectancy that the next cast will bring a fish. You will make over 2000 of them during the match, and your belief must be just as strong after the trout have let 1999 of them pass unnoticed.

You need to be fresh to keep going at full intensity on that sort of day — and if you do you may win your team the match with that two-thousandth cast.

The England captains I have seen in action have all led by example, all been expert fishermen. They have to keep requalifying like anyone else, and it is a measure of their skill that in the first 15 matches after England re-entered international competition, only four captains have been needed: Don Fulcher, Tom Bilson, John Ketley and Bob Draper.

Bob Draper's record of success is indeed remarkable. Despite having to qualify in the Midlands, where the competition is fiercest, he made the England team eleven of the last twelve internationals. When Bob is fishing in a qualifying match other boats drifting by ask anxiously how many he has caught. If they are up with him their hopes of qualifying soar. Bob is always easy to spot, not so much by his jet black hair as by his 11 ft 3 in rod, which will be casting a longer line than anyone else.

The first time I fished with him was on an early season practice for the team at Rutland's press day, when they kindly invite the international team to participate. The only description he could give me of his special ability was that his fishing success was 'like a gardener's with green fingers, a mixture of instinct, and of learning by experience'. Some have the knack, some don't. All can improve by practice, but practice alone will not make perfect at fishing. You need the 'instinct' as well. Bob clearly has that special feeling of where and how to fish at any given time.

There is technique as well. His long casting gives him the edge on most waters, except Irish loughs, and on most days except when the short-lining method is at its best on windy days. The advantage he sees is 'if I see a fish move far from the boat I can still cover it instantly.'

There seem added gains, however, in the length of time Bob's flies are in the water. He false casts very little before shooting out that great length of line, and must on average 'fish' longer than most in an eight-hour day. Again the favoured position in a boat is the bow, since this usually drifts slanting a little ahead of the stern angler. As a result the bow-rod's flies are normally seen first by any wandering fish keenly on the look-out for food. With Bob's casting, even from the stern, his flies are likely to land further out, and be seen first. Such long casting inevitably pulls the rod far down on the forward throw. The supreme testimony to his expertise came in the alteration to the international rules which can only have been made because he was thought too successful. The current rule forbids lowering the rod beyond the horizontal, a quite unnecessary further restriction designed to limit the long caster, and as difficult to 'monitor' as the rule on speed of draw.

Bob was bred a fisherman. His father, Perce, is also a noted Midlands angler, and brought him up to catch trout in the well-stocked reservoirs of Pitsford, Ravensthorpe, and Grafham. Perce Draper fished with his son in two internationals in 1976, when nearly seventy. It made me feel younger when I fished the Leven 1981 international on my sixtieth birthday to have seen Perce accompanying the team, and outscoring most of us in the practice days.

Bob Draper's surplus of skill — or instinct — which rises above any twists of fortune was well illustrated at the start of that year. He had qualified by winning the national at Draycote the previous September with pounds to spare. In his first match as captain he then won the Draycote international for his side with his team's biggest bag — twelve trout for 11 lb $10\frac{1}{2}$ oz. For the third time he was therefore doubly qualified for the next international, by coming first on both those occasions. He is apt to suggest that ought to give him three 'free' places at some future date! I was merely grateful that his double qualification allowed me to slip into the last place in our Leven team.

Bob Draper's approach to the competitions is typically forthright:

> There are two types of competitive angler. One goes all out to win or qualify as his first priority. The other goes for the fun of it, with good performance a bonus on the side. I'm in the first category. If you compete, and particularly if you are part of a team, you should always do your best. If you are confident in outlook, purposeful in method, and fish hard throughout the eight hours that is half the battle. Since there is always some luck in fishing a few 'drifters', even the occasional 'no-hoper', may get through to a final. But it is very rare to find an international who is not an able fisherman and properly competitive in outlook.
>
> The main problem in international fishing is to adjust yourself to a wide variety of waters. You may qualify on an English reservoir with well-defined catching areas and

drifts. Then you find yourself representing your country on a vast Irish lough with little knowledge of such fishing. Until you have built up the experience of all competition waters you need to follow simple rules.

In the Irish loughs you need in the main to look for trout close to rocks, or the shore, or in shallows. You either have to put implicit trust in your boatman, or ensure that you drift to likely looking islands, or round rocks. If you are drifting in deep water with no sign of activity, ask to be taken to shallower areas. That is even more important at Trawsfynydd. In some ways that Welsh lake is like English reservoirs. But if you are not fishing near the bank, or in very shallow water, your chances are slim indeed. That is particularly the case when it is known to have been stocked for an international, and the bait-anglers on the bank have ground baited heavily to attract the fish close in.

In the English reservoirs it is essential to know how fish circulate after stocking, and what their likely distribution is. It is a fair bet that they will have been reasonably stocked before an international. So a crucial decision is whether to aim at catching smaller stock fish, or the quality ones which may be harder to lure. That may well depend on weather conditions. If it is a good fishing day, you do best to go after a heavy weight of good fish. If it is bright, and windless, then your main hope is uneducated stock trout and you need to plan accordingly.

Never change for the sake of change, and keep your flies in the water as long as possible. But be alert for any alteration in the feeding pattern of the fish. I prefer using a floating line and that is the first thought there should be in your mind. But don't let it be a fixation, if you want to be a consistent catcher of fish. On the same day, the trout are likely to be feeding near the surface at times, down deeper at others. You have to try and assess which is the depth of the moment, and use the sinker whenever necessary. In one of my most profitable international days I started to fish Leven with a sinker and did well on it in the morning. But by the final hours of the competition the fish were moving closer to the surface and I caught a lot at the end, having reverted to a floater.

Some years back Leven was the best competition water of them all, and its brown trout are a joy to catch, unrivalled for quality. But hooking them has become something of a lottery of late. The disappointing way in which it fishes means you have often to consider using a sunk line. Indeed, with traditional methods not appearing to work there any more, at least by day, you have to experiment to keep hope alive.

Some purists frown on the sunken line method. That is mere affectation. If it is the method you find effective, you should use it. Those who speak slightingly of it are often the ones who can't throw a long line, don't know how to work the flies well when sunk, and so don't command any success when using the technique. Anyone calling himself an expert fly-fisher ought to have mastered all types of sinking line as well as floaters. Making the right choice of which to use is part of your skill as a fisherman.

The captain in my other international was John Ketley, another effective angler. Living in Dulwich and working as a partner in a large advertising agency his main fishing lake is Chew Valley:

> I always think one of the fundamental pleasures of our sport is the diversity of hard-held opinions among its practitioners. Two friends can be fishing side by side in two very different styles, each convinced the other has it all wrong. For this reason I seldom mention my interest in competitive fly-fishing as it tends to polarize people even more sharply than nymphs on a classic dry-fly water. Nevertheless, I am still surprised that so many are unaware there is a contest between England, Ireland, Scotland and Wales twice each year. To many, fly-fishing epitomizes a period of contented solitude, stalking some ancient and wily brownie in a sleepy chalk stream. I, for one, love that side of our sport, but it is only one side.
>
> If you have ever fished our rumbustious public reservoirs like Rutland or Chew Valley, then you may have experienced the other end of the spectrum. But even that is some way from the concept of a competition, as by definition this makes it important who catches the greatest weight of fish. Happily, I can promise you that who wins such a contest is of secondary importance. There are two non-competitive fishing days prior to the competition, where everything possible is done to encourage the anglers to mix and enjoy each other's company and very successful

it is, too. The rules also put a particular accent on behaving in a considerate and gentlemanly manner. Their purpose is to ensure that the best traditions of loch-style boat fishing are the criteria by which we compete.

Any readers who have fished the competition waters will realize the international takes place during the more unproductive hours, as it misses both the morning and evening 'rise' times. This explains why the numbers of fish killed in these events is often quite small, considering the effort put in. Any team with an average of two-fish per man on a brown-trout-only lake has a great chance of being the top team of the match.

Having fished in about a dozen internationals, and had the honour to captain the English team for three years, I have witnessed many special moments, some amusing, some sad, but all rather charming. The prime factor in creating these special moments, surprisingly for such a normally gentle sport, is the tension created by the occasion. While all of us go fishing to catch fish, we normally have an inexhaustible supply of 'reasons' why we didn't really want to catch lots of fish that particular outing, most of which we believe ourselves by the time we reach the pub. There are no excuses in an international. If you have an off-day you feel you have really let your team down.

With such a prospect facing every international angler, it is hardly surprising there is a certain air of tension noticeable in the hotel breakfast-room on the Big Day. It is at this time that the captain gives each member of the English team a red rose for his hat. On my first stint as captain, passing from table to table, I noticed twelve untouched eggs and bacon glaring up at twelve white and pinched faces as my gallant lads gave me a strained smile of thanks. On arrival at the water, as we tackled up, I suddenly noticed the majority of the team crouching in various positions of agony behind a bush as the anxiety of the moment fetched up even the odd slice of toast they had forced down at breakfast.

The tension is exacerbated by the publicity given to the international. Everyone sees exactly what you have caught, to the last half an ounce, but no one mentions the monsters the boatmen did not manage to net after you held them splashing on the surface for what seemed minutes. Every fish killed is carefully measured and weighed, then your personal total is chalked up beside your name — unless you have the ultimate horror, when a simple dash is put in place of the weight. That little mark stands out from all the pounds and ounces, highlighting your shame for all the Angling Press to faithfully record, and for the TV cameras to pan across as they zoom in on the winning basket. The prospect of such personal and public degradation is enough to make the strongest of characters as nervous as any virgin on her wedding night. Unlike the virgin, though, this daunting prospect doesn't seem to go away once you have done it. Even if you succeed in qualifying for the next international the pressure is, if anything, worse the next time.

My friend Bob Draper is perhaps the most classic example of this ongoing pressure as he is without doubt one of the most consistently successful anglers on the international circuit. Yet Bob, above all my team members, was the most wound up and he has fished in over a dozen internationals. It has taken many years of gentle persuasion to get him to take over my role as captain of the team as he seemed to feel the dual responsibility would be unbearable. Happily, he finally agreed to be captain and started with two very successful internationals.

Despite all this, allow me to recommend competitive fly-fishing to any of you who feel the desire to put your fishing talents on the line. The awful days will be awful, but the great moments will remain golden memories for the rest of your life and you will, I promise you, meet some of the nicest people in the world. As a bonus, your fishing will be sharpened up, you will fish waters you probably would not have visited on your own, and you will learn more about fishing in the three days an international lasts than in all the preceding season. But, be warned, should you qualify for a national and then qualify for one of the teams, you will almost certainly be caught by the competitive bug.

John Ketley has the distinction of having made the heaviest individual catch ever recorded in internationals with the method he describes:

In most sports, tactics play a part and, on occasion, they have helped me get rather more than my share of the fish caught in an international.

During the practice days at Trawsfynydd in 1978 the organizers of the international asked all boats to keep out of a particular area until the day of the match. On the day, I asked all the English team to stay in this area as long as they could, assuming the weather was suitable and we were catching some fish. As it turned out, only three boats remained there for the whole day and they were the three top boats of the international. I was most fortunate to catch nearly 21 lb of fish.

It was a wild and wet day and practically every fish came in the wildest and wettest part of the drift, right on the shore line. Once I had a four-pound plus fish on the top dropper and simultaneously one over three on the point; all in two feet of water.

My Irish boat partner showed great sportsmanship by picking up two landing nets and boating both fish, while our thirteen-year-old boatman struggled manfully with the boat as it beached itself among the weeds.

In really rough conditions, and such shallow water, there is nothing like a small muddler on the point for big rainbows. It also helps keep the other flies off the bottom.

On the top dropper I fished a Blackie (a local fly that is similar to a Red Tag) and as this broke through the crashing waves, the rainbows rushed through the shallows, back fin out of the water in their eagerness to help me win the coveted Brown Bowl.

In the days of the English International Fly-Fishers there were many outstanding anglers, like the Secretary, Sidney Taylor, or one of the later captains, Radley Searle. But there are two captains, B.C. Hall and Bill Milne, who epitomize their success.

For fishing Leven or other waters, B.C. Hall put his trust mainly in a floating line. 'It is how you present the fly that matters. The harder a water is fished, the smaller your flies should be. They want to be lightly tied, too, and preferably hackle only. In my view trout like to see through a fly, not to register it as a muddy blob near the surface. So I don't like wings on my flies or to have a heavy dressing of hackle.'

Short-lining and the art of working the dropper were also important for Bill Milne, as was the use of a long rod to help bob the fly on the surface, and work it close in to the boat: 'The points continually stressed in our team meetings were to keep your flies in the water for as much of the eight hours as possible, and to keep fishing hard to the last minute. I used to fish fairly fine at Leven — 2x gut casts. These were usually about 10 ft long. We mainly fished 16 or 18 doubles, but went to larger flies when we wanted to work them a little deeper.'

The natural link to captains of a later period is Tom Bilson. He is himself a member of the English Fly-Fishers, captained England in 1977, and has been team manager from 1979. His quiet, benign influence on English fly-fishing has been further extended through his past chairmanship of the powerful Midlands Federation of Fly-Fishers (Anglia), and of the Mid-Northants Trout Fishers' Association. This latter club of over 200 members is one of the oldest in the Midlands, and was formed by some of the great names of trout-fishing there — such as Tom Ivens, Cyril Inwood, Charlie Dickens, Colonel Miller, John Rowe and Billy Bell.

Tom's own method was taught him by one of them:

> My own casting length is about fifteen yards, and is modelled on the style of the greatest drift fisherman of all time, Cyril Inwood. I fished with him a lot, both in internationals and for pleasure, and this is the distance he taught me was the optimum casting length. Cyril would always ignore rising trout at more than this distance saying they would move towards the boat and needn't be chased. There is no false casting involved, just one throw forward, then three or four short pulls, then let the rod work the flies skipping over the water right up to the boat. Short-lining is the caviare of trout fishing, something to be relished. The top dropper is the most important fly and you should try to make sure it always leaves the slightest of wakes as you retrieve the flies slowly towards you. Some prefer 11 ft rods, but I have always found 9 ft 3 in is quite long enough. It seems established now for many that white lines cause flash, while some think ice-blue is the ideal colour for them. Personally I play safe, not using white or orange, and putting my trust in mahogany-coloured lines. At least I feel happy with them, and that is the main thing as with your choice of flies. The double taper No 7 mahogany-coloured line gives me that essential confidence.
>
> There are arguments about standing up in boats, but I can't imagine why anyone should want to. Cyril Inwood

would often crouch down with only his head showing and flick his flies out from there. He thought it important to be as inconspicuous as possible, insisting also on drab clothing, and not permitting you to fish with him in a white shirt or sweater. As he caught many thousands of trout with his loch-style fishing I have no doubt he was right in his views, and have followed them successfully myself.

The most important quality of all for the fisherman is that instinct which no textbook can teach, and only the gifted few have in exceptional measure. One such was Evan Owen, the captain who never was. As Moc Morgan recalls he broke every rule of good fishing:

> Evan was the most remarkable fly-fishing competitor it's been my privilege to meet. He was a collier, who lived for his fishing. His tackle was a disgrace, fit only for the junk-yard. Yet in Evan's hard, blue-stained hand that tackle regularly took fish when the rest of us were struggling. He couldn't cast much over ten yards and his flies and his theories were both absurd by normal angling standards. Yet he just went on catching fish when others failed. It is Evan Owen who has the second heaviest individual basket ever caught by a Welshman in an international with his 18 lb 15 oz on Leven in 1968.
> For many years Evan fished with distinction in the Welsh team. He seemed devoid of all the qualities expected of an efficient angler — except the crucial one of catching fish. Evan's outstanding service to the national team was finally rewarded by appointment as captain. For him that was an honour valued above all else, a life's ambition achieved. Yet a cruel fate snatched the prize from him, scything him down before he could enjoy that proudest moment of all — leading a Welsh team in an international.

CHAPTER 6

WINNING WAYS

> Fish (fly-replete in depth of June
> Dawdling away their watery noon)
> Ponder deep wisdom dark or clear
> Each secret fishy hope or fear.
>
>   Rupert Brooke

How can you tempt them in the bright days of summer? How give yourself the best winning chance in competition? What are the methods of those who win the Brown Bowl or keep qualifying for international teams? When Brian Peterson was the winner in my first international at Chew with over 17 lb of trout one of our team asked: 'Is he good, or just lucky?' That was answered immediately by the angler who had been his boatman in practice: 'I wasn't surprised to see him win the Brown Bowl. He had that quality of alertness which marks the good fisherman. Even if a fish rose outside his line of vision he would sense it, and cover it immediately. He was always on the watch, had a reason if he changed flies or methods, and was aware of the birds, in case they led him to rising fish.'

With that recommendation, it was worth finding out how Brian planned his competitive fishing:

> My approach to fishing a local club competition is quite straightforward. As I know most of the usual 'hot spots', the flies to use, and the best method, my only preparation is to try and visit the water a day or two before the match to see the level, note the fly-life, if any, and get the latest information.
>
> A major match on the other hand requires much more thought. International, national, and other big contests are very competitive. My preparation for fishing in an international starts at the end of the year, soon after I am notified

of the date and venue. At once I start to sift through all the books and magazines trying to build up a dossier on the water concerned. If I am lucky enough to know a fellow angler who resides in the area, I keep in contact to gain up-to-date local knowledge on how it is fishing.

The couple of days prior to the competition are official practice days. It is during these that I put into operation all I have heard or read, experimenting and evaluating. At the end of the day we pool our information and work out a plan, and it's important to make your full contribution to the team's knowledge. Sometimes the plan works well, sometimes it doesn't. But in the long run you only get consistently good results if you take trouble.

I very rarely let myself drift away from my own style of fishing, which is the traditional loch method with floating line and small flies. I feel it is bad practice for an angler to alter his own basic technique, especially at a time of pressure and when the end result is vital. Once or twice I have used a slow sinker when the evidence suggests it. Just once I used a fast sinker. That was at Leven when most of the fish caught in practice were being caught by this means. One thing I never forget is that I am fishing as part of a team, not for myself. So when the need dictates, I will alter, but only when it is essential.

I seldom vary my choice of flies; I believe in using the patterns in which I have most faith. I tie all my own, and have one rule of my own. I always tie up a variant, which includes as many as possible of the local killing colours. If all else fails, I tie this onto my cast. On several occasions it has landed trout, and the prize. It is embarrassing, however, when one of these flies does well, and angling correspondents ask its name. For my name for the variant is itself a variant of the word 'illegitimate.'

The only other policy I have is to remain calm and relaxed before, and during, the competition. There is nothing worse than getting worked up, and worried. It destroys your rhythm, it ruins your planning, and upsets the pleasure of your fishing. Sometimes it just isn't possible to stay cool, but you still have to do the best you can.

One who must have found it hard to stay cool was Brian's boat partner at Chew. While Brian hauled in the trout, his English rival had a blank. As he commented:

'At first I hardly had time to fish in case I cast across one he was playing. The more he caught, the more anxious I became. Nothing would go right for me, while it seemed he couldn't go wrong. When he hooked a two-pounder on the dropper, one of four pounds or so promptly seized his tail fly. That was his first bit of bad luck as it happened. The two large fish tore off line so fast his finger was burned and the biggest finally straightened the hook and departed. But he caught the other all right. When I did hook one myself it promptly got off, probably because I was overanxious to catch it.'

Trevor Hirons has a long history of successful fishing for Wales. What have been the most interesting lessons for him from his internationals?

On Lough Conn in 1963 I was missing a lot of fish when the old Irish boatman told me I was fishing the bob fly wrong. He said that the point of the hook should be facing outwards to give the best chance of catching the fish. I took his advice and don't lose so many now.

When you are taking trout on a good drift, play your fish as quickly as reasonable to the back of the boat. This lets your partner fish on unhindered. Don't advertise you are into a fish. Keep sitting down until it is ready to net. Otherwise you will soon have company!

Always give your boat partner every consideration, even if he is your 'rival' on the day. Don't stand up in the boat or do anything similar which many put him off. Remember he can cast your side if you are not fishing, so let him know when you are about to start again after changing a line or a fly.

Vic Williams is one of the most experienced of Welsh internationals, an 'old-timer' as he calls himself. Commenting that older anglers like himself are apt to get set in their ways, his advice to the young is never to be dogmatic about anything in fly-fishing: 'You can keep learning and improving if you remain alert. Observe, act, memorize are the three golden rules for making the most of your own experience. Like successful performers in other sports, you should be able always to do the simple things perfectly, and at the right time.'

Time was when the divide between bait-fishermen and fly-fishermen was so deep that they hardly recognized each other as being the same kind of sportsman. A couple of sentences from Andre Maurois *The Silences of Colonel Bramble* aptly illustrate the then distance between them:

> 'Bombing open towns is as unpardonable as fishing for trout with a worm.'
> 'You must not exaggerate, Parker,' said the Colonel calmly. 'They are not as bad as that yet.'

Now each can appreciate the skill of the other and many share a common interest, and practise both types of fishing. Fly-fishermen will not wish their own competitions to become as highly commercialized as match angling with its big sponsorship, its large prizes, and its league structure. They have to recognize, however, that it has led to the top match anglers developing an expertise and technical skill in advance of the majority of fly-fishermen. Have they anything to teach us about competitive fishing? I certainly thought so as I watched Dave Thomas come top on two successive days of the World Freshwater championships with twenty countries participating. England was runner-up in the team championship which they have never won in the twenty-five years of its existence. But Dave's catch beat all other ninety-nine competitors that day, qualifying him to fish with thirty-nine others in the individual championship, which he then won to confirm his skill. That made him *The Observer* sporting personality of the week, and gave me some insight into his 'champion' qualities. It was only the second time the world competition had been fished in England, with the Avon at Luddington the venue which drew nearly 20,000 spectators. That was good fortune for Dave, but no other member of the England team of five made home advantage count. This was Dave's view of it:

> I had some preparation for the experience as I had considerable success a fortnight before in the Courage-Ladbroke bank-holiday weekend competitions which attracted crowds up to 10,000. As I won the main individual event, and came second in the other two, I had a large following behind me. But it was nothing compared to the atmosphere, and pressure of the world championship. That really made me nervous at the start when I lost two good chub, and the sigh of the crowd deepened my own disappointment.

> One loss was particularly galling. The crowd alerted me to a branch floating towards my line and I evaded it skilfully enough by pushing the tip of my rod under water so that it passed over without tangling. Then for no reason the hook came out just as I was ready to net the chub. As an experienced match angler you learn not to let such mishaps disturb the rhythm of your fishing or your intense concentration. Once I started catching regularly the cheers of the crowd doubled the pleasure.

What makes a champion angler in Thomas' experience?

> Attention to small details is very important. There are perhaps fifteen items that need to be just right, the type of float, the hook size, and so on. Get one shot out of place and it may be the difference on hard-fished match waters between a blank and 10 lb of fish.
> Equally important is instinct. There are perhaps a hundred options in the way you fish — at what depth, with what bait, in what area — and you need the instinct to choose right. I am never totally wedded to a preconceived plan. Fish react differently on different days and at different times on the same day. You may start catching them one way, then they dry up on you. To be a winner you have to get the right "feel" at the start and choose right when you have to change method.

A much closer relationship between coarse and fly fishermen has led to less unthinking disdain on one side, less reserve on the other. Some may still scorn the others' methods, with artificial fly one of the specifically banned baits for world championships; but we can still share the fellowship of angling and learn from each other's winning ways.

Dave's namesake Brian Thomas is a friend of his and an experienced English international fly-fisherman. That is Brian's first love, but he is equally at home hunting 'coarse' fish, and has represented the City of Nottingham in a match. As he puts it:

> This allows me to fish the year round if I want to, with only two or three days when the close seasons in the waters around me don't overlap for the two different branches of the sport. As with match angling, competitive fly-fishing improves your ability and makes you fish your best. To do

well you have to prepare well. The first need is to take the right selection of flies, and be ready to tie up new ones. Standard patterns do well enough on most competition waters, except the Irish. But you do need to be aware of variants, and prepared to tie them up for the day.

The obvious examples of this are the success of the yellow-tailed Greenwell at Leven or of variants of the Dunkeld. On English waters a variant of the Grenadier is often very effective. I used to rely mainly on the Soldier Palmer, which is always a useful fly on the bob. After being introduced to the Grenadier at Chew it was not long before I found a variant caught many more fish for me. The standard fly had an orange-red body with long hackle at the front. We tied up some Palmer fashion instead, and they proved very productive at Rutland as well as Chew. Indeed last season this variant Grenadier even outscored my favourite Soldier Palmer at Rutland. An adequate range of flies for all seasons are these two plus the Wickhams (winged and wingless), Invictas (standard and silver), Mallard and Claret, and the Bibio.

For Irish waters, however, you are wise to take local advice as the bright coloured flies popular elsewhere rarely seem to work there. The Connemara Black and the Black Pennell are more likely to be effective unless it is the mayfly season. In one international there I did see success for a fly with a bright yellow body. Len Wheddon caught a lot of big browns with this in practice at Conn, and I tied up a number for various members of our team. It was certainly effective as we were only a few ounces off winning the match, coming a very close second to the Irish. In practice I had moved very little, but with this fly I had top weight of the English team, and it was the most effective on my cast. However, it was a Connemara Black which caught the winning basket, and that is undoubtedly one of the best flies for Ireland.

Before my son John fished his first national at Grafham I arranged for him to have a day there, a week or so in advance, with Clive Greenaway, a much more successful international than myself, and very knowledgeable on that water. What did John learn? 'The most important was the concept of working the fly right up to the side of the boat even if you cast long, because a number of fish followed and took at the last moment. After a long draw it is particularly difficult to strike home so close in. Clive showed me how to do it, by thrusting the rod straight up with one hand, and pulling down the line with the other. There is then difficulty in maintaining contact at the start, if the fish doesn't run, but this type of strike should set the hook so well it doesn't matter. Then there was a useful tip about the playing of big fish. It is better to tire them out playing deep, and only bring them up to the net when ready. If you bring them in too early, they are apt to thrash on the surface and throw the hook.' Sadly that didn't work for him on the day, but it was the right advice for playing the large ones.

Perhaps the best and most successful fisherman in Southern-Region competitions is David Porter, winner of the English national in 1979. His favourite flies are Black Pennell and one not often used in competition — Watson's Fancy: 'This was deadly fishing in Kenya and I've found it very effective in home waters. My own tying is with a black wing, a black-and-red body, black hackle, a golden pheasant tail and those important junglecock cheeks, which give it a hint of the Dunkeld.'

When he won the national at Grafham, David was fortunate only in the conditions, with a big wave on the water to suit his favoured method.

> When it's windy I fish a slow sinker rather than a floater, which tends to make the flies skip unnaturally across the trough between the waves. I don't cast very long, and draw in quickly enough to keep the flies working only a few inches below the surface. On a day like this I am always expectant, and find it easier to observe the essential rule of keeping your flies in the water for as much of the eight hours as possible.
>
> I never eat or drink, except when motoring back for another drift, and that's when I try also to make any necessary change of line, cast, or flies. For the same reason of avoiding any waste of fishing time I never false cast.
>
> I also try to make maximum use of each cast by quartering the water, rather than just casting straight ahead to the area covered by the previous cast. It is usually the diagonal casts to right or left which prove the killers. The flies fish better across the wave, and on the angle are visible to a wider range of fish during the draw than is the case with the simple straight-ahead cast.

David Porter classes himself as typical of most fly-fishermen, who by preference enjoy the solitude of the river bank, or the relaxed companionship of a friend in a boat:

> But I enjoy competition as a change. It makes you think more about your fishing, and improves your skill. You also meet a number of very good anglers from whom you learn new techniques, or who stimulate you to review your methods. I've been particularly impressed by the best of the West Country fishermen, the Chew experts. They seem in any conditions to be in a class of their own for reservoir fishing. It didn't surprise me when, even on Rutland, five of them took the leading places in the 1981 national. Fishing with someone like David Lovelace, who came second then to Chris Ogborne, has been a revelation to me, especially in the catching of fish in calm conditions. As often as not these experts go down to tiny nymphs, perhaps with only one on the cast, and twitch it along slowly, tightening firmly the moment they see the line move away or off sideways. They are very skilled, too, in deciding the depth at which fish are feeding in these conditions, and adjusting to this by shortening or lengthening their cast so that the nymph is either just subsurface or several feet down. They thrive on windless days, while without some breeze I tend to lose all confidence and concentration. The highest skill of all is to catch fish in apparently hopeless conditions, and I have a lot to learn from them.

David Mussell, though fishing as England reserve, had the heaviest bag of the international at Draycote with eighteen fish weighing $15\frac{3}{4}$ lb. As when Adrian Ashness, also fishing as reserve, won the Brown Bowl at Trawsfynydd in 1980, Draper was the leading scorer in the official English team. David's Draycote win was in his eyes a simple matter of building on success:

> At Draycote it was a question of getting first in the queue chasing large numbers of highly unsophisticated stock fish, having a first-class boatman who knew the water and worked unremittingly, and, as usual, having some luck. As far as choice of fly was concerned I started with a Soldier Palmer, a black creation of my own, a Dunkeld, and a Red Tag. When the Soldier Palmer caught the first two fish, I attached another one, and then another

so that the Dunkeld was the only other fly to remain for reason unknown, and without effect. The Soldier Palmers took all eighteen. Logically the point is simply this — if a fly catches fish and you can use more than one fly on the cast you multiply up for maximum return. Most of us, after all, have used a team of buzzers on occasion, and in competition the name of the game is quantity rather than quality, industry rather than art.

Somewhat diffidently, if the likes of Bob Draper, Tom Bilson, and Adrian Ashness are contributing, I can add some practical points I have found valuable in competition, and most of them in ordinary angling as well. *Do* listen to the locals, but *don't* be afraid to come to a contrary decision. *Concentrate* throughout the eight hours. Most of us tend to fish relaxed, and with mind wandering. In competition a high degree of intense concentration is essential, and that is absolutely untypical for most of us on ordinary fishing days. Keeping an eye open for moving fish in casting range is vital, and it is wise to enlist the boatman's help in this. They are all skilled anglers themselves and enjoy assisting in the look-out for rising fish.

This 'seeing' fish is a skill you need to cultivate. The difference it can make was driven home to me when I acted as boatman at Chew to a very good angler, the Irishman John Byrne, and an outstanding one, the Scot, Bob Veitch. Bob 'saw' more fish than John or myself. As a result he also had more rises to his own flies, coming out with a fine bag of fish. He also habitually struck parallel with the water, striking to the seen rise, rather than to any felt pull. This way he missed fewer fish.

There are a small number of anglers, among whom unfortunately I am *not* numbered, who seem to have a telepathic understanding of the movement of trout. Some obvious examples are Bob Draper, Brian Peterson, Christy Deacy and Bob Veitch. They seem to have the ability to detect infinitesimal changes in the behaviour of the flies or the look of the water around them, and to read into this some fishy activity which most of us would miss. They react immediately when others would either see nothing at all or react too late. Whether this stems from the intensity of their concentration I know not, but I do know that perhaps one day in twenty I note, and feel, things which I do not on the other nineteen. Draycote fortunately was one of those twentieth days, and became a day in a million for me.

You need also to take misfortune in your stride. My worst moment came after hooking a good fish when Brian Peterson was my boat partner. The trout headed for him, and quick and generous though he was in taking his line instantly off the water, the confusion as I tried to avoid him, and he tried to avoid me, ended with a broken cast. As I was disconsolately repairing the damage Brian promptly caught one under my nose!

In such times you have to retain your sense of humour, and in internationals there is usually a comment or two to cheer you on your way. With the boat bouncing up and down on a typical Irish 'nice wave', lifting the anglers off the seat on the up, and smacking them into it on the down into the troughs, Willie Patrick of Scotland observed, 'This is awfu' haird on the airse.' On another match day my boatman, who had been known to take a drink or two, commented 'I'm on the dry today — I had two bottles of Bushmills yesterday, and the break will give me a taste for it in the evening again.' I also on another occasion heard an English angler enquire of Moc Morgan: 'What does Llyn Trawsfynydd mean? The lake of the tailless trout?' I had better not repeat Moc's answer.

Since England's return to international competition no one, except Bob Draper, has qualified more frequently than Stan Wood, who fished in seven internationals between 1975 and 1982. This has been his method of success:

> You have to have sound basic technique and the ability to adapt to any condition and to use any method from long-lining to the dabble near the boat, from fast sinker to floater. That means fishing tangle-free in any weather up to a howling gale, and adapting not only to the method water conditions dictate, but to what your boat partner is doing. If he is long-lining it may be unproductive fishing close to the boat, when he has covered most of the fish first, putting down or catching some which might otherwise have been yours.
>
> I usually fish with a cast four-feet longer than the rod. To help the line slide easily through the top ring, I use a needle-knot to tie eighteen inches of 14 lb nylon to my

weight-forward line, carrying on with 8 lb to the first dropper, and 5 or 6 lb thereafter. I always have a couple of casts tied up complete with flies, and immediately replace any which gets in a serious tangle. I never change a fly unless there is a good reason, as it is flies in the water that catch fish. Above all I try and pick up, and store in my mind, any local snippets of information, however insignificant they appear.

A good example of the value of such information occurred in my second international at Sheelin. On practice day I overheard a chance remark of 'watch for the sea-gulls'. I still can't see how the trout should relate to sea-gulls, but when I noticed a large flock in the corner of a bay as we were motoring up I insisted on fishing there. The boatman did not want to stop, but it was my period in charge and I decided on a drift. And there the trout were, rising all over the place. We fished there all day, and I had five beautiful brown trout weighing $7\frac{3}{4}$ lb. They won me the Grafham Trophy, and nearly the Brown Bowl as well.

Your boatman can of course be of great help to you, though you have to take final decisions yourself, and one quality of the outstandingly successful anglers, like Bob Draper, seems to be an ability to sense where the trout are. In a national at Draycote I had a remarkable experience with my gillie for the day. I was playing a small rainbow, which took fright when the boatman put the net in the water and darted round the end of the boat. An exclamation from the boatman made me look round and there he was with a fish of about a pound in the net. He answered my query with, 'I saw it swimming past, thought it was on your line, and netted it.' A pity it couldn't count!

Location of fish is vital to success. In English competition waters the wandering rainbows outnumber the more static browns. Following the normal trail of stocked fish is one way to find them. Another is deduction from water temperature as international John Snelson has found:

> Rainbows' best feeding temperatures are 58–62°F, and if the wind is blowing steadily this only applies in parts of the lake in early season. If the wind is cold, the rainbows will be at the top where the wind first strikes before it has chilled the surface. If the breeze warms up, then they may

move quickly downwind, affected by a matter of a 2° change in temperature.

May to June can be a difficult time for location as water temperature near the surface may be the same all over. But you still have pointers to the best places. If a warm south wind blows, the trout may soon be found over by the north bank. That was the case for the May international at Draycote. The south wind blew over to the Toft area, and that was where the concentrations of feeding fish were.

If you are unfortunate enough to get a really hot spell, the fish go back to the top of the wind where the cool water lifts up from deeper down. There you are likely to get a gathering of trout, mostly close to the bank.

On practice days you should pool information on the depth and times the fish are on the feed. With temperature added in you can have the winning knowledge to ensure you drift over the highest density of trout when they are on the move, and that your flies are at the level where they are feeding.

Moc Morgan, the Welsh Secretary, has been involved with national and international competition for over twenty-five years. He has seen how important temperament is for the competitive game angler. Some are stimulated by the challenge of competition to develop from good anglers into outstanding performers. Others, excellent in normal conditions, fail miserably under match pressures. In his view, they are the ones who too easily let themselves be thrown by some early mishap, and who cannot accept the advice to fish normally and stay calm. In competitive fishing you need a team of people who grit their teeth if things go wrong, and let nothing interfere with their concentration. In fishing, as in most sports, the great competitors achieve the impossible balance between being tense and being relaxed. Throughout the eight hours they are intent, but never taut.

This is what Moc wrote for *Trout Fisherman* on the making of such winners:

> A competitive angler is a man apart. He thrives on opposition and the better it is, the better he performs. Angling's Steve Ovetts, though not so flamboyant, are just as dedicated and just as fired with the determination to win.

What makes the good competitive angler? One of the most prolific winners of contests over in Ireland is Mike Tolan. Could it be his local knowledge which brings him his many successes?

Eric Campbell of Scotland always does well on that most testing of fisheries, Loch Leven. Could his particular secret be his direct manner and unflagging concentration?

Gwynfor Jones of Wales can always be relied on to come out in the top handful in any competition. Is it his excellent temperament which pushes him on to win?

Bob Draper has served the England team equally well. Is it Bob's long casting, and confidence in his own ability which makes him a most dangerous rival? Somewhere in all of them is that single quality which drives them on to the top. Not all of us have the guts to work hard enough at winning.

No wonder Moc Morgan rates Eric Campbell as Scotland's best. The record confirms it, as Eric has represented his country fifteen times. Only Alastair Nicoll has fished more often for Scotland, but a number of his caps were awarded ex officio in his capacity as the Scottish National Secretary as well as the International Secretary. Eric Campbell has always had to qualify and the one other person to have done that fifteen times is Harry Wilson. Both are regarded by visiting teams as expert anglers and entertaining companions, and by the Scots as couthy characters. Eric's competition career began just over a quarter of a century ago when he was aged 21. By 1982 he had fished in 304 club competitions and won 97 of them! Fishing for two clubs, C.I.S.W.O. and Tullibole, he competes in about a dozen club competitions each year. These are not for prizes, but for points which tot up over the season to provide a champion to represent the club in the Scottish national. On twenty-eight occasions he has been a club champion, and he has won both the Scottish national and the Loch Leven Championship. These have been Scotland's two major championships outranking even the *Daily Record* champion of champions contest, which doesn't as yet appeal to some top clubs as the rules allow too much latitude in method of fishing.

As an international Eric's *annus mirabilis* was undoubtedly 1977. In his first match as Scotland's team manager, his country won at Grafham and he himself won the coveted Brown Bowl. In the other international that year at Leven he also had

Scotland's best basket winning the Phoenix Salver twice in a season, the only time this has been done. So his views on competitive fishing techniques are as authoritative as anyone's, and encouraging for everyone, since he starts from the belief that he is not a great caster, or a technically expert angler, but one whose main attribute is that he never gives in.

On his winning ways Eric comments:

> My philosophy is to fish really hard no matter how bad the conditions. There is always one stupid or unlucky trout which may get itself caught. In one club competition on Loch Leven, for instance, I kept going under the most depressing conditions and eventually caught the only fish taken all day. And what an unlucky trout that was! It had been tagged for research during the previous season and my tail fly, a size 14 double, got hooked in the wire holding the tag to win me the competition.

Eric Campbell follows five golden rules for competitive fishing, which are just as valid for the non-competitive angler who wants to do well in his pleasure fishing:

(*i*) Fish as if you expect to catch a fish every cast.
(*ii*) Never fall into a set routine of casting and retrieving. Vary the style and speed of retrieve until you find a successful method.
(*iii*) Fish the flies in which you have faith.
(*iv*) Always be aware of your boat partner's style and tackle. If he is having more success than you, try to see why, changing your own method if desirable. At the start arrange, if you can, to swap knowledge as two can discover more than one.
(*v*) On away venues, or waters you don't know well, try and get information from local anglers. They are generally delighted to help even if they are your rivals!

On that final point Eric gives an example illustrative not only of its value, but of the fraternity of fishermen which makes even internationals the friendliest of sports: 'In 1977, before going to Grafham I wrote to an English international, Peter West, for advice and what he told me helped me win the Brown Bowl for which I have always been grateful.'

Amid those many successes Eric has of course suffered those occasional days or moments of frustration most of us know so well. When everything goes right in practice, it is maddening if it then all goes wrong on match day. He experienced this in the 1978 Spring international at Trawsfynydd. On the Friday he caught four rainbows with the two best weighing 10 lb 8 oz. On match Saturday he took five — but together they weighed just 3 lb 12 oz!

Then there is that deflating moment when you come in convinced you have a winning bag, only to find yourself well down the list. In a Scottish national on Leven Eric once weighed in a fine basket of twenty-one trout without even getting in the top twelve to qualify for Scotland!

Competitive fly-fishing is so often an odd compound of disappointment and happy achievement. Eric's best example of this came at Trawsfynydd in September 1974:

> This was the first international to be fished with inter-country pairings. I was partnered by Trevor Hirons with Norman Hampson as boatman. With two top Welsh internationals as company I was well placed for 'inside information'. Before embarking Trevor told me the 'killer' fly was a small Invicta and asked if I had any. I had just started tying my own flies and on searching through my box found two size 14 Invictas, which were the first I had ever tied of that pattern. I gave Trevor one, and put one on myself in place of my tail fly. After the starting gun we rushed up to the dam-end where I hooked a trout with my third cast. When it had been worked round to the back of the boat it slipped off for no apparent reason. On examining the cast I found the fish had gone off with my Invicta. Nervous as always at the start of an international I had not tied it on properly in my haste and excitement. Now I found in my fly-box a rather similar Invicta that I had bought at some time, but it brought no immediate response from the trout. Using 'my' Invicta Trevor proceeded to catch five in the next ninety minutes while I was still blank. Unfortunately for him the hook was broken as Norman removed his fly from the fifth trout (Thank heavens, thought I!).
>
> By this time I was fishing a team of four shop-bought Invictas, hoping the trout would find one of the different patterns attractive, and cursing myself for not tying more

size 14 Invictas of my own. Breaking that hook did in fact change Trevor's luck and mine. During the rest of the day he only took three more, while I had eight to end level on numbers. So I weighed in feeling very lucky to have salvaged something after that disastrous start.

As usual Eric's persistence paid off. That he regards as also being a main attribute of two of the best Scottish anglers with whom he has fished:

> Mike McKinnell is one who would certainly top me as a successful fisherman, having won the Scottish national three times in five years. It was misfortune for Scotland when he emigrated to Australia in 1975 missing the two internationals for which he had qualified that year. But he is back now and will captain Scotland in 1984.
> Another is Dr James Cuthbert who won the Scottish national twice, once with a catch of thirty-two trout weighing 27 lb 11 oz. I was privileged to fish with him in an international practice on Loch Leven in 1977 when we landed twenty-five which is, I think, the last time I had double figures on that loch. Back in 1974 I asked the late Tom Stark, who was top boatman then, whom he regarded as the best angler to fish with him. He replied that Dr Jim Cuthbert was certainly the most dedicated as from the time he started to fish his eyes *never* left off watching his flies. He would chat to boatman and partner, but *never* turned his head to look at them when fishing.

There's hope for all of us if we try hard enough.

Mervyn Williams has been one of Wales' outstanding fly-fishermen. Not only is he the only person ever to win the Brown Bowl twice in succession, but he has been within an ounce or two of taking it on a couple of other occasions, and has fished eighteen times for Wales since his debut in the team in 1968. His first Brown Bowl typified the friendly cooperation in internationals with the story starting the year before in the autumn match at Trawsfynydd.

During that week one of the Scottish team, Jimmy Robertson, claimed to have been broken in Tyntwll Bay by an enormous rainbow of record proportions which had gone off with his Dunkeld. The following day Mervyn fished this bay and landed a $3\frac{1}{2}$ lb rainbow with a Dunkeld in its jaw. Everything tallied except the reported size, and when Jimmy reclaimed his fly he had a barrage of caustic comment to endure. As compensation, however, this same Dunkeld caught him a lot of fish on the following days, and Jimmy promised to give Mervyn Williams one when he came to Leven.

On the way to the boat pier at the start of next autumn's international there, Mervyn called to Jimmy Robertson to ask where his fly was. The Scot was back in a few minutes with two Dunkelds, size 12 and 10, and both played their part in Mervyn's win. As captain of Wales he was teamed with Eoen O'Sullivan, the Irish captain, and had Gordon Hutchinson as gillie. This is how he describes the day and its unusual climax:

> Practising earlier on the North Deeps I had seen a good shoal of large trout move in the mornings and late afternoons. Eoen agreed we should try and locate this shoal. I got off to a reasonable start with two trout, one on a Dunkeld, the other on a Kingfisher Butcher (with blue hackle!). Then we spent the next four hours trying to locate the shoal in the area between North Deeps and Scart Island.
>
> A good gillie makes a lot of difference and Gordon was one of the best, working hard for us throughout. At intervals, I stood up in the boat to try and spot the shoal, but it was late afternoon before I saw them as we moved from Factor's Pier towards Castle Island. Allowing time for the run home there was only just over an hour's fishing left as Gordon responded to my request to take the boat upwind of the fish. By this time both Jimmy's Dunkelds were on my cast, the 12 on the point, the 10 as top dropper. We were soon into fish with Eoen bringing a good Leven trout of over 2 lb to the net. Then I had four in rapid succession.
>
> With only about ten minutes left before we had to motor home, and many other boats now congregated around us, I hooked two large fish at once, one on each Dunkeld. The trout on the point was over 3 lb, the other around 2 lb. To play both of them on a 4 lb cast and land them in time demanded quick thinking, positive action, and good team work. Gordon stood by with the net, and Eoen with a pair of scissors, while I applied the pressure. As soon as I slid the smaller fish over the net Eoen did the rest by snipping off the dropper. That was number seven in

the bag, and with the pressure maintained number eight came into the net just in time. Instantly, Gordon started the engine and raced us back to the pier with just three minutes to spare. Those eight trout weighed almost $17\frac{1}{2}$ lb, and a beautiful sight they were.

The following international was Sheelin in May 1976 and again Mervyn was the winner. His partner that day was Bob Draper on his debut, his first-match nerves heightened by having to watch Mervyn pull them in, as he records:

> Sheelin gave us one of our best week's fishing ever in Ireland. There was a steady wind, a good fly hatch, and plenty of fish moving. The size limit was 14 inches with many tantalizing fish being caught of around $13\frac{1}{2}$ inches. On the Friday I fished the Ross Bay area out towards Curry Rocks and Curry Point. My bag limit was six trout for $9\frac{1}{2}$ lb to give me confidence for match day. Fine fisherman though he is, Bob Draper by contrast was understandably anxious. His special style of fishing is not best suited either to the Irish trout which are so swift in rejecting the fly. He was casting thirty yards or more, and moving plenty of fish. But because of his long line he had difficulty in hooking them.
> Good flies for me were the Duck Fly, sizes 12 and 10, and the Black Pennell, size 12. But on match day the best of all was a size 16 Black Zulu — fished on the point !! Of the six trout weighing 8 lb $8\frac{1}{2}$ oz which won me the Brown Bowl, four came to the Zulu.

On two other occasions Mervyn was very close to the Brown Bowl. In that dreary Llyn Alaw match in 1972, he was one of only three fishermen to catch a trout. Again at Menteith in 1973, when the top three rods were all Welshmen, and all with five fish each, he was one of the three. Indeed, had he been more selfish, he might well have won on that occasion. He was teamed with fellow-countryman Norman Davies, and had four trout while Norman stayed blank. Then he saw a fish move which he could easily cover, but called instead to Norman to try it. Davies' spirits were lifted when he hooked and caught that trout, and later in the day Mervyn pointed another rising fish which Norman rose and missed. Had he covered them himself would that have won him the Brown Bowl he wonders? 'Would those two fish have come to my fly I ask myself? Possibly, but it would have meant Norman would have gone in "clean". Better he ended happy, than that I won the prize.'

Mervyn's most unusual catch won him another kind of prize. In the week of the Leven international in 1980, he was fishing near the bottom in the shallow Beech Hedge area when he hooked what he thought was a coil of wire. It turned out to be the coils of a line which still had rod and reel attached. By the look of the split-cane rod from J.A. Walker of Alnwick and the Hardy reel, they had been some years on the bottom. If the previous owner recognizes the description, he knows where to apply! Until then, imagination can work on how the tackle came there. Was it jerked from the fisherman's hand by a monster trout? Or did the present frustrations of Leven cause some unfortunate to rebel against fishing — to paraphrase the classic description of mutiny in the Army Act did he throw down his rod and equipment saying, 'I'll angle no more'?

As with all branches of competition, it can be a case of 'there's naethin' for't but drinkin',' when you've won, as well as when the trout are lauchin' at you. Winning methods may have a helpful bonus in this regard when fishing in competition on the Lake of Menteith. A number of the stock fish there are tagged. If you catch one and return the tag your prize may range from a free day's fishing to a bottle of whisky for a White Horse tag. As the advertisement says, you can take a White Horse anywhere!

Scotch has indeed figured in some international post-match celebrations as well as dealing with pre-match nerves and sustaining competitors through the long day's fishing. After the first-ever Irish victory on Leven in 1933, the English invited them to celebrate at the Green Hotel. During the course of the evening a piano mysteriously made its way through a large window. The Irish have been a little cautious about visiting the hotel since.

There was a time after an international in Ireland when the Irish ganged up with the English to see what effects might be achieved on the victorious Scots by a steady but alternating supply of whisky and whiskey. Which brand was responsible for several being transported home in wheel-barrows and perambulators is not known.

The English International Fly-Fishers often had a rule of no spirits and early to bed on the eve of the match, whatever might happen after. The ban did not, however, extend to the officials. Bill Milne recalls a time when many of the team in a dormitory-type bedroom were kept awake by the revelry below. Finally their President came unsteadily to bed, clutched the wash-stand with one hand, and with the other knocked out the bowl of his pipe on the forehead of the only team member sleeping at the time.

The Welsh have not always been immune either. After winning in Ireland not so long ago they celebrated well at the dinner. The hotel was twenty miles away and half their team set off with some of the others to go back by coach. In due course a stop was requested and a number disappeared into the darkness. One of the Welsh team failed to notice nearby roadworks — and vanished down an open manhole. There were a couple of anxious hours of waiting for the rest of the group until he had been rescued and repaired.

As Negley Farson — and many others — have found, there is more to fishing than fish, and that is true even when the size of the basket determines the result. Conviviality after the matches is usually a simple expression of the friendship they generate. Their general atmosphere is indicated by Adrian Ashness:

> Why do fishermen take part in these competitions? They are faced with the effort and expense of eliminating contests. They incur considerable expense in travelling, in staying four days at the agreed hotel, in paying for three days' fishing and the dinner. But all that is of little account compared to the personal satisfaction of representing their country. There is also the pride of being one of the few who has won through in competition. The reward is not the 'silver' or 'gold' medallion. It is in an experience you never forget.
>
> The friendship built up among our own fishermen of recent years, and between the teams of the competing countries, is the key to that experience. After the Leven international of 1981, which we won in hard fishing conditions, the dinner was over, the 200 or more guests dispersing. One young member of the English team sat on alone. I went to ask if he was all right. His answer summed up the spirit of these occasions: 'I just wanted to savour every moment of it'.

CHAPTER 7
THE DOUBLE INTERNATIONALS

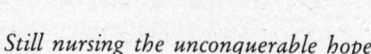

Still nursing the unconquerable hope
Still chasing the inviolable shade....
                           Matthew Arnold

The smooth routine of the international contests was changed and shattered in the seventies. The first significant alteration was to make the autumn 'friendlies' into official internationals. Some felt that it had been an unfair advantage for the Scots always to be fishing at home, even though it was the English who had won most matches, and there was still universal respect for Leven.

So the present rotating system was introduced in 1971 by which two internationals are fished each year, with the venue changing round all four countries in turn. The new series began in June at Killarney's Lough Lein, a beautiful setting guaranteed to ensure a happy start. To emphasize the change, the next match was fished in Scotland, not on Loch Leven, but on the Lake of Menteith. That, too, was a productive and enjoyable match with England beating Wales by 6 oz and the total bag of 235 trout indication of the excellent fishing.

Already, however, there was some concern among English members about mounting costs of fishing at international level. Two events sharpened the criticisms. The first was a disastrous match at Llyn Alaw at the start of 1972. The four national teams put fifty-six expert anglers on the water, but in 448 man-hours of fishing these experienced men caught just four small trout — so small, indeed, that they weighed ony $2\frac{1}{2}$ lb between them. It was thought farcical that Ireland should come second with a catch of $6\frac{1}{2}$ oz, while England and Scotland kept no trout at all, except one taken by a Scottish reserve who only fished because B.C. Hall was ill and England let him take the spare place.

The two countries had to toss to see who held the wooden spoon for the first six months, and there were strong opinions that the fishing had been an expensive waste of time.

The next matter to niggle the English was pressure to form an International Association as the overall governing body. Previously each country had run its own international association with coordination achieved through a committee to which each sent three elected delegates. The English saw no need for change, and felt that a central association would diminish independence, and add unnecessarily to cost. They also thought that the 1951 constitution, which had been the model for the constitution of each country's own international association, was still adequate. That had been drafted by competent lawyers who were top-class fishermen as well, and the proposal to bring in an outside lawyer to draft a new constitution added to their anxiety.

England, then, was firmly wedded to the status quo. They argued that there was no need to alter a system which had worked so well for so long, and produced such pleasant relationships. The English International Fly-Fishers' Association had in fact over 450 members, and was open to anyone to join for a nominal fee. It was select only in the sense that out of this larger membership only about 100 in fact wished to be considered for the effort and expense of international fishing which also involved competing in the annual national match on Leven. It had also failed to attract significant interest from the bulk of fly-fishing clubs, despite many of their members also belonging to local clubs and associations, and despite an open offer to fellow members to join the international association.

So there were rumblings behind the scene when the next international was staged at Grafham. All might well have been restored to normal there, for the water provided excellent sport as usual with a sunlit day ending in a victory for the Scots with their Bill Small also taking the Brown Bowl. There was, too, an entertaining end. One Scottish pair fished the last few minutes close to the landing stage, and as one of them was reeling up to motor in he hooked a 4lb rainbow. The furious fight which followed was cheered on by all the other boats as they passed, and to everyone's satisfaction the large trout was netted just in time. Indeed so pleasant was the day that a Welsh boat came in twenty-five minutes late, and had to be disqualified when the only reason they could give was that they had been enjoying themselves so much they had forgotten about the time and the competition!

But sadly the arguments had continued, offence was taken at what was seen as a slighting comment, and an English committee meeting, hastily summoned between the finish of fishing and the dinner, only cooled down just in time to avoid withdrawing on the spot. Instead the matter was later debated with calmer logic at an extraordinary General Meeting, but with the same outcome. By a 96.8 per cent vote in favour, the English International Fly-Fishers' Association decided to withdraw from future internationals. Their resignation was tendered on 1 October 1972.

Reflecting on this on the eve of his 98th birthday, B.C. Hall was able to look back in tranquillity:

> It may well have been the right time for change. We had had such happy experiences in the past, we may have got in a rut or become apathetic. Times and attitudes were changing, and the old traditions becoming hard to preserve, and perhaps due for review. My one concern was that we should leave without altercation or rancour. When I first fished for England, it was drummed into me that fishermen should always behave as gentlemen to each other, and that this was doubly important when representing your country. That's how we tried to behave to the end, spurning recrimination, and aiming to maintain the many true friendships we had forged.

There was, however, just one hint of harder feelings. Most English donors of international trophies followed B.C. Hall's lead of instantly agreeing that they remain for those competitions. The main Cup, when the matches are staged in England, is still the magnificent silver trophy B.C. donated at the first Grafham international. One donor, however, withdrew his trophy for the reason that he did not wish it to go to anyone fishing in a more 'professional' manner, a comment which pointed to another latent fear which had prompted the defence of the status quo.

For three matches the English remained unrepresented with the fourth team being an invited 'President's' twelve. Among those urging an end to that sad state was Jack Thorndyke in his editorial in the influential *Trout and Salmon*. That gave further stimulus to the forming of a new 'Confederation of English Fly-Fishers', which might take over the baton, and provide an international team selected on performance in wider qualifying matches.

The real drive to this end came from the Midlands, where the club structure was most highly developed. In February 1974 the

Confederation was launched at a meeting in the Soar Valley School, whose Head of Community Education, John Canning, was also Secretary of Leicester Fly-Fishers.

The most important decision taken there was to organize a selection committee with representation from the four regions into which the country was divided, before the Midlands later split into Severn and Trent Region and Anglia Region which fairly recognized the preponderance of Midland anglers.

Two contributions to the meeting express the spirit in which the Confederation was set up. Peter Tombleson, Secretary of the National Anglers' Council, pointed out that any body formed as a result of the meeting must be fully representative of all English fly-fishers, and that, although the rules of the International Association were not in accord with Olympic rules on amateur status, the Olympic rules were in course of revision.

Don Fulcher, chairman of the East Midlands Federation, then made it clear that there was no wish for fly-fishing to get involved in big money prizes.

Alastair Nicoll, representing the International Association, replied that prizes *were* offered for qualifying matches in Scotland, but the money was won by clubs, not individuals, and was often used for charitable purposes. Following that assurance and Colin Harms' suggestion that the meeting organize regional selection procedures, Bruce Jones of the English Association proposed 'that this meeting form a steering committee to decide on the best method of choosing a representative team to fish for England, and to negotiate with the International Association.'

Less than seven months after that was passed, much active work in drafting and organizing culminated in an England select team competing against the international team on Trawsfynydd.

During the same period a meeting of regional representatives making up the Confederation attended a meeting at The White Lion Royal Bala with Don Fulcher in the chair. The proposed constitution of the Confederation was accepted, and an immediately following meeting of the International Association 'considered and accepted the application and constitution'.

So England was back in international competition, but inevitably it took time for the new organization to settle down. In the next two internationals England took the wooden spoon. Perhaps that was not surprising when the selection problems of some regions are taken into account. It was fine for the Midlands, with its club structure and its experience in such matters. But at the other end of the scale was the South, a region of dry-fly experts for whom such competitive ideas were a novelty.

Tom Carter, the current Southern Secretary, was one of those primarily involved in the awakening of the South — and what hard going it was!

> We had a phone call from Colin Harms, who ran Damerham Lakes, asking if members of the Salisbury and District Angling club would attend a meeting about a competition. Gordon Topp and I went along expecting to discuss a casting competition, which was the only kind we had ever heard of. In the end the follow up action was left to the two of us together with Pat Russell and Colin Harms. We arranged broadcasts on local radio with the theme: 'A representative gathering of fly-fishermen from the South has determined that the South be properly represented in future in the English team. The aim is simply to select a truly representative side to fish for England in the internationals.' We told people how to apply for the qualifying competitions. Such was the combined power of local radio and the angling press that the total response amounted to one twelve-year-old boy!
>
> So we fell back on the old adage that every angler knows at least three others. We organized the Southern Federation largely by letter, and word of mouth. We threw in the stones and the ripples spread rapidly, reaching an ever-widening circle of interested fishermen. Not all approved the idea, however. Our own club's newsletter drew a heavy response, but there were nearly as many against international competition as were prepared to be involved.

The Confederation was not organized in time for England to enter a team in June 1974 for the international at Menteith. Their first re-appearance was at Trawsfynydd. This was Tom Carter's impression relayed back to his Committee: 'The general tone of the match was anything but frantic, and there is no taint of the big coarse fishing circuits. Apart from the serious fishing it was a social and friendly gathering.'

Tom's own first impression of international fishing centred on the lake itself. Llyn Trawsfynydd was a novel experience for him as was match fishing:

There is an eerie atmosphere about the lake, until you get used to it. That great nuclear power station broods over it, towering up like some monster guardian of the water. It has a mysterious silence, no smoke, no noise, no discernible movement, and yet you know that immense force is being generated. Then there is the hot water it spews out into the lake with an occasional wisp of steam rising beside the current of its flow. For me it was a strange experience to be casting into hot water, or searching for cool areas.

On competition day the action was all down at the far end in the shallower area beyond the bridge, which spans the neck of the lake. My Irish partner had a marvellous new Hardy rod he had won in a salmon-fishing contest. That unnerved me a little, as did his habit of immediately changing any fly on which he took a fish. I thought it an established principle that you at least kept in your team of flies any one which was catching trout! Then there were the bait fishermen on the bank with whom we were in competition for the stocked fish, many of which they seemed to have enticed close in with ground bait. Some of them must have been careless with their equipment, too, for as the boats converged ever closer together we watched a sea-gull keep circling over us, trailing some twenty yards of thick nylon.

Tom also fished in the next match, and Viv Church gives this account of that 1975 Lough Conn international:

> Sixteen intrepid English fly-fishermen left East Midlands Airport on 21 May to do battle in Ireland against the traditional enemies. We were not dismayed, despite our task having been likened to that of the English cricketers faced by Lillee and Thomson, and the end result proving much the same.
> Our team of twelve was captained by the buccaneering and bearded Don Fulcher. We also had a team manager, Stan Page, two reserves and one solitary supporter. We were indeed a motley collection from North, South, East and West and from sixteen totally different occupations. From the start, however, the team jelled into one large friendly party without disagreement or dissension.
> The journey to Lough Conn was swift and comfortabe, the only difficulty being at the airport where our strange gear played havoc with the metal detectors. This

didn't surprise those of us who had seen the size of the lures Peter Dobbs usually carried! We stayed at the Downhills Hotel, a most lavish and comfortable establishment, and were greeted there by Colonel Moylett of the Irish team who kept us entertained with endless amusing stories throughout our visit. On our first evening we paid a visit to our Scottish 'enemies' where the whole insidious business of sabotage by alcohol began.

On practice day we drove the fifteen miles by coach for our first sight of Lough Conn, which makes Grafham look like a puddle. It is set amid beautiful scenery and has a fascinating variety of bays and islands. The majority of the boats were long, narrow, and very sea-worthy, though a little cramped for the bow fishermen. The boatmen were all knowledgeable and completely charming, all been fishermen and capable of maintaining a drift with an oar in one hand a rod in the other.

Our captain instructed us that on the first day we should all 'do our own thing' — whatever he meant by that. We soon found that fast sinking lines were quite useless as were most of the flies we had been instructed to take.

The mayfly season had just started — a new experience for me. The most successful flies were small yellow, or yellow and orange, mayflies fished wet, and a strange sedge-like fly called the Green Peter. The hatch of fly was sporadic, perhaps because of the appalling weather with a bitterly cold wind and bright sun. Despite these adverse conditions fish were rising most of the time, and provided we were drifting over comparatively shallow water 'takes' were frequent.

Initially I found it hard to hook fish, since unlike Grafham trout, they never hooked themselves. My boatman came out with a classic 'Irishism': 'You're much too slow, Sorr. You must strike five seconds before you see the boil.'

After this I handed over my rod and watched him take four trout from four rises. His method was to cast about twelve yards dead straight in front, retrieve rapidly for about four yards, then cast again. In this way he was always in direct contact with his flies. Any kind of 'belly' in the line clearly resulted in a missed fish. These Conn trout are not large with the size limit then only ten inches, though for the competition it was increased to eleven. However, they are beautiful fish and very fast. On practice days several 2–3 lb ones were caught, and each of the other teams had a salmon as well.

One evening was happily spent being entertained by the Ireland Fisheries Trust, where the alcoholic sabotage continued, and we also suffered and joined in with a great deal of Welsh singing. For the competition the English team shared boats with the Irish, which was an excellent arrangement. Scotland won with fifty-one fish, and we came last with thirty-seven. That was not as important as the friendships made, the really good fishing and the company enjoyed. If this is competitive fishing I, for one, only hope I prove good enough to be selected again.

That gives exactly the flavour of the international matches which England had re-entered. Seriously as the competition is taken by all the competitors, there is much more to it than fish caught, or results achieved.

Results might be secondary, but the English team, which had never before been beaten by all three other countries in an international, had now come fourth in its first two matches after re-entering. The first attempts at wider selection based on performance had failed to produce teams with the experience of those chosen under the traditional method.

From that dismal restart as regards performance, England has steadily improved to record four successive wins in the matches which ended at Trawsfynydd in 1982. So those who support selection by qualification and those in favour of freedom of selectorial choice have no conclusive argument from the results. The 'new' England has so far maintained the lead handed over to them by the 'old'. But I have much sympathy with one of Bill Milne's comments: 'We find it odd to have a system by which you can be good enough to be captain one match, and may then be dropped because of one unlucky day. Indeed we used to have a saying that the captain was entitled to come in blank — and often did!'

Don Fulcher might see the sense in that. Before the Leven 1975 international in which he captained England, some of his team were commenting that it was all a matter of luck anyway. 'Not so,' said Fulcher positively; 'it is all a matter of skill. If any of you fish in the match tomorrow and come in "clean" you are unworthy to fish for England again.' On the day, only one member of the England team came in without a fish — the captain, Don Fulcher.

From a cross-section of experience of the internationals which followed, Don Webber recalls his impressions from the next one at Leven as England began to get in their stride again. Don had been primarily a bank angler entering the qualifiers, and winning the Northern eliminator. So a large, windswept loch like Leven was a new and slightly awesome experience for him; particularly when on his first practice day he was greeted by three-foot-high waves. The sturdy Leven boats rode them well, but with the pitching of the boat he missed a number of rises while his experienced Midlands partner netted four good trout. The final practice day was also blank for him for seven hours. Then: 'I hooked and landed my first Leven trout. It weighed $1\frac{1}{2}$ lb, and I could have kissed it. Breaking your duck on a new water, as all anglers appreciate, gives a wonderful feeling of exhilaration.'

At least it gave him some confidence for match day — but not much. The Scots were reported to have had a fabulous practice day, landing some seventy trout weighing well over 100 lb. Don was not then aware of the adage that a good practice day is usually herald for poor performance in the match itself, and assumed they were certain winners. Anxiety gripped him well before morning:

> I had slept badly, and my breakfast went untouched so nervous was I feeling. At the lochside there was a large crowd apparently confident of a home win. The captain's wife pinned fresh red roses on our hats and lapels. We wished each other 'tight lines', had our photograph taken, and went to our allotted boat pursued by weak jokes like 'we'll need the Grimsby trawlers to help us out today.'
>
> A grand old Scot named Charlie Johnson, an experienced international, was in the boat with me. From the start he was most friendly and helpful as was the gillie. Our captain went from boat to boat wishing us luck, and soon we were being cheered away by the crowd.

Charlie Johnson soon had a fine trout of over 2 lb, and Don's nerves quickly settled when he netted one of similar size. When he soon had another the boatman began to talk hopefully of the boat prize coming his way. That was not to be as they had no further sport, while others began to score heavily. No matter. There was still pleasure in the fishing, excitement in the return for the weigh-in: 'The crowd waiting to greet us on the jetty had grown to great size. To add to the spectacle a pipe band in kilts gave us a rousing welcome back, and the captains were there to shake us by the hand, and thank us for our efforts.'

Stephen Marsh-Smith was the leading Englishman with a splendid basket of eleven trout weighing $15\frac{3}{4}$ lb which helped his side into second place. The Welsh, however, were easy winners, led from the front by their captain, Mervyn Williams, who took the Brown Bowl with an even weightier catch of $17\frac{1}{2}$ lb, in happy contrast to the English captain's unfortunate blank.

For a Scot's view of this fishing at the top, their present Loch Leven champion of champions recalls incidents from his experience. Modestly skating over his own Brown Bowl success at Chew Brian Peterson concentrates on incidents in various matches at Trawsfynydd:

> My second international was fished there with Peter Medlicott of Wales as my boat partner and another Welshman, Tony Bevan, later to be an international himself, was our boatman. I asked where we should head, and was told that as I had been catching them on practice days (word gets around!) that was up to me.
>
> Fortunately I guessed well, and we were both soon catching trout. Before long I found myself helping my rival. Peter had hooked a good fish, but his top dropper became caught through the top eye of his rod. After several abortive attempts I finally managed to free it without breaking the cast, and the fish was netted. We each had nine trout for the weigh-in. A nice equal result you might think. The snag from my viewpoint was that Peter's weighed 18 lb 1 oz, while mine only turned the scale at $7\frac{3}{4}$ lb. The same misfortune seemed to envelop the whole Scottish team that day as the Welsh made home advantage tell.

Peter Medlicott's catch was the third heaviest ever by a Welshman in international competition. He watched Brian boat two before he struck into one on the second drift. But what a starter that was, a rainbow of 5 lb. It was on that second drift, too, that Peter's fly became caught in the ring, and he was relieved to catch the fish:

> I thought Tony Bevan was joking when he first told me. Then I realised why the fish was keeping the same

distance in front of the boat and not running. By the time it was ready to net we were drifting onto shore and it was a tense moment as my landing net was just a small bank one. But Tony lifted the fish out very expertly at first attempt, even though it overhung the net by several inches. I was grateful also for Brian's assistance in releasing the offending fly.

My three flies were an olive-coloured Green Peter on the tail, an Invicta as top dropper, and a variety of flies as middle dropper starting with a Zulu. I don't know why I put the Green Peter on the point as I had never fished it there before. It also seemed that the olive colour was important. Gwynfor Jones also had success with it in this position, but others I spoke to hadn't had much luck with it, perhaps because they used the more popular dark-green bodied fly.

Brian had a Green Peter similar to mine and moved a large number of fish. He was unlucky in the size of those he caught and in being broken, when we struck a shoal of fish. More than once he had two on at a time and ended with his team's heaviest bag of the day. The weigh-in was especially exciting. England were first and set a very high standard with their catch. We beat them in the end by 5 lb 7 oz, but that was close on a day when 5 lb fish were being taken. It was their turn when I fished at Draycote and in a high scoring match they won by a few ounces.

At Trawsfynydd again some years later, when fishing on practice day, Brian Peterson drifted into a wide bay:

> On the shore an elderly gentleman, dressed as if for a hike through the jungle, was playing — or being played by — a large trout. After a time he had to sit down exhausted as the trout headed off where it pleased. Then he staggered up to resume the fight. The cycle was repeated several times before he landed the rainbow when both seemed at their last breath. There was an instant ripple of applause all round the bay now filled with several watching boats. We weren't sure who was the more exhausted by then, fish, fisher, or the spectators who had fought his battle with him.
>
> Shortly after that incident, we saw another bank angler in apparent difficulty, and heard him calling to us

for assistance. Rowing towards him we found he had a fish on, but his dropper had caught in a piece of submerged wire too far out for him to wade and reach. To have my hands free to unhook his fly I cast out behind the boat. Before I could lay down the rod a good trout seized the fly. So we backed off again to get that in the net, watched by the bemused bank fisherman. Then we rowed in to free him, and let him land his own fish. Clearly that was a case of one good turn having been repaid by another.

The competition day that year was blistering hot, as it had been all week. The sun beat down, and the fish sulked. Several boats were drifting slowly along close together on this quiet and windless day. Behind me there was a sudden splash so shatteringly loud I thought someone had risen 'Jaws' himself. Turning round expecting to see a rod bent double, and a record fish being played, I saw team-mate John MacDonald floundering in the water. We held our breath until he was safely back in the boat, then the questions began to echo over the still water:

'What are they feeding on down there? Did it get away?' and some ruder comment as well. In reality many of us envied him his cool plunge.

The self-confessed culprit who caused the ducking was English international Roy Laver, whose single trout of just over a pound put him third in his team that day:

> My partner was John MacDonald, father of Linsey, the Olympic sprinter. We stood up together to cool ourselves and ease our bottoms — the fibreglass boats at Trawsfynydd are small and cramped. Suddenly I decided to change my line, mentioned this to John, and sat down very heavily on the side seat of the boat. He crouched to retain his balance, and pitched into the water, still curled up, without touching the side. Among the other boats near was one with an Irish priest. The shouted comments included requests to him to carry out the baptismal service, but he claimed to be unable to do so without 'the book'. Our boatman (just call me Morgan) laughed continuously until the end of the session.

On the same day Bob Draper was among those becalmed not far away:

All we were doing was going through the motions without any real hope. Along came the eager team manager, Tom Bilson, in one of the official boats to enquire how we were doing. A nearby boat answered him with a spirited imitation of Terry Wogan singing 'Blankety blank, Blankety blank', with some expressive additions. At once my rod bent over, and I had a nice rainbow of $1\frac{1}{2}$ lb. This ploy was tried several more times during the day, but without further success.

That it pays to keep fishing to the end was rubbed into me in one Conn international. I caught nothing on the first practice day, nothing on the second, nothing for seven hours and twenty minutes of the match. But I kept at it without slackening, and suddenly I was into a fine fish. That $2\frac{3}{4}$ lb brown trout, taken in the last few minutes of fishing time, put me in second place in the English team, fourth overall, and had it only weighed a few ounces more would have won us the match. Keep right on to the end is the first rule of competitive fly-fishing.

I even had to bear that in mind on one of my best ever days in an international, so disastrous was my start at Leven in August 1977. Our boatman ignored warnings, and managed to run us aground in muddy shallows near St Serf's. I was the one who had to do most of the hauling and sweating as we struggled to pull the boat clear. More than an hour had passed before I had my first cast of the day. Perhaps rage gave my hand a good imitation of the Harris shake, and helped attract the fish. For once in action, I had six by one o'clock. There was a quiet period in the afternoon. But once we dropped back to Castle Island for the closing hour of the competition I realized the trout were now moving again, and were near the surface. So I changed method to fish on the top, ending with several more to bring my bag to eleven weighing $16\frac{1}{2}$ lb. The day that began in misfortune ended with my taking the Brown Bowl, England the gold. No need to look back in anger on that despite the early stranding!

If I had to pick the worst hour of my whole competitive career that would not be difficult. For my first international at Sheelin, as we launched away, blind panic struck me and I was shaking with stage fright. Within ten minutes I had a good take, but was so nervous I struck too hard and the dropper broke off. While I fumbled with nerveless fingers to tie another my fingers became ten nerveless thumbs quite unable to cope with that simple exercise. As I struggled in vain my Welsh boat partner expertly extracted two trout to complete my feeling of inadequacy. What a start to my international fishing!

But I've had my luck, too. In one international I hooked a fish on the top dropper, but as it twisted and turned the cast tangled round it. When I brought it towards the net, I was startled to see all three flies hanging loose, and the trout now held only by the cast wrapped round it. The next thirty seconds seemed like half-an-hour before the fish was safely in the net. On another occasion I left the dropper in a trout's mouth, but the tail fly caught him in the belly. The fish was netted, and both flies recovered — fools for luck again.

Bob Draper may not know that his match-winning bag on Leven was also in part fool's luck. Viv Church was his team manager, and in a burst of efficiency he had circulated his team with a list of flies they must have for the loch. Unfortunately his typist was not conversant with these fine-sounding names, and at the end her attention wandered. So instead of the final two being typed as Silver Invicta and Dunkeld, the list as sent ended with the Invicta and Silver Dunkeld. A number of puzzled team members sat up late tying their version of this unusual fly. And the Silver Dunkeld did indeed prove a killing fly that year. It was known as the 'Typist's Variant', and Bob had fish on it.

Bob's was not the only boat in trouble on Leven that day in 1977. Viv Church came on another, also at St Serf's, in which the motor had failed. A very diminutive boatman was struggling to row into the wind the heavy Leven boat which requires at least two strong men to pull it by oar. Viv offered a tow, but the two fishermen were by now so disgruntled they ignored him as if he was demanding salvage rights, instead of trying to help. All conversation had to be conducted through the boatman, who eventually negotiated their agreement. Viv then towed them back to the pierhead for repairs without a word exchanged by the fishermen whom misfortune had betrayed into a rare breach of the spirit of these matches.

Bob's first two matches as captain were memorable for him since his team won the gold on both occasions. His personal experience could not have been a greater contrast in fishing fortune. At Draycote he had the heaviest basket of the team with twelve trout of 11¾ lb. At Leven he had a blank.

That poor fishing on Leven made Bob reflect that fishermen, like farmers, are never satisfied. The previous catch of 232 lb from Draycote's well-stocked water might be thought a happy contrast to the hard fishing at Leven. Some, however, were just as critical as Bob recalls: 'More fish were caught in this international than in any other outside Leven. The comment on this in the Angling Press was "if anything, there were too many fish". The Fishery Officer, Commander Dunn, must have been left pulling out his few remaining hairs after his efforts to give us a good day's fishing. For us at least it was a pleasant change from many other dour international fishing days, and made for a good contest, too. Some anglers are never satisfied, always critical.'

Mrs Wynne Kirkby had blazed the trail for women to fish in internationals, but most of the lady qualifiers thereafter seem to have come from Ireland. Mrs Hannen was the first to fish after the Second World War, representing her country at Leven in 1960. Sadly the Irish team came last, though catching forty-five trout weighing 43 lb, with Mrs Hannen contributing one of a pound to that total. Later Mary Radley Searle, whose husband was such a successful international himself, fished effectively for Ireland. Mary is the only lady ever to fish in a winning team in an international. She was in the victorious Irish team of 1979 at Lough Conn and her one trout was important in tipping the scales in a close contest. Her partner that day was the usually successful Peter Medlicott. For him at least a lady in the boat did prove something of a 'Jonah', however pleasant the company. As he puts it: 'It rained most of the day. I was cold and wet, caught nothing and was outfished by her. The Welsh team fared badly, too. It was a Conn!'

Only the Irish team has ever been captained by a lady. In 1978 Roy Purves unexpectedly found himself paired in the Trawsfynydd international with the Irish captain, Eileen Timmins, wife of the Secretary of the Irish Trout Fly-Fishing Association:

> Eileen should have been paired with our captain, John Ketley. However, in error the printers had put my name at the top of the English card because I was holder of the Grafham trophy from the last match. John graciously conceded the privilege of fishing with Mrs Timmins, which proved bad luck for her. On match day John Ketley had the largest individual bag in the history of the internation-

als, while I caught one small trout, and Eileen had a blank. At least it was a most enjoyable day for me as she proved a delightful companion, although my usual fruity epithets, when I miss a fish, were less in evidence.

I had met Mrs Timmins first at Sheelin, when I fished the competition day in her husband's boat. The previous day my boatman was Pat Foley from Monaghan, who has become a great friend. Pat is an angler of extraordinary skill whose as yet unfulfilled ambition is to fish for Ireland himself. Whenever the mayfly hatch is on he frequently leaves the running of the Garda to his fellow constables!

The Irish seem to get their priorities right, and another heading for the boats at that time is likely to be a certain clerical gentleman taking a short leave of absence from his pastoral duties! It has been one of the great pleasures of international fishing to make such firm friends and meet such splendid characters, with the friendliness and hospitality of the Irish quite outstanding.

Success in national competition is not always followed by equally effective performance in the international. That certainly was Terry Waite's experience as he records:

> Though I live in Salisbury, and am primarily a dry-fly fisherman, I had been to Chew often enough to relish the thought of the 1978 national being fished there. It is my nearest sizable reservoir, and one of the few where a floating line regularly outscores the sunk. Indeed, at Chew I usually grease the cast as well as the line, which is pleasant practice for a lifelong chalk-stream angler. The lake also has a particular attraction for me, because it is the only place where I have yet to have a blank!
>
> In the 1978 national Chew was particularly kind with a very happy ending for me as a 4 lb rainbow obligingly took my size 12 Wickham in the final few minutes. With all other boats converging on the landing stage, I had a large gathering of onlookers as it came into the net to top up my bag to the winning total of the competition.
>
> My favourite fly on Chew is the Wickham tied with a Palmer body which I often fish on both the point, and the first dropper. The Soldier Palmer is another excellent fly for the lake. That day my cast was a combination of these two, though at other times I use a Red Sedge, Mallard and Claret, or Pheasant Tail nymphs.

None of these worked well for me, however, in the following international even though this was fished at Chew. For boat partner I drew the Scottish captain, John Stirling, who proved a most charming companion for a nervous novice cap. Unfortunately we got onto the outside of the 'fleet' drifting down past Herons Bay, and this took us outside the 'hot' areas by Wick Green. It was frustrating to see the other rods bending there while little was happening to us.

But not to worry. While I should have been acting as 'host' on home waters it was the hospitable John Stirling who supplied the ideal antidote to disappointment. Three small tumblers soon appeared to be frequently topped up from his bottle of excellent Scotch. So passed an enjoyable day, though we had only one fish apiece.

At least I carried out my captain's instruction to outscore my boat partner as mine was a few ounces heavier. Yet even had I caught as large a bag as in the national, Scotland would still have had a sweeping victory, so well did Brian Peterson and his colleagues perform. And we thought *we* knew how to fish Chew!

That was my first national, too. As a team we had put in six days of practice. The first two were get-togethers on the Press opening days at Rutland and Draycote. Then we had a couple of relaxed days practice on the 'Test-Match' pitch at Chew a few week-ends before the international. To fish the Saturday I had to persuade *The Observer's* Sports Editor that *the* Benson and Hedges match of that Saturday was Somerset v Minor Counties South at Taunton. As I anticipated, it was all over by 3.30 p.m., and I was drifting round Chew by five o'clock.

For that practice captain John Ketley sent us this advance note on Chew:

> Tom Bilson has booked boats for us on 19 and 20 May. This is two weeks before the actual competition, and should give us all a great opportunity to experience Chew together.
>
> Ideally we will meet at 9.30 a.m. at Woodford, pair off into boats, and fish the day through until 6.0 p.m. when we can meet up for a meal and chat somewhere. We can then fish Sunday until 6.0 p.m. followed by a farewell meeting before we drive off to our homes. It will be a relaxed, friendly couple of days and we will all be responsible for

our own expenses. From past experience a weekend like this just before an international can add tremendously to the team's confidence and ultimate success.

For those of you not familiar with Chew this is a particularly pleasant Fishery. It is perhaps the most consistent in the country because it has hardly any large areas of deep water. Fish rise (usually) very well, sometimes all day and are fairly catholic in their taste. Apart from the first fortnight of the season, sinking lines are seldom used by the regulars.

Stephen Pope, a member of the team, has fished Chew virtually every day of his life and is, I know, a great believer in the floating line, the long leader, a thirty-yard cast, and a fast retrieve. His team of flies usually seems to have a Grenadier on the bob (on occasion three of them) with a Silver Invicta and a Mallard and Claret of maximum size for the international (between 8 and 10).

That certainly gave us novices more information about fishing Chew and allowed us to get to know our team-mates better. They ranged from 23-year-old Stephen Pope to 69-year-old Adrian Ashness, Chairman of the English Confederation, and also Secretary of the Macclesfield fly-fishers. Adrian proved an expert in short-lining technique and the working of the bob fly. He is also an expert dry-fly exponent of fishing the Dove, that stream beloved by Izaak Walton. The captain, John Ketley, was partner in a London advertising agency, and a past winner of the national. Terry Waite, the previous season's winner, was an Army communications expert.

The rest ranged from Ian Greenwood from Southport, second in the previous match at Trawsfynydd to Clive Greenaway from Kettering, hairdresser, expert angler, and the humorist of the party. Humour in fact was always lurking on the edge of the serious endeavour. In the lengthy tactical talks each evening, as we analysed the results of the practice day's fishing, it was decided the Welsh had had a winning run of late partly because they could call to each other where and how they were catching fish without others understanding what they said. So we were to devise a system of signals. Indicating how many you had caught by fingers displayed was obvious enough. The key information of the fly being used was a more complex signal. The eight favourites were alphabetically listed and learned in order. Raising the arm once meant success with a

Bibio, twice with a Dunkeld, up to eight times signifying a Wickham.

On the day most of us forgot all about it. One in particular failed to interpret the signals when he saw them. 'I can't remember what it is he's signalling,' he said to his boat rival. 'He's telling you he's caught two on a Soldier Palmer,' his Scottish opponent told him. Word does get around! In my own case, it slipped my mind in the concentration on catching fish until late afternoon, when I found myself drifting down on my captain. Pulling myself together I signalled two fish with my fingers, then gave the wash-out sign to indicate the muddler fly on which they were taken was not on the list. In case he hadn't got the message I signalled again. Echoing over the water I heard John Ketley comment to the Irish captain in his boat. 'I wonder who that is waving his arm about and scaring the fish. I hope he's not one of our team.' Signals went out of fashion after that match.

The Irish captain was Canon Gargan, a striking figure, broad of build, white of hair, and with a ready smile and a fund of stories. In fishing terms his spiritual home seemed to be Lough Sheelin. In his own words: 'When I preached my first sermon it was so long-winded one listener commented, "If that man's got a message he'd better write it in future." He wouldn't have made the same comment if he'd heard me preach just after being told the fly hatch had started on Sheelin. Knowing the great trout would soon be cruising up to suck them down my sermon was one of the shortest on record.'

Our final instruction from John Ketley was: 'You will feel real tension at the start of the match. So it's best not to take coffee and sandwiches with you. Rely on a bottle of lucozade, and a couple of bars of chocolate to sustain your concentration. Don't forget these matches are usually decided in the last hour so all of you must keep fishing hard to the last minute.'

When we gathered at Woodford Lodge, checked over our tackle, had our final briefing from Tom Bilson, and waited to go to the boats, it was Clive Greenaway who was the joker in the pack to dispel the mounting tension: 'Tell you a story. An Irish angler went out yesterday and was struck by lightning. At once he turned round to see who was taking his photograph.

'Then there was the Welshman who kept extending his arms to the limit to show the size of fish he'd lost. Last night we bound his wrists to stop him. Instead he put his fingertips together, made a circle of his palms like this, and said "I lost a fish so large its eye was *this* big." Then there was the Scottish angler....' But by then we had to hurry to the boats.

The partner in mine was Roy Jones, a fishery manager from Betws-y-Coed. It was his sixth international, and he had already been a Brown Bowl winner. I fished a floating line drawn fast. He short-lined working a Green Peter on the dropper. I hold my breath as trout follow my flies swirling beneath but not taking. Then he hooked and landed a nice rainbow. A change to a Muddler brought me an instant take and that welcome first fish. Through the day we continue totally concentrated on the fishing, sometimes swapping stories, occasionally hooking a trout. One of mine circles round to the back of the boat, and Roy Jones passes my rod round to help me land him easily. At the end of one drift, he asks the boatman to motor back just as I see a fish move ahead. At my request he lets us float on and I rise and miss the fish. At the same moment he hooks and lands one. That was a proposal which rebounded against my team! We both end with three good rainbows, and each lose two to cement the friendship of the day with an equal catch. Brian Peterson had the largest catch with $17\frac{1}{4}$ lb, Canon Gargan shared with him the heaviest weighted fish at 3 lb 2 oz, and at the end of the rapidly conducted weigh-in a great cheer soon announced a handsome win for Scotland. Ian Greenwood was the best of the English with 9 lb of trout, with Peter Heddle, Clive Greenaway, Brian Thomas, and Stephen Pope close behind as we finished third. At the dinner afterwards the Welsh promised to relieve the Scots of the Cup at the next opportunity then invited us to join their singing as a happy close to a memorable experience.

On that day Peter Heddle had good reason to record that his strongest impression of nationals and internationals is the good fellowship. He was paired with Gwynfor Jones in the international and soon had to watch him net three good rainbows all taken on his favourite Green Peter. Heddle had only one by then and he remarked that he wished he had that fly in his box. 'Tell you what I'll do, Peter *bach*,' Gwynfor said, 'I'll catch one more trout on it, then you can have the fly.'

He landed another some ten minutes later and was as good as his word. Such spontaneous help to a rival makes fly-fishing something special in international competition. Certainly it assisted Peter Heddle to take another four trout though Gwynfor still stayed well ahead of him. And it confirmed his happy view of such competitions: 'What a great feeling it is to be fishing for one's country! The sense of occasion is terrific. But you can still say to yourself — "Right! Now let's have a good day's fishing!" With rivals like that how can you fail to enjoy it.'

In my last international at Leven in 1981, the winner of the Grafham Trophy, Richard Webb, had been my boat partner on a productive practice day. This is his account of a successful first international:

> Fished with Tony Pawson in practice. Hooked a trout on a size 14 Wickham. It made two great leaps, then a third towards the boat. Tony relived his Kent cricketing days and made a magnificent slip catch to keep my 3 lb brownie in the boat after just thirty seconds. At team conference in the evening, we were asked how the fish were playing. Said mine was like hooking David Hemery.
>
> At eve-of-match tactics talk all went quiet as we began to worry about the morrow. Start panicing about possibility of letting team down. Decide to tie a few more flies. Sit up to midnight tying a dozen or so to add to the 300 I already have to confuse my choice. Wake early and go through tackle for fiftieth time. Try and eat some breakfast, but find international fishing is world's best laxative. As teams march down to quayside succeed in getting my rod and flies tangled with captain's. Wonder if Bob Draper is doubting wisdom of my being in team.
>
> Another panic as no sign of gillie with only five minutes to start. Fortunately he arrives just in time carrying a bottle of amber-coloured liquid. I lose the toss and my partner leaves it to gillie to decide drifts. Conclude it's not going to be my day. Feeling confirmed when he heads for St Serf's while everyone else makes for the North Deeps. Confirmed again when I find my tail fly has become so firmly embedded in my barbour jacket that the gillie has to cut it out before I can start fishing.
>
> On the second drift my boat partner has a rise. Excitement mounts. I make a long cast and feel a faint 'take'. Tighten firmly and am in to a good fish. Start praying. Work fish round to back of boat and pray harder than ever. Land it after five minutes which seems a lifetime. What a magnificent feeling! No blank! Confidence improves one hundred per cent with a fish in the boat. Take another good one in afternoon to end as top rod for England — and in the winning team too!
>
> The first fish was taken on a size 14 red-tailed

Dunkeld, the second on a 14 Burleigh: probably luck or the gillie's skill in taking us to the right places. My own tactics and equipment might have played a part. I used a long rod of 11 ft length and an aqua-sunk line. Finding the depth at which fish are feeding seems to me more important to discover first than their fly of the day. So I always start with a sinker and vary the depth of the fly from close to the surface to many feet down by varying the speed of retrieve. And, of course, it was good sense to use the gillie's local knowledge of the best areas to fish given the difficult conditions of that day.

1982 was celebrated as Jubilee year of the four-country internationals with Llyn Trawsfynydd in May, Lough Conn in September as the match waters. At Lough Conn, a special commemorative competition was also arranged between invited teams. The future of these internationals, the focal point of interest for so many, has been made more secure despite rising costs, by sponsorship.

Competitors willingly accept the expense of travel, accommodation, and fishing, high though this now is particularly for the Irish teams. In the early fifties, Bill Milne used to budget under £15 for his week at Leven with another £3 for the petrol for the journey. You would be lucky to do it now for twenty times as much. Costs of organizing have gone up proportionately, and neither national nor international associations have much cash reserve. In the Southern region of the English Confederation Tom Carter puts it succinctly: 'We have no money problems. We just don't have any money.'

For the first time, in this fiftieth year of the competitions, the decision was taken to attract a significant sponsorship. Knowing of the National Westminster's concern for social and sporting projects of value to the community, they were my first thought as an appropriate sponsor. Through their community affairs department a happy arrangement was soon completed with Mike Childs acting for the International Association and Barry Collins for National Westminster.

In cricket, the National Westminster took over the sponsorship from Gillette, and the first year of the Nat-West Trophy provided the most sensational of semi-finals and final, each decided on the last ball. While fly-fishing internationals can't reach the same dramatic climax, it is to be hoped the first sponsorship brings equally close and sporting contests. The

National Westminster International Fly-Fishing Championship is an appropriate title for a contest in which the individual prize has only been won twice in succession by one man — Mervyn Williams, their accountant at Llanrwst.

CHAPTER 8

IRELAND'S INDIVIDUAL INTERNATIONALS

> *Imagining a man*
> *And his sun-freckled face,*
> *And grey Connemara cloth,*
> *Climbing to a place*
> *Where stone is left under froth*
> *And the down-turn of his wrist*
> *When the flies drop in the stream.*
>
> W.B. Yeats

Ireland has taken the lead in arranging fly-fishing competitions open for international entry primarily on an individual rather than a team basis. The three major events are those on Loughs Mask, Conn and Melvin.

Lough Melvin was the venue for the only international fished between Ireland and England. That was back in 1937, but the modern Melvin individual 'international' competition is only two-years-old. Much longer established is the Lough Conn 'inter-continental' contest, or the Crossmolina Angling Festival as it is now called. But the most prestigious is probably the Lough Mask 'world cup', fished annually since 1965.

This is how Alan Pearson, noted catcher of large trout, experienced the lough and the competition:

> To the English eye, more attuned to the limited acreage of such reservoirs as Rutland, Grafham and Bewl Bridge, Lough Mask can prove an awe-inspiring spectacle. That is the way it should be. Situated in Ireland's County Mayo, and by no means the largest of the limestone loughs, Mask is nevertheless a dangerous water to the uninitiated. High winds can sweep unexpectedly down from the mountains, causing great white-topped waves to march endlessly

across the immense sheet of water, while jagged-tipped jumbles of rock lie concealed beneath the surface ready to rip the bottom out of recklessly handled boats. Even in mild weather, this is a lake to approach with caution. Treat Mask with the respect it deserves, and you will find it safe enough and productive enough to satisfy even the most demanding angler.

The brown trout seem to have divided themselves into two sub-species or races; the ordinary brown trout of excellent configuration and colour, and the more heavily built and brilliantly coloured gillaroo, which tends to occupy the rockier shallows where snails are numerous. Occasionally one catches brown trout that have more of the appearance of sea-trout, being very silvery and possessing just a sprinkling of black spots. These are normally taken only in the immediate vicinity of the mouth of the Carra River, the overspill from Lough Carra, and are in fact typical Carra brown trout, which have migrated downstream. Lough Carra is highly alkaline, blessed with exceptionally clear water, and it is this environment which creates the unusual colouration of its trout. Indeed, if a perfectly normal brown trout was introduced into Carra, it would only take a relatively short time before it was indistinguishable from native stock.

Mask is a noted water for very large brown trout, most of which are taken on trolled spoons, and at one time was rightly famed for the numerous monster pike which it contained. Some years back the Inland Fisheries Trust concluded that the numbers and size of pike must be having adverse effect upon trout stocks and instituted an intense programme of trapping and netting to eliminate these predators. Many who know Mask well think this operation was misconceived. The extinction of pike has allowed a population explosion of perch, and echo-sounders reveal the presence of shoals of this species which are unbelievably vast. Not only do the perch compete directly with the trout for available food supplies, but it appears likely that they devour far too many trout fry. This has led to trout stocks declining; and in order to attempt to correct the balance, massive injections of farm-produced brown trout are taking place. After they have acclimatized to their new environment, they seem to settle down to a normal, territorial pattern of behaviour, but in the interim period they are prone to show up in restricted locations, at unusually high density.

It is not easy to fish the fly from the shoreline, but it is easy enough to fish from the banks of most of the many islands scattered across the lake's surface. In these conditions the trout seem willing enough to succumb to the temptations offered by a variety of nymph patterns. Out in the open lake it seems fruitless to do anything but follow the lead of the expert local anglers, who use a team of from two to four traditional wet flies when fishing the drift.

Perhaps the most favoured pattern of all is the Green Peter, although other local favourites include the Brown Peter, variously coloured Murraghs, Bibio, Soldier Palmer and, of course, a 'wet' mayfly. On occasion, trout seem willing enough to take a biggish pattern of nymph fished as point fly and the main criteria seem to be that it should be darkish in colour, have a silver or gold metallic rib, and carry a little lead or copper wire in the underbody which permits it to fish slightly deeper than would otherwise be the case. This concept of a weighted point fly can also be very useful as a means of counteracting conditions of high wind and maintaining control of the performance of the bob fly, which on Mask is normally the most important by far of any of the flies.

Mask is a water where one could, with advantage, be the possessor of eyes which work independently, with one to watch the retrieve, the other to scan the water in search of a rise, or more usually, a 'little brown wink in the water'. This is not an unusual event when drifting across rocky shallows, and an accurate cast over that 'little brown wink' will often induce an offer from a good trout. It is probable that the phenomenon is caused by a trout opening and closing its mouth as it takes food, but that the white lips take on a brown tint when viewed through peat-stained water.

Generally speaking, it is the shallower reaches of Mask that are the most productive, unless the mayfly is up. In this case, trout appear to be feeding everywhere, and it is at such times that the trolled spoon is likely to entice a monster brown trout. Normally, these giants take up residence in deeper water, probably around the 25–30 ft contour, but when so many smaller, 'bite-sized' trout throng to the surface to gorge the mayfly, they follow them up to indulge in their own feeding orgy. This, at least, is the theory of Ballinrobe's Robby O'Grady, one of the area's most successful anglers. On three occasions Robby has taken two trout over 10 lb in the day, and his total catch of these specimens numbers close to fifty.

It is very rare for such trout to be taken on the fly, but many fine specimens in excess of 5 lb are taken on the drift each year, and dapping with natural flies or grasshoppers produces several more. Because of the ever-present possibility of contacting these larger fish, local anglers do not believe in using fine leaders, and it is rare for anything less than about 6 lb breaking strain to be used; many prefer to fish heavier than that. Bearing the colouration of the water in mind, this seems a reasonable proposition, and does not militate against excellent catches being made. Fishing experimentally with leaders down to 2 lb breaking strain appears to have little or no effect on the numbers or sizes of trout caught, but certainly increases the risk of being broken.

I first competed in the World Open Wet Fly-Fishing Championship in 1979, after having conducted a reconnaissance of Lough Mask over a two-week period in June of that year, and having been shown the ropes by that Lough Mask master, Robby O'Grady, the only man who so far has won this most important championship twice. Any ideas I may have held regarding possible 'Irishisms' in the organization of the 'world cup' were very rapidly dispelled.

Arrangements are complex. Entries are received from very many countries of the world, and each entry has to be awarded a place in one of the qualifying heats which take place on consecutive days, with final day taking place on the fifth day. Each entrant shares a boat with another competitor, who must not be a close friend or relative, and wherever possible local competitors are not drawn to fish together. Although there are a good number of boats permanently based on Mask, there are never enough for this massive competition, so other boats have to be brought in from nearby waters. Each boat has to be controlled by a boatman, who again should not be too closely connected with either of the two competitors for whom he is gillying, and since the majority of these boatmen are themselves competing in the main contest, this creates additional complexities.

The total of competitors has to be broken down, bearing the above points in mind, into four approximately equal groups, for entry into each one of the heats. At the end of each heat, a formal weighing-in is conducted in public, and supervised by a senior official of the Garda (amongst others) to ensure impartiality. Competitors' weights are listed in descending order, and only the top quarter will qualify for the final. Competition is so keen that it is considered a major triumph for anyone, let alone an overseas visitor, to achieve qualification.

In addition, records of largest individual specimens, weight achieved by each boatman, and total weights of 'team' entrants have to be formally recorded in order to determine final placings in those other sectors of the competition apart from individual performance. For instance, the 'team' competition is an added bonus, if one is fishing with friends. Before the start of the contest, the organizers must receive in writing the notification that a group of four named anglers wishes to compete as a team, as well as individually. There is a separate section for the ladies, for overseas anglers, and so on, so that this is by no means a simple affair to administer.

The social side requires careful attention, too. Entry fees, which vary around the £20 mark, include all fishing costs of boat and gillie for the qualifying heat, and, should the angler enjoy success, for the final also. In addition, there is a dinner each night of the heats for that day's entrants, which is also included in the price. For those who are good enough to reach the final, there is a banquet on that night at which prizes are awarded.

The prizes themselves are lavish; the winner receives a perpetual silver cup, a Waterford glass replica of that cup, and a very substantial money prize. There are numerous other valuable prizes and trophies, too.

My first entry to this contest was fraught with disaster. The day prior to my qualifying heat I somehow acquired a 'flu bug. It was as much as I could do to drag myself down to Cushlough Bay at the start. The whole morning disappeared into a feverish mist from which I did not emerge until lunchtime to find myself sitting on a small island, alternately suffering attacks of the shivers and profuse sweating, while my boatman and fellow competitor consumed their lunches. I gather that I had missed little of event during the morning, because the trout had been particularly sullen and uncooperative. Perhaps they, too, had a virus infection.

The afternoon seemed better from my point of view. At least my head had cleared and I could actually see the occasional rise to my team of flies, even if my reactions were too slow to make connection. As time passed I began to improve by leaps and bounds, and when I saw a dimpling rise amongst some scarcely covered rocks, I essayed a longer cast, and achieved startling accuracy. One pull on the line, and there was a savage, boiling rise at my Claret Murragh bob fly. The strike was good, and I connected with a very large trout which fortunately elected to come straight out of its rocky lair and fight in the clear water in front of the boat.

It did fight, too, lunging first in one direction, then in another, and seemingly untiring as the long minutes passed. Then it made a long, straight run at the boat, but veering off at the last moment, and passing to my left so that it was now behind me. As it changed course, I caught sight of the length of it, and the breadth of the heavy shoulder, and I knew that this single trout would qualify me with ease, and doubtless would secure the prize for the biggest of the competition. It was a whopper!

It is a fact of life that you cannot fight a trout if you are sitting facing the other way, so I was obliged to stand up and turn to continue the flight. I managed to get up on my feet, whereupon my legs buckled at the knees, and I ended sitting in the bottom of the boat, still facing the wrong way. No matter how hard I tried, I could not scramble up again. Shortly afterwards, all necessity to do so had departed, along with the trout which had gladly shed the hook. So I ended that fateful day as I had started it, with a dry net.

My second 'world cup' was very different. I had designed a new carbon-fibre rod, eleven feet in length and weighing under three ounces. With this I had teamed a very expensive, ultra-light carbon-fibre reel loaded with a short, single taper line. In practice I had found this the perfect answer to a certain physical disability of the shoulder with which I am afflicted, and I was in no doubt at all that with this featherweight gear I could complete six casts every minute of every hour for the entire duration of the competition. That really is essential: to fish every second, never to pause for a breather, or refreshment.

It seemed I could do little wrong this day. Trout rose obligingly, and I missed none of them. Some had to be shaken off because they were below regulation size, but my tally, increased very satisfactorily through the day until the last ninety minutes, when suddenly the water went dead. Still, I knew I had a big enough weight to qualify with ease, and as we approached the pier at Cushlough Bay, I happily threaded my catch on the string provided for that purpose and affixed the label bearing my name and competitor's number. As I bore, so proudly, this excellent catch to the weighing-in point, numbers of my Irish friends clapped me on the back and declared their certainty that I would head the qualifiers for the day. I thought so, too.

Alas for fond hopes. It seemed that about sixteen of us had enjoyed really superb sport, whilst the other forty had not. In the event, my catch came fifteenth in weight order — and there were to be just fourteen qualifiers on that day. The extra weight that I needed if I was not to have missed the cut was just 0.02 of a pound. Ah well, I thought, there's always next year.

Alan isn't the only one to have lost a large trout during the 'world cups'. Robby O'Grady himself hooked the largest of his many double-figure fish in one match. In the deep water it played so hard and strong that time began to run out on him. So the boat was worked back towards Cushlough, which proved a costly mistake. For in the shallows there the trout exploded into violent action. Somewhere between 15 lb and 20 lb is the estimate of the trout which proved too violent in the shallow water for even Robby to master.

Apart from Mask, the best established competition is the Lough Conn Intercontinental Trout Fishing Competition. The three-day event, open to overseas competitors, has been staged each Whit weekend from 1964 onwards with rapidly rising numbers of entrants and amounts of prize money. For the first time in 1981 more than 200 took part, and the first prize is currently £1000.

Patrick Langan is the Secretary and this is his view of the sport to be had at Conn: 'The lough has a fine stock of natural brown trout ranging up to 5 lb. The fishing was damaged in the sixties by a large drainage scheme, but has now fully recovered as is reflected in the excellent baskets in recent competitions. Stocking takes place regularly, organized by the Inland Fisheries Trust with the transfer of natural brown trout from the feeder streams to the lough. Conn trout, like Mask trout, are free-rising and an angler would expect to catch half-a-dozen on an average day.'

That has certainly been the case on finals day of the Intercontinental with typical winning catches in the last three years being eleven trout for almost 10 lb, and nine for $9\frac{1}{2}$ lb, reflecting a normal average of a pound a fish. The starting point of the competition is Gortnor Abbey at the Crossmolina end of the lake with boats setting out at 11.30 a.m. in the two heats, and 10.00 a.m. in the final to return by 6.30 p.m.. The prizes for the overseas angler and the best lady angler are judged on weight caught throughout, the rest on weight taken in the final.

International anglers are well versed in competition on Conn, which is the most frequent venue for the matches in Ireland. Inevitably some of the local experts qualify for the Irish team. Outstanding recently has been Michael Tolan, who captained his country to victory in the 1979 Conn international.

Alan Pearson has also been a competitor in the Lough Melvin individual international and gives this appreciation of an unusual lough and contest:

> Lough Melvin, situated on the border between Northern and Southern Ireland, is a fascinating water. Some nine-miles long by an average of one-and-a-half miles in width, its surface liberally bestrewn with small islands, it is fed by a number of small streams and springs, and drains out to the sea at Bundoran through the four-mile-long Bundrowes River. An excellent spring run of salmon occurs, while grilse averaging 5–6 lb seem to run all through the summer, and in the autumn a massive seaward migration of eels takes place. Some of these eels are of incredible size, and it is not at all unusual for forty or fifty over 10 lb in weight to be taken in traps during the two weeks of the year that they are set.
>   The lough itself is of variable depth, ranging from rocky or weedy shallows down to as much as 150 ft or more. The use of an echo-sounder reveals the presence of large shoals of fish around the 90 ft contour, and all

available evidence suggests that these are Arctic char, of which the largest authenticated specimen weighed $7\frac{1}{2}$ lb.

Higher in the water, around the 30 ft contour, massive shoals of perch are easily located, perhaps too many for the ultimate good of the trout fishing, since they provide direct competition for the trout in respect of the available food supply. That this may already be having adverse effect upon trout stocks is suggested by the very large numbers of very small trout which are currently present in the lough.

The trout themselves are fascinatingly varied, and would obviously repay a detailed scientific study by biologists with open minds. Irish waters are notorious for containing a variety of alleged trout 'species' which scientists tell us are just simple, ordinary brown trout that just happen to look slightly different. I always used to believe the scientists, but nowadays I am far less certain than I used to be on this topic, particularly after spending time examining the Lough Melvin trout. The locals insist that four quite separate species are present: the normal brown trout, the gillaroo, the sonaghan and the ferox.

The normal brown trout of Melvin is a nice enough fish, but unremarkable, being an ordinary specimen of that ilk, not endowed with bright colours. It looks just what it is, an 'ordinary' brown trout of reasonable build and slightly dingy colouration such as one might catch from any unremarkable fishery. It seems not to appear in specific types of location, unless one can postulate that middling depth water is a specific location. In terms of dietary preferences it is unremarkable, and contains mainly the nymphal and adult forms of the aquatic flies that populate the lough.

The gillaroo is a totally different sort of trout, possessing a good, humpy back, deep belly and thick shoulder. The colouration is invariably brilliant: golden flanks and belly liberally splashed with carmine and dark spots. Just as in many other Irish waters, it appears to have a preference for shallower waters, often with an irregular rocky bed, and can also appear in great numbers over shallow, level reaches in close proximity to massive reed beds. Stomach contents invariably include a high proportion of snails, of which it appears to digest the shells with ease, plus a much smaller proportion of nymphs, shrimps and adult flies. It is 'known' locally that the gillaroo has a second stomach, or gizzard, to assist in the digestion of snail shells and, indeed, some people call it the 'gizzard' trout. I have performed quite a few autopsies, but have so far failed to discover this gizzard, although I do gain the distinct, if unscientific, impression that the stomach wall of the gillaroo is thicker than that of other brown trout.

The sonaghan is a very strange variety of brown trout. It is slimly built, more so than the 'ordinary' brown trout of the lough, and resembles a brown trout of perfectly normal colouration that has been sprayed all over with a thin coat of transparent black varnish. The tail is disproportionately large and powerful, and is also very dark in colour, as are the other fins. It appears to be very much a shoal fish, cruising in large numbers over the deeper water, and behaving in every way as a shoal fish, as opposed to an accidental grouping. Remarkably enough for a brown trout, it is a plankton feeder, and examination of stomach contents invariably reveals that the greater mass is that peculiar greyish jelly which we expect to find in the rainbow trout feeding heavily on daphnia, as it does for much of its life. Just like the rainbow, the sonaghan seems to rise and fall in the water with the daphnia clouds, with the effect that on a bright day, they are feeding deep, and on duller days they move higher in the water, at which time they can also be induced to accept a nymph, or fly.

Finally, we come to the ferox trout. We all 'know' that the ferox is just a brown trout that is on the downward path, either from age or illness. The traditional picture is of a dark, lank-bodied trout with a disproportionately large head, which has resorted to cannibalism because it is unable to support life in any other way. Unfortunately, the Lough Melvin ferox trout does not fit this preconceived notion. I have not seen very many, but those I have seen have all had the ugly head, with savage, well-toothed jaws. The bodies have not been dark and lank though. They have evidenced the plump, bright appearance of a fine, healthy fish, and in size they have ranged from a few ounces up to a couple of pounds. These look fiercely, healthily predatory, and stomach contents invariably include numbers of small fish, both perch and trout. Most of those I have caught, or seen caught, frequent ideal ambush areas on the fringes of the areas in which one would expect to locate the gillaroos, or the ordinary brown trout, or indeed, shoals of perch fry.

The colouration is not particularly unusual, but is clearly different from any of the other three 'races' of brown trout that inhabit the lough.

So there you have it: like it or not, there does seem to be four distinct races of brown trout present, inhabiting largely different ecological sectors, having disparate physical appearance, and preferring quite distinctly different diets. Fortunately for the angler, all are more or less willing to take the fly fished in the traditional manner. Local anglers fish teams of two, three or four traditional patterns, and follow the classical short-lining technique of fishing the drift. Everyone has a different idea of the best team to use, but many insist that the Gosling, or one of its variants, is by far the best bob fly for the water. Being heretical, I experimented freely on my first and second visits, and came to the firm conclusion that although the Gosling will work well enough on its day, the use of a Green Peter (tied full) as the bob, will consistently rise a great many more trout. And I am far from certain that a lightly dressed ginger or black Woolly Worm can be bettered as a point fly.

One thing that is very disconcerting about Lough Melvin is that it seems to enjoy many more periods of flat calm than the majority of big loughs, which can be disastrous for traditional angling methods. The first time I fished the Lough Melvin competition, in its inaugural year of 1980, this very difficult condition of weather persisted for the entire competition. I had no spare tackle in the boat with me, and could not change my floating line for a sinker, or sink-tip, so had to rely upon using a very heavy point fly to get my imitations down deep. I missed half-a-dozen indeterminate takes, and landed just one sizeable trout — which put me into fifteenth place. My companion, a very experienced local man, opted for a sink-tip- line and very long casting, and appeared to have won the contest hands down. In fact, if I'd been a gambling man, I would have staked a sizeable sum that no one could beat Thomas Kelly on that day. At the weigh-in, after several re-checks, the winner was decreed to be Robby O'Grady of Ballinrobe by about a quarter of an ounce — and Robby had remained faithful to the floating line and a Gosling bob fly. How he had persuaded the sullen trout to rise to the surface is something I shall never know.

Lough Melvin is a most beautiful, mysterious and exciting water, but it can be one of the most exasperating I have ever encountered. On a day with a good 'lop' on the water, and not too much sun, the trout are more free rising than in any other water I have ever fished. They will smash at the bob, or leap into the air and smash down upon it, in order presumably to drown it, and then they will come back and give it a healthy tug. Something unseen will pull violently at the dropper, or the point fly, and wrench the rod tip round with its savagery. You cannot miss such suicidal trout — but you do, over and over again. On my first-ever visit to the lough, I had just a short afternoon to spare, and went out with another fine local angler, Vini Battisti. As I recall, he was amazed at the way I was inducing rises, not less than forty in that brief period of time. I actually hooked and landed about four!

I have improved on that ratio since, and I think I can say with some confidence that for every six trout I rise, I will catch one, and I'm very proud of that average. The problem is that the fish are so very fast, that unpractised reflexes just cannot react speedily enough. However, there is a major advantage in honing one's reflexes on Melvin. If, after three or four days, the angler is beginning to connect with trout, he can then, with absolute confidence, take himself off to another big lough where he will find himself making contact with every trout he rises, and if he misses any it will be because he is striking too fast.

The main statistics of that Melvin competition were over 200 trout caught in the two preliminary heats, with the Fiery Brown the most successful fly overall, closely followed by the Gosling, the Connemara Black, the Invicta, and the Mayfly. The competition winner, Tony O'Brien, was so overwhelmed by his triumph that the local press reported him as commenting that Melvin was 'the least unpolluted lake in the British Isles'.
The intended compliment that it is in fact the *least polluted* has been endorsed by Dr Ferguson from Queen's University who has made detailed research of a lough which 'has interested scientists for over 150 years since it is unique in Europe in holding these four strains of trout. The large deep-water ferox feed on char, which only come into the shallows at spawning time. If the water was to become polluted the char would be the

first species to succumb and their presence in large shoals indicates the cleanness of the lough.'

Melvin has its marvels for the scientist, but its main attraction is for the fisherman, with Brian Geraghty adding the reason for its special appeal to him as he recorded for *Trout Fisherman*:

> It was a Saturday in mid-June when Melvin and I began our love affair. At the end of the day my friend and I counted twenty-five trout in the boat. Mostly they were on the small side and sober-looking fish, but a number boasted a beautiful speckled cloak. Four stood out and reflected the sun's fading light as if they knew they were that bit special. They were gillaroo, beautiful thick trout, redder in colour than any other. Their stomach walls were plump and thick like the gizzards of fowl. The gillaroo haunt the shallow rocky shores, and on opening them we found most of their food was molluscs. It was possibly this that prompted the sometimes poverty-stricken Irish to call them *Giolia ruaidh*, and 'Red servants' they must surely have been in times of want.
>
> The lough has since then given me as much enjoyment as any I have fished. It is a pretty lake, eight miles in length, partly in Fermanagh, but mainly in County Leitrim. With hills rising all along its southern shore it runs south-east towards Lough MacNean, the lake of the bird's son. Melvin is a lough of great variety with the shallows divided between the stony and off-times rocky bottom to areas of golden sand. It has also a good supply of thickly wooded islands, and a tree-lined northern shoreline. Between it and the islands there are shallows, all too numerous in low water to judge by the number who go aground.
>
> In the shallow you find gillaroo, and those great little Melvin brownies which ounce for ounce have few equals on the end of a tight line. When you see most of them are only $\frac{3}{4}$ lb you can't believe it. Gillaroo on the other hand grow big. Over the years I have had many of 2 lb size, and one up to 4 lb. Each season the different angling clubs around the lough organize a series of wet-fly competitions. During one held in September 1980 John Martin landed a magnificent $8\frac{3}{4}$ lb gillaroo.

B.C. Hall was catching gillaroo in Melvin back in 1937 in the international. He was fishing close to the river mouth with a couple already netted, when a keeper rowed up and demanded payment for a licence as they were 'salmon fishing'. Hall pointed out that everything was already covered as part of the competition, and they couldn't in any case waste time catching salmon in a trout competition. That had no effect and despite requests to go away, and not interfere with the fishing, the keeper rowed round splashing his oars. As an expert shot, Hall finally took out his catapult and scored a couple of bullseyes on the keeper, who at last made off at speed. Such was the interest in the competition, however, that the Garda apprehended the keeper for creating a nuisance, not Hall for assault.

The Irish won that competition by just 2 lb and Melvin, as usual, won the hearts of those fishing there.

Among the international trophies awarded after each match there is the oddly named 'Melvin Murderer'. That is no reference to Hall and his lethal catapult, but to a vast and shaggy fly tied in jest and 'won' at each international as a side contest between Ireland and England — a happy reminder of the location of the only international solely between the two countries.

Lough Melvin is also becoming Northern Ireland's one competitive water of significance, as the North has not yet shown the same initiative in developing any open events on its many interesting lakes. The only fly-fishing matches have been those organized privately by individual angling clubs, mainly those affiliated to the Ulster Angling Federation. A very successful competition has, however, been recently started on their side of Melvin and was first fished in August 1980. Not surprisingly, Benson and Hedges also picked Melvin as the venue for the Northern Ireland heat of their national club championship with the first heat fished there on 26 June 1982.

It is to be hoped that Ulster will soon appreciate the great boom there is in competitive fly-fishing and make wider use of its assets. Already the province is highly organized for coarse match-fishing and expert at staging such open events. This has paid off in Ulster having the privilege of holding the World Freshwater Coarse Fishing Championships of 1982, in which twenty-one countries compete, on their Newry Canal.

Development of such open competitions might also be the encouragement which would let more from the North qualify for the Irish team in the home fly-fishing internationals. Ulster fly-fishermen may not have the chance of making the same record catches there as do the coarse anglers, but they do have some fine trout waters. These give them the potential to develop open competition in game angling just as has been done in coarse match-fishing. That certainly is the expressed view of Larry Nixon, their best known writer on game angling. In that fifth of Lough Melvin which lies in Ulster they have the best possible setting to start the development of such open competition, since this is a lake with special attractions for any European fly-fisherman.

CHAPTER 9
THE SPREAD OF COMPETITION

> *Give me the sunlight, give me the water,*
> *give me the trout, — and leave the rest to me.*
>
> Frankie Vaughan's theme song as Patshull
> Park fly-fishing champion 1981

From small beginnings 150 years ago, competition fly-fishing is now so popular its adherents are numbered in hundreds of thousands. There is nothing new in the phenomenon, only in the recent and continuing explosion of interest. An ever wider variety of contests capture the imagination of growing numbers of fly-fishermen in Britain and Ireland. Some competitions are serious in intent, some social. Some entrants are competitive by nature, some enter for fun. Some look for prizes, some for contacts, some to learn by fishing with those more expert than themselves. Most fish in the Olympic spirit that the taking part is much more important than the winning.

To the first organized fishing club goes the honour of the first organized fly-fishing competition. The Ellem club founded in 1830 is acknowledged as marginally senior to the West of Scotland Angling Club. It was formed by a number of Berwickshire and Edinburgh Gentlemen, fishing in that border area which was to play a significant part in developing the international matches. W.R. McCreath, for instance, who was both a leading instigator of the 1928 international, and England's captain on the day, was an Ellem member who twice won their rather different type of river fishing competition. Under the Presidency of Lord Home of the Hirsel the current club captain is Henry G. McCreath, and to emphasize the continuity he, too, has twice won this competition confined to the Whiteadder river and its tributaries.

Nothing much has changed, except perhaps the winning baskets, from that first competition in 1831: 'The members having roused themselves by time proceed in their several ways.

At seven o'clock, the hour appointed for the commencing of the competition, a spectator from an adjoining hill might trace hickory and casting lines flickering through the fog in many a distant glade.

'About four o'clock in the afternoon the competitors might be seen emerging wet and weary from the different valleys which surround the tavern each oppressed with the weight of an unusual quantity of trout'.

Half-an-hour later, at closing time, the eight competitors had lodged their 'well-stored baskets' for the inspection of the Preses. Presumably a certain amount of talk and drinking followed since the count was not complete until sunrise with George Trotter a narrow winner from Mr Secretary Girvan. The weights were not given, but it is recorded that in 1834 'the new beam-scale was tested with a weight which served as sufficient proof of its temper and strength.' The winner was J.P. Trotter with 103 trout weighing 19 lb 7 oz, beating Mr Michellson's eighty-one trout weighing $17\frac{1}{4}$ lb.

The aims of the Ellem club still include 'to encourage and promote angling in Scotland with an emphasis on loch fishing'. Whoever has done the encouraging, there has certainly been no lack of that type of competitive fishing with Leven as the centre of attraction. Even before the start of Scotland's national competition in 1880 the loch's waters were quartered by a formidable armada of competitors. Records of 1873 show 463 anglers taking part in twenty-six different club contests there. Between them, they had a total bag of 2431 trout weighing 1814 lb, averaging five trout each. The most prestigious and select competition, however, was the Loch Leven championship in which the nine expert competitors caught forty-four trout weighing as many pounds.

Sixty years later club competitions were so numerous that the private angler had to book well in advance to have much hope of a day's fishing. No less than 3,823 rods took part in 1933 in competitions on Leven during which more than 11,000 trout were caught. That growth rate was also reflected in the Loch Leven championship which now had sixty-two entrants. Those experts' catch rate was in no way remarkable, but at least it was double that of the 'boatmen's' competition.

Even then competitive fishing was a sport for all classes, with Sir J. Calder's employees having a much higher average catch than the 'Bench and Bar', or the 'Edinburgh and Perth High Constables'. The 'Perth Artisans' also scored more heavily than the Glasgow Conservative Club. The Perth and Kinross Police, however, were clearly better at catching criminals than fish. Their 'Constabulary' team of ten recorded the only blank in that season's contests.

Most of the competitions were serious sounding, like the long-running Patron's Prize competition with its twelve selected entrants. Then there was one of those inter-city contests between Edinburgh and Glasgow, which still excite such interest. In recent years that has developed into a triangular contest to include Dundee, whose fishing club has been so successful.

At the end of the list of Leven 1933 competitions are two with that delightfully informal air, which characterizes a host of small local competitions throughout Britain at the present day. The 'Casual Boatmen' and the 'Occasional Anglers Club' hardly smack of cut-throat competition. Yet those who approach their matches in relaxed and cheerful mood often have the largest bag. The 'Occasional Anglers' certainly turned in one of the best results for all that year's Leven competitions.

Scottish fly-fishing clubs have been so well developed for so long that it is natural to find Scotland organizing national club competitions earlier than anywhere else. The first competition in 1973 attracted sixty-two clubs to enter their teams of three chosen champions. It took only nine years to reach saturation point with the 1981 entry of 196 clubs the largest that can be handled. That number still required fourteen heats to cope with the 588 anglers, apart from semi-finals and final.

The final was fished on Leven with Argyle triumphant to maintain the competition's record of a different winner each year. That can't last forever, but one of the 1981 season's records may. In a heat on the Lake of Menteith Scottish international Bob Johnson of Oakfield took the heaviest fish, a massive rainbow of 10 lb 1 oz, the largest yet taken in national competition in Scotland. That is a nice record to hold in a country where competitive angling has been a dominant feature of the fishing scene for so many years. In this particular competition it may never be exceeded, at least as far as counting weight goes. To catch one such fish shuts the door on other competitors, and in future the rules may be changed to limit the poundage which any one fish can count towards the total. But don't such rare and exciting catches deserve to win matches? Bob's certainly did:

It came in the flat calm of evening near the end of the competition hours. I was fishing a sink tip with a very slow retrieve. The fish took a Woodcock and Mixed size 12, about two feet below the surface. The breaking strain of my nylon was 6 lb, and it was fully tested. The rainbow fought just like a salmon with many runs and sideways lunges. The real difficulty, however, was in the netting. Mine was too small, and another boat, coming to watch the battle, offered theirs. But that was too small, also. My boat partner had followed the fish on the oars, and after some ten minutes it was quite played out. Then we managed to net it finally, sliding the net up from the tail.

In that same Scottish club championship Menteith provided some other large trout. Kelvinside Academicals angler Tom Neil had one rainbow of $5\frac{1}{2}$ lb in a qualifying heat. In the semi-final he went one better, landing a six-pounder.

Perhaps the most prestigious fly-fishing event outside internationals is Scotland's champion of champions competition. This is sponsored by the *Daily Record* and fished on Leven between 120 nominated champions. The 1981 winner was that very perceptive fisherman, Brian Peterson. The autumn morning was chill and calm, the afternoon icy cold under a fresh north wind. In such conditions Leven was at its dourest, and Brian alone caught two trout. At least the few fish taken were of prime quality with J. Breen of Aberdeen and W. Farrell of Upper Annandale each catching three-pounders to come close to Brian's winning total of 3 lb 12 oz.

Where Scotland had led others were again to follow. In 1982 Benson and Hedges, in conjunction with the Salmon and Trout Association, inaugurated the first national club competition to involve all four home countries.

Seven regional heats were arranged, Scotland's on the Lake of Menteith, Wales' at Trawsfynydd, Northern Ireland's on Lough Melvin, England's on the Kielder Reservoir, Rutland Water, Bewl Bridge and the Wimbleball Reservoir. The encouraging number of entries for the inaugural competition gives promise that this will grow and flourish as Scotland's national club competition has done. The winning club from each of these seven regions sent its team of six to the final at Grafham, fished in the dead days of August when skill was at a premium. With Benson and Hedges putting up over £4000 in prize money, sponsors are clearly beginning to appreciate the explosion of interest in competitive fly-fishing.

Fishermen, of course, are mad enough to enjoy the challenge of catching difficult fish, and Leven has given them plenty of opportunity. But it is in danger of becoming too hard, and of losing its attraction even with competition to give the extra stimulus. In the past any club which had once fixed a competition on Leven automatically continued it for fear that if they dropped out one year it might be impossible to get back another. For the first time for years now clubs are considering other venues, and Leven having to tout for custom rather than select who fish. That may be the stimulus its management need to improve the fishing.

The English scene is less highly organized than Scotland's, with a less highly developed club structure, except in the Midlands. Qualifiers for the Scottish team can only come from clubs. In some English regions, like the South, the entry is by individuals unaffiliated to any club. But there is perhaps a wider diversity of competition for that reason. Bob Church looks at some aspects of English competition of which he has been an interested participant:

> The real boom in stillwater fly-fishing for trout began with the opening of Grafham Water in 1966. However, it wasn't until the early 1970s that clubs and associations began to form in each town and city throughout the Midlands. These became so many that the Midlands Federation of Fly-Fishers split into two sections, the Anglia Water Authority area, and the Severn and Trent area. There were three other regional areas covering the whole country as the Confederation of England Fly-Fishers was formed, but none has been quite so active as the Midlands.
>
> One of the competitions I look forward to most each year is the Midland Federation bank match. This has been run for five years since the Hinckley Club put up a fine shield trophy which is fished for annually. It is a team event of six-a-side. The Northampton Specimen Group have won the shield three times, Leicester once and Peterborough once.
>
> For the first four years Rutland was chosen as the venue, but after patchy results it was decided to give Farmoor II a try in 1981. Farmoor is merely a concrete bowl, but it provides some of the fairest and best bank-

fishing on any of the reservoirs. This is due to its constant deep water around the whole of the perimeter.

I believe a main reason competition fishing has become so popular is that the organized clubs enjoy three or four days out fishing together each year.

It is interesting to note that most of them keep to the 'gentlemen's rules'. This is known as loch-style drifting, or short-lining. The method is to fish in front of a broad-side drifting boat. Usually traditional wet or bob flies are used on a floating line, but the rules do allow for the use of a sinking line.

As we moved into the eighties trout fishing competitions were becoming more and more popular. This was not because of any offers of vast prizes. Usually the reward of winning was a trophy of some kind, and a 'well done' from those who took part. It was a matter of interest rather than possible profit.

The international rules are in process of alteration, but until this period they had firmly banned anglers like myself who are involved with the tackle trade. We were classed as 'professional' and were not eligible for national or international competition. This ruling was made by the international body many years before, when it was felt that the Mallochs or Hardys might profit in their business through personal success in this level of competition.

Since the English fly-fishers had also ceased to compete at international level, but, like myself, enjoyed fishing international rules, I approached Bill Milne in 1978 about a competition. The idea was to organize a competition, fished to international rules, between his English International Fly-Fishers' Association, and my team of selected 'professionals'. Many fly-fishers were keen to take part in the first match organized that year at Rutland Water, and inevitably known as the Pro-Am, though my 'selection' is wide.

The English Association came out winners in that first match. In the three years following the 'Pros' have won equally handsomely, and this is now an annual event with team places eagerly sought. There is a silver trophy team prize, and a very valuable silver cup held by the person who takes the heaviest fish during the competition. It can also be said that the competition has led to the forging of many new friendships on both sides.

Surely the country's oldest active fly-fisherman must be B.C. Hall, who was still competing this year, and seems to take eight hours in a boat in his stride at ninety-eight. He fishes each year with the 'English' team and is the envy of us all. Some very well-known names have appeared in the Pro's team. They include John Wilshaw, editor of *Trout Fisherman*, Dave Wotton and Peter Gathercole, famed professional fly-dressers, and old experienced fly-fishers like Frank Cutler, and Dick Shrive, who were practising the gentle art long before Chew Valley and Grafham had been planned.

In these competitions Viv Church always fished with Hall, and had a close view of the old master at work; this is Viv's eye view of him:

> His enthusiasm is tremendous, and he makes sure his flies are always in action. When things are dour he will suddenly shout, 'Come up you blue-nosed bastards' — which leaves the trout unimpressed, but keeps us awake.
>
> He has friends all over the world, and a fund of fishing stories from every continent. One that amused me was of catching vast rainbows in Argentina. He had been given one black fly, which seemed the only thing they would take. Then a monstrous fish broke him, and he had to try and manufacture another as they would not look at anything else. This entailed going through all the feathers in his pillow until he found a few black ones, and then acquiring some jet-black hairs from his landlord's daughter. With this material he tied up a couple more of these 'special' flies and was back in business.
>
> B.C. is a great exponent of short-lining. The first time we fished together he caught three fish so close to the boat I thought he had hooked the bottom of it. He never false casts, and usually fishes less than ten yards out. A remarkable man, and a fine angler.

A variant of the Pro-Am competitions are those fished at Patshull Park Fishery. In this beautiful setting, with the winding lake well stocked, it is impossible not to enjoy oneself. The competitions are not too hidebound with rules, though taken seriously by the invited competitors. The 'Great Lake', narrow and curving, does not lend itself readily to having twenty-five boats drfiting in a high wind. So anchoring is allowed, as is any normal method of fly-fishing. This was my first experience of the competition, the second of the year, fished at the strangely late date of 25 November. For *The Observer* I recorded the experience, and the surprise winner for those who were unaware of his fishing ability.

Frankie Vaughan proved himself as adept at charming the trout as the ladies by winning the Pro-Am fly-fishing competition at Patshull Park, near Wolverhampton. His bag of sixteen rainbows, averaging a pound apiece, put him far ahead of an armada of fifty anglers, including such leading fishermen as Alan Pearson, John Wilshaw, and Bob Church, who himself caught a heavy enough weight to have won most matches. Frankie and his boat partner, local expert Alan Barker, took the prize for the most successful boat, and it was a welcome change to find sportsmen who were 'over the rainbow' about winning.

The only fortune the pair enjoyed was in locating feeding fish in a little bay screened off from the rest of us. Usually in competition others are quick to notice bending rods, and edge in close for their share of the pickings. Frankie may have owed it to his partner that he selected the right spot, and used the right fly, specially tied by Barker, but he himself was expert enough to catch twice as many as his mentor.

Frankie is one clear convert to the new concept of fly-fishing for rainbows the year round. Past practice has been to enforce a close season from the end of October to March, and a contest like this, at the end of November, would have been unthinkable. Innovations in the gentle art of angling usually stir fierce controversy. This is no exception.

Unbroken fishing for trout has been practised for years in places like California, but David Fleming-Jones puts the case against in these forcible terms: 'Current pressure from some quarters to have trout fishing for non-reproducing rainbows all the year round is undesirable. Although Fishery Officers, under pressure from finance departments, argue that there is no biological reason, where rainbows do not reproduce, for having a close season, the fact is that they do go through an 'unclean' period, when it is wrong to take them. Some Water Authorities and private fisheries are moving this way in order to maximize their revenue from indiscriminate anglers.'

For the fifty of us who fished Patshull's 'Great Lake' with the November sunshine gilding the natural setting this was a day to savour. The fish were eager and mostly in prime condition with many plump silvery rainbows and only the occasional one darkening in colour with the sheen of summer turning to a misty film. In general my own view is that fish and fishermen are better for a long break, with perhaps an occasional late day like this as an enjoyable exception. But it is a development likely to stay and fill a need for those compulsive fly-fishermen who seem to wither away in the winter months when denied their favourite sport.

My initiation to Patshull Park confirmed it as a pleasant fishery ably run by the energetic Naughton Dunn. For Frankie Vaughan it now has a special attraction. This year he is their double champion, winner of the major competition, and catcher of the season's largest fish. Inevitably there is a story to that:

> I've been hooked on trout fishing for twenty-five years without ever catching a five-pounder before. That ambition was heightened when my son, David, caught a trout over 7 lb and had it hung on the wall where it appeared to leer down at my own incompetence or ill-luck. Then, this May, before a visit to Patshull, I dreamed of landing a monster trout. Alan's son, Neil, was taking me out and I told them both that this was the day. Fishing one fly only, a green nymph, I was soon into something very solid. The great trout made some heart-stopping runs, particularly when it came towards the boat, and all I could think of was keeping its head up. When it tired and rolled on its side we saw for the first time how large it was. Alan got so excited he shouted to his son not to net it in case he made a mess of it. Neil sensibly took no notice and netted it smoothly first time. There was a breathless wait to weigh it, and then I found I had my first double-figure trout — 10 lb 8 oz.
>
> I had to go straight off to perform at the King's Club, but all I could think about was that huge fish, which was in truth a dream come true. What that poor audience must have suffered! I was probably singing 'Give me the sunlight, give me the water, give me the trout,' and was lucky not to get the bird instead.
>
> How could anything in my life ever top those moments of elation in landing that fish?'

Considering the Frankie Vaughan success story in show-business that is quite a statement. You need to be a fly-fisherman to appreciate he means every syllable of it.

The following February Frankie and Alan Barker fished a sponsored contest at Patshull against Eric Morecambe and another local expert, Barry Brooks, raising a large sum for charity. Eric is an equally good angler as you need to be if you practise the sport mainly as a dry-fly fisherman on the Test at Stockbridge and Kings Somborne. He enjoyed sea-fishing with his father as a youngster, but not until he was forty was he able to realise an ambition to be a trout fisherman: 'It's an absorbing sport which totally relaxes you. And all the fellow fishermen you meet are nice people. That's so different from other individual sports like golf or tennis where you come across a few real nasties.'

Eric appeared at the boat dangling a fly considerably larger than the Melvin Murderer, its dressing the size of his hat, its hook looking suspiciously like the head of a gaff. There was nothing funny about his fishing, however. The contest was in a private part of Patshull, specially stocked for the occasion. He matched his expert partner's 15 lb of rainbows and, though their boat was just beaten, he himself caught a slightly heavier bag than Frankie: 'He's a good-looking lad, but he'll have learnt a thing or two from me today' was Eric's parting shot.

The other thirty-four of us fished a separate competition in the wider and less populated expanse of the Great Lake. Fortunately, I was paired with another knowledgeable local angler, John King, who found a shoal of rainbows and gave us a flying start before Bob Church and John Wilshaw arrived to clean it up with us. That purple patch enabled John King and I to win the best boat competition. The sponsors had kindly supplied a cup for each of us. So now the first such trophy I have won since the junior mile at Winchester nearly fifty years ago is inscribed 'Porky Scratchings Invitation Charity Trout Match'.

Inter-Services competitions began in a somewhat haphazard way with the Navy's greater interest and superior watermanship making them the initial champions. Their run was broken when the English international, David Porter, took the Army side in hand, passing on some of the lessons learnt at that level.

The first occasion he turned up to fish for the Army, by casual invitation, was in 1978 at Eyebrook. The match verged on the farcical. His team came second, largely because the RAF had a late breakfast, and missed the best fishing of the day.

With the Navy winning yet again, David Porter decided it was time for the Army to take a proper interest and treat the fly-fishing competitions as seriously as any other sport, such as cricket or soccer. The top brass soon gave backing, and the way was open for him to apply his experience in international competition.

First he persuaded the others to fish at a venue where there were adequate boats available for sizable teams to compete. Rutland was an obvious choice. Lying so close to the AI it is central for those coming from Scotland or the South.

He then organized a qualifying contest for all Army hopefuls with twenty-five turning up, and twelve selected. Next he arranged a pre-match practice, so important a feature of international preparation. In the event all his team caught fish, and went confident into the match.

On the day they averaged five fish each, as did the RAF. But David Porter's team had just the heavier weight to record the Army's first victory. With the RAF also well-organized now, this has become a highly competitive match, staged annually at Rutland, and taken very seriously by the participants.

A variant of the many types of competition is the charity fishing contest. The Thames Water Authority's Inter-Reservoir Charity Trout Fishing Competition, described by Dr Brian Hughes, is a typical example:

> The idea of bringing together teams of anglers from its trout reservoirs first came into the heads of the Thames Water Authority's officials in 1980. There had been a number of Press days in years before, but these had only really benefited the Press anglers: what was needed was something which the regular reservoir anglers could enjoy. So the competition came about. Press anglers would be invited to form teams as well, and to make the whole thing even more worthwhile each competitor would be invited to raise money, through sponsorship by friends, neighbours, or relatives, for some appropriate cause.
>
> Invitations for the first competition went out in the spring of 1980 and on 1 July, a cold, wet and blustery day, nine teams with six anglers per team gathered together at Queen Mother Reservoir. The fact that fishing was from boats only was a novel experience for many of the anglers (although it was rumoured that some teams had been having secret practice sessions the week before!)
>
> The team from Queen Mother Reservoir, naturally the favourites to win, set off for the far side of the reservoir in

search of 'the big ones'. Since the competition for the team prize was to be judged on weight they had it figured that one or two of the reservoir's well known 'whoppers' could be all they needed. The other teams settled down to fishing closer to the clubhouse (and bar!).

Despite the weather, which seemed to get worse rather than better, the anglers persevered until the finish at 4.0 p.m. In all 211 trout were caught, the best individual bag being fourteen fish and the best individual fish being a rainbow trout of 3 lb 6 oz. To everyone's surprise, the winning team was from the Walthamstow reservoirs with an average weight of 7 lb 2 oz per angler. And the team from Queen Mother reservoir? They finished ninth — 'the big ones' obviously weren't feeling very loyal that day!

In all, just over £200 was raised through sponsorship and was donated to the Atlantic Salmon Trust.

In 1981 the event was repeated, but at Farmoor Reservoir near Oxford. This time it was bank fishing only, and the ten teams (seven from the reservoirs and three from the Press) set out on 7 July, a very hot and sunny summer's day, with high hopes of good fishing. Yet again the home team were the favourites, but yet again it was the team from Walthamstow that took the team prize — by a difference of half an ounce. A total of fifty-five trout were taken with the best individual bag being four trout by local Press angler Syd Brock. The best trout was a brownie of 2 lb $6\frac{1}{2}$ oz. Bob Church logged his first blank of the season on this occasion, although he put the blame fairly and squarely on the weather and not on the fishery. Since that day he has returned and made good the shortfall.

Since this was the International Year for Disabled People it was decided to donate the money to the British Sports Association for the Disabled and just over £350 was raised. Tony Mills, deputy Director of the Association, presented the prizes in the clubhouse, kindly made available by the Oxford Sailing Club, before the competitors sat down to think how in 1982 they could possibly prevent the Walthamstow team from winning. One suggestion was to hold the 1982 competition at Walthamstow!

Typical of many local events which attract a number of leading anglers is the Peter Brown Challenge Cup run each year at the Church Hill Farm in Buckinghamshire. For good reason this is Alan Pearson's favourite fishery, one which he designed and which Tim Daniels keeps well stocked with large fish. Departing anglers are apt to foregather at Mursley's Green Man where the ones that got away grow larger with each pint. The landlord, Peter Brown, is himself a keen angler and his challenge cup is contested by invitation only, an event which many of us enjoy. The final results are judged solely on the weight of the first four fish landed.

Bank or boat fishing for brown or rainbow trout is the basis of most fly-fishing competitions but the range is much wider than that. Ireland not only stages great individual international competitions, but has a wealth of others. The Irish team is selected as a result of inter-provincial, and national contests. Most big loughs stage a number of local competitions for their clubs as at Conn, Corrib, or Melvin. But there are many other varieties, too. One of the rarer forms is a sea-trout competition, such as Brian Thomas experienced at Lough Currane in County Kerry:

> The Waterville Angling Association introduced me to this fascinating match in which only sea-trout count. It is fished much like ordinary trout competitions, drifting two to a boat. A local gillie both supervises and plays an expert role in putting you over the likely lies of these very sporting fish.
>
> The lough is rightly famed for its sea-trout, fine-looking fish, and formidable fighters. It is a real experience to hook one of them, a matter of surprise and delight. The first you see is the heavy boil, and then the line tears off the reel, if you have struck lucky. You fish the same method as for brown trout, except that it is rare indeed to see a fish rise. So you cast blind all the time. The first you know is that firm pull, coinciding with the appearance of the boil in the water, as they soar up from the depths. Or so it seems, though the best fishing is perilously close to the rocky pinnacles, which threaten to rip the bottom of the boat. Your gillie's knowledge of where to fish is essential to success.
>
> The same patterns of fly predominate with the Black Pennell and the Connemara Black as favourites, along with the Bibio or the Sooty Olive. Sizes tend to be larger too, with 10 or 8 the normal, and none of the usual limitations applying to trout fishing.

ABOVE: The England team before the 1933 international at Leven won by Ireland.

BELOW: B. C. Hall hands out his motor at the end of the Leven international in 1969. Sidney Taylor is behind him.

OPPOSITE ABOVE: The start of the 1952 friendly international at Lough Lein in Ireland.

OPPOSITE BELOW: The England team with local support before the only international between Ireland and England in 1937 at Lough Melvin.

RIGHT: Vic Williams with the catch which won him the Brown Bowl at the Lake of Menteith.

BELOW: Cliff Harvey of Wales plays a fish at Trawsfynydd in the September 1974 international. S. Hughes waits to net, watched by J. A. W. T. Macdonald of Scotland.

RIGHT: Gwynfor Jones with his fine basket at the Chew international 1979. *(Photo: Len Gilborson, Brendon Studio, Bristol.)*

BELOW: Brian Peterson and Canon Gargan hold up the two largest fish caught at Chew in the 1979 international: each 3lb 2oz. Brian also had the heaviest individual catch. *(Photo: Len Gilborson, Brendon Studio, Bristol.)*

LEFT: E. G. Wright fires the cannon to start the 1979 international. *(Photo: Len Gilborson, Brendon Studio, Bristol.)*

BELOW: The 126 anglers assembled before the start of Scotland's centenary celebration match at Leven 1980. David Biggart is third from the left in the front row, Alastair Nicoll (in glasses) is fifth from left, the author is eighth.

OPPOSITE ABOVE: Mary Radley Searle with some of the international trophies.
OPPOSITE BELOW: Bill Milne catches a large Lough Conn trout.
ABOVE: Bob Johnson's 10lb 1oz rainbow from the Lake of Menteith, the largest trout to be taken in over a hundred years of Scottish competition.
BELOW: A tense moment as a catch is weighed at the end of a Welsh national.

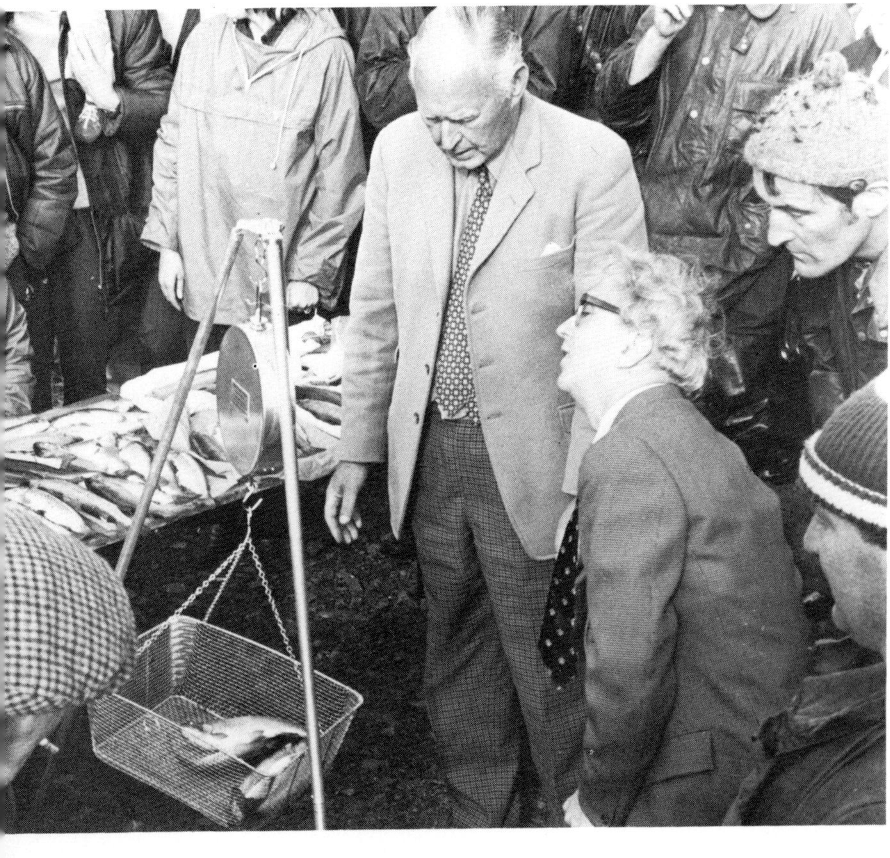

OPPOSITE ABOVE: Action from the Disabled Fly-Fishers' international at Llyn Brenig.

OPPOSITE BELOW: Making light of crutches, Brian Foster lands one of his bag of a dozen rainbows by lunch at Linch Hill Fishery.

ABOVE LEFT: Alan Pearson holds up his record 19lb 8oz rainbow caught at Avington. *(Photo: Courtesy of Angler's Mail.)*

ABOVE RIGHT: John Wilshaw at Avington with his 9½lb cheetah, the largest to be caught up to 1982.

OPPOSITE ABOVE: The competitors speed up Rutland Water at the start of the 1981 English national.

OPPOSITE BELOW: Competitors at the 1981 English national at Rutland.

ABOVE: Bob Draper with the eleven trout which won him the Brown Bowl at Leven.

ABOVE LEFT: Chris Ogborne with his winning basket at Rutland in 1981.

ABOVE RIGHT: Percy Smythe with the 12lb 2oz rainbow which won him the Merrydown Cider trophy at Bayham Lake in Kent.

ABOVE: The top rods at Draycote; *from left:* Mark Thomas, Joe Barry, Dave Mussell (Brown Bowl winner) and Douglas Stockdale.

LEFT: England captain John Ketley ties up some flies before the international at Chew.

BELOW: Adrian Ashness studies the map of Chew as the England team plan a practice day.

ABOVE: Eric Morecambe and Frankie Vaughan in competition at Patshull Park.
BELOW: The start at Trawsfynydd.

ABOVE: Top rods on a difficult day at Leven in 1981; *from left:* Ken Bowering, James L. Sidey (his trout of 3lb 5oz won him the Brown Bowl) and Richard Webb.

BELOW RIGHT: Mervyn Williams with Brown Bowl winning catch.
BELOW LEFT: Mervyn Williams *(left)* with the other catch which won him the Brown Bowl at Leven in together with Trevor Hirons.

The Scottish team is piped to the boat before winning at Grafham in 1977.

The Coppal River mouth provides an unusual setting for one of the best drifts, and it was here I took my best fish. In my first competition the sea-trout were active on an autumn day with a fair breeze which helped me take three fish about $1\frac{1}{2}$ lb each. My boat partner took two, but there were many heavier catches.

Then I fished again in spring of 1978 on a bright, though windy, day. The glare of the sun seemed to keep the fish down, and there was a glazed look to our fishing late in the afternoon. Then in the river mouth there was a sudden large boil, a fierce take, and a screaming reel as a three-pounder gave me a fierce fight before being netted. On that dour day the one big fish was enough to give me third place in this competition involving sixty boats and 120 anglers. Catch a sea-trout like this, and you hanker to come back for more. You are hooked on yet another of the intriguing variety of fly-fishing competitions, which add a little extra spice to a delightful sport.

A very different type of sea-trout competition is run on many Welsh rivers. Even the name of the fish is different, for here they are called sewin, though they are still the same thrilling fighters and often much heavier than you will get in Irish loughs. The timing is different, too, for the night is when the sewin are really on the feed in these Welsh rivers. John Cronin describes one such competition as experienced by a visiting Englishman:

> The Llandyssul Angling Association Sewin competition takes place every Wednesday night throughout the river Teifi's season, which runs from 25 March to 17 October. This stretch of the Teifi is wild and rugged, and you are often fishing under overhanging trees with a backdrop of sheer rock. Even by day the back cast has to be accurate, your fishing controlled and precise. The sea-trout your traditional wet-flies may hook are the most exciting fish to enter any river. Better eating than salmon, they are also much more spectacular fighters, spending much of their time in the air. A large soft-mouthed sewin fresh from the sea will give you a fight to remember and break free as often as not, even when you can follow his every move. Add in the dark and the competitive element and you have a recipe for the most thrilling of all fly-fishing competitions.

Visitors holding a weekly comprehensive permit are eligible to enter the Llandyssul competition which is in three parts. There is an award for the first three places on any night. Then there are trophies for the heaviest fish of the season and for the heaviest overall bag throughout the whole season. This last, the Arcade Shield, is the most prized, making the winner the Teifi Sewin Champion of the year. The other, the Cyril Thomas Cup, is a more recent trophy, commemorating a great angler with whom I was fortunate enough to fish in the past. Cyril represented Wales in the international contests on lake or llyn, but his great love was catching sewin on the Teifi.

Anglers entering the competition meet at 8.0 p.m. at the appropriately named Half Moon Hotel. If fewer than twenty-five take part you can choose your own beat, with local knowledge of great importance. Otherwise there is a draw for beats. Any fisherman new to this type of the sport has a lot to learn, but the first rule is to respect the knowledge and traditions of those who fish there all their lives, and whom you will find most helpful. If you haven't tried night fishing before, be prepared for many tangles, particularly if you use more than one fly. So carry one of those small torches which you can hold in your mouth, leaving your hands free to tie on a new cast, several of which you should have prepared in advance. *Don't* shine the torch towards the river, but walk some way with your back to it, and make sure you screen the light from the water.

Walk the river bank by daylight in the area you will fish, noting the currents, the river width, and any prominent trees or rocks, which will make good landmarks. In the evening you can be at the river bank by 9.0 p.m., but you will be wise to wait until the light has gone before starting to fish. Meanwhile check the distances carefully and make sure you've measured the maximum amount of line to use. As it darkens the opposite bank can look further away than it is, and you don't want to hook into that! Pick out a landmark there to give you direction for casting and fish your chosen spot systematically. The fish move around freely, so you don't have to.

While there is still light enough, make sure you arrange your landing net and bag to be handy and available. *Don't* be tempted to start too soon — not even when you hear the splash of a solid fish. When the light has faded, and the bats begin to wheel round you, then is the moment to begin. As you move to what had seemed a deserted river, you will hear the swish of other rods going into action, the frantic splashing of hooked fish, the scream of reels, the occasional curse as a monster is lost. For you may come that heart-stopping moment as the sewin takes, perhaps with a gentle pluck, perhaps with a savagery that nearly wrenches the rod from you. And in the eerie darkness you will battle with the bravest fish that swims. So absorbed will you be in your fishing that as you finally leave for the midnight weigh-in (11.30 p.m. in months other than June and July) you will be startled to find how black is the curtain of night through which you must move. Keep to the river bank as the rules instruct you and don't try short-cuts.

This is a competition on the most beautiful of rivers, in the most exciting conditions against the greatest of fish. It's an experience to savour. Even if you have little or no success on your first few trips, you will know yourself better and rekindle your own sense of adventure. And you will meet a lot of new friends in this friendliest of all sports.

My own night fishing for sewin has been on the Cothi near Llanwrda where they run up to 8 lb or more and where you may even catch a salmon at night — that rarest of angling experiences as they are said to be catchable only by day. In non-competitive situations you can choose your spot for the night, put white tape on a bush on the far side as your marker, then measure the length of line which will enable you to cast exactly within inches of the far bank for hour after hour. Remember sewin tend to feed more in the shallows at the tail than the deep water in the middle of pools — and that from 3.0 a.m. to dawn is as good as from dark to midnight. It is one of the most exciting forms of fishing whether or not the challenge is heightened by competition.

Some other competitions run on throughout the year, such as those for the heaviest fish caught in a particular lake or river during the season. Typical of them is the Merrydown Vintage Cider Trophy awarded annually to the Bayham Lake Kingfisher Club member who takes the largest trout of the season. This Kent fishery competition was won in 1981 by Percy Smythe of Staplehurst with a fine rainbow of 12 lb 2 oz.

An unusual one in this category is the Glorious Tweed Festival Fishing Competition. This autumn contest coincides with the run of heavy fish as was evident in the results of the first ever competition in 1980. This was organized as a joint venture by the Borders Regional Council's Tourism Division and Angler's Choice, the tackle shop in Melrose. The salmon section was won by Major Hon. C. Dalrymple of Dalkeith with a splendid salmon of 33 lb from the Rutherford beat. Even more impressive was Mr E. Pemberton of Harrogate winning the sea-trout competition with a specimen fish of 19 lb. Seeing that the British record is open for claims at 15 lb or more, it could have been his had he activated the claims procedure.

Later still in the season of 1980 a novel type of fly-fishing competition was staged by the Wiltshire Branch of the Salmon and Trout Association on the Avon. It was a grayling contest with simple rules. These were: 'Dry fly or upstream nymph; no wading; all trout to be returned unharmed and all grayling to be killed. Fishing to stop at four o'clock.'

The Salmon and Trout Magazine gave details of this competition fished on 4 October on the Piscatorial Society's water at Lake on the Avon between a team of eleven locals and eleven Yorkshiremen from the Leeds branch of the Association. The grayling were catholic in their choice of fly taking the Treacle Parkin, Sturdy's Fancy and Grayling Witch as eagerly as Tups Indispensible, Hare's Ear and the Pheasant Tail, or nymphs and grayling bugs.

Yorkshire were handsome winners with eighty-three grayling weighing 40 lb compared to Wiltshire's fifty-four scaling 22 lb. Man of the match was clearly Yorkshire's Oliver Edwards, known as a champion amateur fly-dresser and clearly able to deceive the grayling with his patterns to the extent that he had thirty of them. With Mr Parker of Wakefield catching the largest fish of 1 lb 7 oz, Yorkshire swept the board, as 137 grayling were taken from what is primarily a trout water. Skillful identification of rises ensured that only eight trout were hooked all day in this very successful and very original competition.

As competitive fly-fishing mushrooms in a whole variety of forms one traditional aspect is dying out. Of all the casting competitions the most famous and the only one on running water was the Usk Valley Casting Club Tournament. This was started in 1929 at Glanusk Park, Crickhowell by the 3rd Lord Glanusk as amusement for his friends. It remained a strictly amateur competition except for one open class. After the war it was revived in 1950 by the Hon. Mrs Cooper who was herself a British Champion. Sadly, the cost of setting it up has become prohibitive and in 1978 it was discontinued.

    Yet another type of competition is fly-dressing for which Benson and Hedges sponsor a major event with over 300 entries by its second year in 1982. If most contests now centre on the art of catching fish, this displays the fascinating craft of the sport, and one in which the gifted amateur can match the professional. In all aspects of fly-fishing occasional competition adds an extra relish, provides the spur to improved performance, and accords with man's natural instincts in this most natural of sports.

CHAPTER 10
GOING FOR A RECORD

> ... to catch a fish
> So large that even I
> In telling of it afterward
> May have no need to lie.
>
> The Angler's Prayer

Any of us, whether it has been our angling ambition or not, may suddenly find ourself playing a fish of record size. My own first encounter with a monster was unexpected and haphazard. The bottom beat of Norway's Laerdal river is noted for vast salmon, but these are meant to have travelled through to higher waters by late August, when I was fishing.

The uninhabited far bank can only be reached by boat or cable car, but the best of the fishing was over there, with a fishing hut for leaving equipment. This was later enlarged into a small bungalow, so that you could live self-contained for a week or more of uninterrupted fishing. On this occasion, however, I was staying at the village hotel. After breakfast I set off up-river for the boat, not dressed for fishing, or with any equipment other than rod in hand. Passing one of the stone dams angled into the current, I noticed some sea-trout moving. With my best shoes slipping on the pointed rocks of the dam, I hurried into position for a few casts. At once I hooked a sea-trout of some 4 lb. With no net it had to be manoeuvred into a crack in the dam, where I was about to scoop it out by hand, when the hold gave.

That encouraged me to cast again and at once there was an explosive swirl, followed by a moment of rocklike stillness. Then the huge fish was off porpoising upstream along the far side of the current. Its broad back gave no indication whether this was a 30 lb salmon or a record sea-trout. On and on it ran up the length of the pool while I scrambled back up the bank and hurried after it. In the rushing, eddying water at the head of the pool it came to a sudden stop.

With the cast only of 7 lb breaking strain, and with two droppers for sea-trout, only limited strain could be exerted. That wouldn't move the fish, nor would stones thrown into the deep swirling water where it rested. For more than an hour we stayed anchored and immobile. By now my host and fellow anglers had arrived, rivetted at first by the size of the fish, soon bored by the lack of action.

We had come to the Laerdal by sea-plane, flying in somewhat perilously below the cable strung across the bottom of the fjord. Now my host was due to return for a business meeting, but felt unable to leave until the contest was over. As he kept looking at his watch my desperation grew with the great fish still motionless. At last it began to give ground and was soon drifting down the current. It even came tamely into the quiet water by the bank, swimming slowly in the clear water below me. Gradually it came nearer the surface until the top dropper was out, the second dropper nearly reached. But as I enquired hopeful about the net, it took off again heading downstream for the fjord with irresistable force. When I tried to turn it the cast parted under the strain, and the largest fish I've ever hooked went its way.

There was no thought in my mind then of a record and if it was indeed a late salmon that fish was not out of the ordinary for the Laerdal. Only once have I begun to worry about what to do should the fish I was playing prove of record size. Thinking about it distracted my concentration on the chunky trout which kept boring down to the bottom, rather than wasting its energy in wild rushes. In the bright October sunshine its humped back was easy to see in the clear water of Avington's third lake, marking it as a cheetah, the cross-breed between brook and rainbow trout. Alan Pearson, who had the United Kingdom records for both these species, had recently told me that the largest cheetah caught in Britain was some 6 lb in weight. And this fish was clearly heavier than that.

Would I lose the record claim if I called for help since I was on a high bank stranded far from my net and with little hope of landing the fish without one? Memory recalled the relevant British Record (rod-caught) Fish Committee's ruling that: 'assistance to land the fish (i.e. gaffing, netting) *is* permitted provided the helper does not touch any part of the tackle other than the leader.' So I gratefully accepted when a fellow angler, who had come to watch, proffered her net, apologizing that it was small for dealing with so big a fish. It had however a long handle which enabled me to juggle the trout in once it was tired out. In unthinking exultation the cheetah was lifted high rather than drawn gently out, so that the handle of the net buckled into future uselessness under the weight. That might have complicated the next part of the claim which requires a witness — other than a close relative — to certify that 'the fish was caught by fair angling with rod and line with a legal hook or lure taken *into* its mouth and that it was played by one person only.' This the lady kindly agreed to, despite the destruction of her net, giving her Inverness address for the record. In particular she was asked to witness that it had been hooked inside the mouth for I was mindful of Alan Pearson's reaction when he caught a rainbow of over 20 lb at Avington. This was almost a pound above his existing record, but he did not claim it, since the monster trout was hooked on the outside of the mouth when landed.

The next step was a hurried weighing, for a fish soon loses weight out of water. Avington is used to weighing big trout as more than a hundred rainbows and browns over 10 lb had been caught there in that 1981 season alone. But it is the pounds the fishermen usually bother about, and the ounce weights took some finding. At last it checked out at 7 lb 2 oz. 'All we need now is a second witness to the weighing so that a claim can be made.' 'Don't bother,' I was told 'Alan Pearson weighed in one of nearly 8 lb a week ago, and John Wilshaw one over 9 lb just after.'

At least that meant there was no need to complete the final formalities of keeping the fish available for inspection by the committee (they advise deep-freezing or immersion in formaline), and sending in a claim to the secretary.

That was in 1981, and even had this been the largest cheetah caught there would have been another hurdle for any claim to surmount. Claims can be made for species not included in the Committee's record list, but there is less certainty of success. By some aberration neither cheetahs, nor tigers, the cross between a brook and a brown trout, are presently included. That was odd because both can be caught on a number of British waters, and are sizeable fish well capable of testing any fly-fisherman.

Certainly they would provide a more worthy record than some accepted fish which are so small they can hardly swallow a hook. The record minnow weighs just 11 drams. Another recognized record is for a pumpkinseed caught in the GLC's Highgate pond and setting the scales aquiver at 2 oz and 10 dram. The sea-fish records include no less than 29 mini-species. Bottom of the lightweights is a sea stickleback of 4 *drams*, narrowly outranking a record big-scale sand-smelt of 5, and a pogge of 10. So it does seem a little absurd to include these minnow fish, and exclude those which gave real sport to a fisherman.

That big cheetah came like all my large trout — out of the blue. I was hurrying on my way to the middle lake when my eye was caught by a shadow in the weeds on the far side. As I prepared to cast the trout suddenly cruised out, close to the surface and heading straight at me. When the Black Chenille fly dropped in front of him his surge towards it was instant, my strike too hasty to get a touch. By then we seemed to be eyeball to eyeball so close was the fish, so clear the water. Yet against all expectation, he took even more eagerly at the next cast to be firmly hooked.

There was another element of luck about that cheetah. After landing two reasonable rainbows in the middle lake, I had hooked and lost a double-figure fish.

A couple of disconsolate casts later, there had been a surge of water humping up behind my fly followed by a fierce take, a fierce fight and a 5 lb cheetah netted. Had that large rainbow also come to the net that would have been my limit and I could not have fished on to catch the $7\frac{1}{2}$-pounder. Yet even that diminished into insignificance against the cheetah taken by John Wilshaw, Editor of *Trout Fisherman*, who describes its capture a few days before:

> The cheetah record was there for the taking. It lay lauguidly fanning itself not a yard from the bank.
>
> Now every trout, no matter how large and crafty has just got to eat sometime, hasn't it? Of course it has. Not this one.
>
> Every nymph in my box was fumbled onto the leader and jiggled in turn within an inch of its nose. It needed only to suck in an extra large draught of water to impel my offering into its mouth. Not a bit of it. Several hours of this frustration had fled by when I realised that Avington's fishery manager, Roy Ward, was standing a yard away watching my inept efforts. 'Big, isn't it? Catch that and your name will go up in lights,' he promised. The smirk on his face was evidence enough that I was wasting my time. I reckoned he'd stapled its lips together.
>
> A month and repeated phone calls to Avington confirmed that the big cheetah was still swimming free in the

second lake. In my dreams it had grown to leviathan proportions. In one it had Bismarck tattoed along its immense flanks.

The standard 9.0 a.m. Le Mans style start at Avington saw me breathless in position by five past. It wasn't there, but a very large rainbow was, and all of 14 lb. Ever tried passing up the opportunity of catching a double-figure rainbow which I knew in my bones was a sitter? By now the later arrivals were settling in the best swims.

The big cheetah was nowhere to be seen. The big rainbow I had left minutes earlier came out as did two other double-figure fish.

Cursing my single-mindedness, I began to cast blindly which is certainly not the correct way to approach Avington's bigger fish. An hour and all faith in my own skills and nymphs had disappeared.

'Have a look in my box then,' offered Ken Clayton. A chunky black nymph sporting a green fluorescent tail sprang from amongst the ordered rows in his well filled box.

A long cast across the shallows and a dark shadow appeared from nowhere. A gentle pluck and then nothing. A chance missed. Cursing the missed chance, the nymph was within yards of the bank when what appeared to be a much smaller cheetah sprinted from its algae umbrella under my feet. The fact that it hooked itself well and truly had little to do with any movement on my part.

Not the one I had waited a long month for, but still, it was a good fish.

'That's big, very big,' said a quiet voice at my shoulder. It was Peter Stone.

Now I had always been taught not to mess about with my food and was piling on the pressure, but the cheetah refused to come. The leader scythed through a mass of floating algae leaving a dripping washing-line of weed strung out along the line's length. Not again, I thought, having lost a big rainbow in exactly the same way only a month before. Caught later that fish scaled $17\frac{1}{2}$ lb.

The weed-festooned leader squeaked through the tip-ring. The first netting attempt was bungled thanks to a flick-up net which refused to do just that.

There was no mistake with Peter's borrowed net large enough to harvest shrimps at Morecambe.

It was big. Not long, but with shoulders like Rocky Marciano.

'Got to be 7 lb, Peter,' I inquired hopefully.

'You've got to be joking. That was 7 lb a year ago, so weigh it now,' he advised.

The scales in the lodge thumped down to $8\frac{1}{2}$ lb. It was the largest cheetah ever caught. Having witnessed the capture of some very large specimens during my time as an angling journalist I could never quite understand the sheer rapture which spread over a captor's face when he was informed of his achievement. Now I did.

'Go back and weigh it again. It's bigger than that,' said Peter. 'You've mis-read the scales. You must have.'

I had. In my excitement I had missed off a full pound. So there I was. Happier than a pool's winner with an ear-to-ear grin Jimmy Carter would have been proud of. A record holder even if it was unofficial. I doubt that my $9\frac{1}{2}$-pounder will ever figure on the record lists. There's another cruising Avington's margins even bigger. It's got a white scar on its nose and I swear that one really has got Bismarck written on its side.

Were that cheetah to be recognized as a British record, it would be only the third such fish to be taken on fly. From over 200 recognized rod-caught British record fish just two have fallen to a fly-fisherman. It is the same angler, Alan Pearson, who holds the record both for a rainbow and for a brook trout.

The official brown trout record is one of 19 lb 9 oz caught on Loch Quoich by Mr J.A.F. Jackson in 1978, but that was taken on a spinner as were many legendary monster browns which have not been accepted by the record committee. The largest ever for which there is credible evidence was the $39\frac{1}{2}$ lb trout from Loch Awe in 1866. That was at least taken on fly, though foul-hooked by Mr Muir, who took two-and-a-half hours to land it. The fish was mounted, but the case later lost in a fire. Then there was the $30\frac{1}{2}$ lb trout reported caught in Lough Derg in 1861 by J.W. Pepper on a spinner, and the 29 lb trout taken in Loch Stenness in 1889. This was a 'slob' trout caught on a hand line and mounted by P.D. Malloch, its weight recorded three days after capture and a cast of it since owned by the Flyfishers' club.

The record specimens of other species which might have been

taken on fly have all succumbed to other lures. The record grayling is one of 2 lb 13 oz taken on that splendid fly water, the Test. But it was caught on a maggot in February 1981. The record char (Salvelinus Alpinus) is one of $1\frac{3}{4}$ lb which fell for a worm ledgered in Loch Insh.

In fishing, as in boxing, it is the heavyweight crown which is most prized, with the salmon record the most prestigious of them all. It must have been disconcerting for those who opposed ladies competing at top level to reflect that this was held by a Scotswoman. Georgina Ballantyne's 64 lb Tay salmon caught in 1922 is still recognized as the record sixty years later. From dusk into the blind dark of an autumn night the small, slim Georgina fought unaided, and finally landed, a fish which was only some six inches shorter than herself and was two-thirds her own weight.

On that September morning the 32-year-old Georgina had taken three salmon from 17 to 25 lb. As the evening was warm her father, James, took her out for a final hour's harling on the Lower Murthly beat's boat pool. Two rods were set up, the lighter with a Wilkinson fly, the heavier greenheart with a revolving brown lure called a 'dace'. Until the moment of hooking the skill of harling is all the boatman's as he takes the trailing lures over the best lies. No one knew these better than James Ballantyne, the Laird of Glendelvine's fisherman.

Georgina was in part fishing with a fly, but it was the 'dace' which was seized so ferociously that the rod was nearly wrenched from her hand. It was 6.15 p.m. and she had suitable tackle for dealing with what she soon realised was a 'very, very heavy fish'. Her father made one comment about 'beauty on one end of the line, the beast on the other,' and then concentrated tight-lipped on his rowing. During the two-hour fight he did nothing to aid her even when a final crisis threatened disaster. As Georgina put it: 'He had the oars to look after and I was busy enough concentrating on the cantrips of the creature.'

The 'cantrips' involved fifty-yard dashes across the pool, then sulking behind a rock, then towing them steadily downstream. Never once did it surface. There was nothing except the great weight, the silent force, the line cutting through the black water. Almost half-a-mile from the boat pool they were forced under Caputh bridge. As James set the boat to pass through the near piling, the salmon headed inexorable for the far one and a certain smash. Tired as she was, Georgina just had the strength to turn him, and with that the battle was won. When the salmon finally weakened, it was too dark to see. With the boat now still, and the line going vertically down into the water, they knew the great fish was close below. Her father had put on her leader and knew how many knots there were in the expensive silk-worm gut he had tied for her. He inched the gaff down the line feeling each knot until it reached the fifth and last. Lowering and turning the gaff he struck home, hauled out the mighty fish and threw himself on it.

Georgina was left to guard it in the silent dark of the river bank while James collected two men to sling it on a pole and carry it to the farmhouse. So quicky did news spread that sixteen witnesses were present as it weighed in at 64 lb and was measured as 54 inches long with a girth of $28\frac{1}{2}$ inches. The Laird, Sir Alexander Lyle, gifted the fish to Perth Royal Infirmary, but it was first displayed in Malloch's tackle shop attracting admiring crowds.

So this oldest of acknowledged freshwater records was well-enough substantiated to meet stringent modern tests. A cast of Miss Ballantyne's fish exists at Glendelvine to add to its credence as a record, unlike the 'somewhat legendary' salmon of $69\frac{3}{4}$ lb said to have been caught by the Earl of Home fishing the Tweed about 1730, or that of 67 lb attributed to poacher Jock Wallace who is supposed to have taken ten hours to land it from the Nith at Barjarg in 1812. Some better authenticated fish also give the ladies a variety of lesser records including the largest fish caught on fly in Britain. This appears to be the salmon of 61 lb caught by Mrs Morrison on the Deveron on 21 October 1924. Had it not been kept twenty-four hours before weighing, this would have been an even closer challenger to Georgina's fish, since some pounds must have been lost in the dehydration. Prompt weighing would also have taken it well clear of the largest fish caught on fly in English waters, the 60 lb salmon taken by Lowther Bridger in 1888 on the Eden and exhibited in the British Museum. The third salmon record which goes to the ladies is for the largest spring fish taken on rod in Britain, the salmon of $59\frac{1}{2}$ lb caught by Miss Doreen Dovey on the Wye at Lower Winforton on 23 March 1923.

Men can't even pride themselves on dominating the sea-trout records, since none are officially recognized in 1982. The British Record Fish Committee has at least put the species as open to claims at 15 lb or more. That ought to give plenty of opportunity to anyone prepared to try for it. In Loch Eilt, for instance, sea-trout are regularly taken up to 17 lb, and there are some well authenticated but 'unofficial' record fish much above this weight from at least three countries. In England it is one of 22½ lb taken by S.R. Dwight on the Dorset Frome on 18 May 1946; in Scotland the Rev. A.H. Upcher had one of 21 lb from the Bothie pool of the Awe on 30 June 1908; and from Wales there was a sea-trout of 20 lb 2 oz taken from the Dovey by T. Williams in June 1935. But for an 'official' record anything over 15 lb is still worth claiming.

The only records with which I have been associated, apart from the near-miss cheetah, are not claimable under any known procedure. The first fish I ever hooked was so large it caught me. I was five at the time, and present at a fishing party at one of the river Nile dams in the Sudan. Someone asked me to hold his line, and a moment later the bait was seized by a Nile perch. These fish can run up to 300 lb, and when hooked they are off with a rush. This one of unknown size towed me over the rocks and into the river. There I prudently let go, and was fished out by a Sudanese. Was I at the time the largest fish-caught human in freshwater angling?

Then there was the occasion in Ireland when I was driving past Joyce's river on the stretch of lonely road leading to Leenane Hotel in Connemara. A car was stranded by the side of the road, the driver waving for assistance. He told me he had run out of petrol, and asked for a pint to get him to the nearest garage. I regretted that I had no spare can, and nothing with which to siphon any from the tank. In an instant he had produced some tubing and the largest can I had ever seen, into which he expertly siphoned the best part of two gallons.

When I reached the hotel and mentioned my Good Samaritan act, the staff were unimpressed. 'Don't say Patrick caught you, too! You fish for trout and salmon, but catching motorists is his kind of angling. He hasn't *bought* a gallon of petrol for months.' Was I also part of the largest bag of motorists on a single road? There are some records you can't claim and don't want to.

CHAPTER 11

THE BIG TROUT MAN

Of fishes that shall have the wit
To make the angler look a fool
Not brainless, puny, darting things
But wise important water-kings
That have no time for hooks and lines.

Edmund Blunden

These are the fish which Alan Pearson catches with such regularity. He holds now, as often in the past, the British record for a rainbow, and also for a brook trout. He landed the second largest cheetah ever caught, being overtaken only by John Wilshaw's great trout. Alan has also landed more double-figure trout than anyone else in Britain, his total now past sixty. Even though many others now know, and follow, the methods he has developed, more and bigger 'water-kings' still seem to home to his fly.

A few envious anglers dismiss his achievements with the jibe that the fish are specially stocked for him, just as some detractors used to say Don Bradman could only score his centuries on a perfect pitch. His bag of record fish caught should be answer enough on its own. Most of them were caught at lakes where twenty or more other anglers might be fishing on the same day, yet it was Pearson's fly that the trout took. For the doubters one rainbow might be conclusive. At Horseshoe lake near Cirencester a very successful local fisherman, P.G. (Tips) Thomas, will tell of a twelve-pounder he had hunted for days without success. When he asked Alan to have a try it was hooked and netted after only a few casts.

Last season I had my first double-figure rainbow in the productive Willow Pool of the Linch Hill Fishery near Oxford. That came out of the blue, the $11\frac{1}{4}$ lb trout taking a small Dunkeld near the surface just as my attention wandered at the day's end. Another almost as large seized my sunk Daddy-long-legs at the attractive little Winter's Hill Lake, fishing on which is controlled through the inimitable 'Scrappy' Hay's 'Rod Box' shop in Winchester.

That rainbow was $9\frac{1}{2}$ lb, and I *had* seen it move. But again my fishing was blind and hopeful, rather than the confident planned approach with which Alan outwits his fish.

I need no convincing of his superior skill in this regard. A week later I passed him at Avington, peering intently through his polaroids into the first lake. We stopped for a chat about Botham's latest feat in wrecking the Aussies, which seemed to focus his attention. In mid-sentence, however, he suddenly flicked out his leaded mayfly nymph, gave a heavy strike, and there was a five-pound rainbow being held hard to prevent that initial rush. Then the rod was jerked so hard the fly flew out, which seemed an astonishing way to try and play a fish. 'Bad luck' I said, thinking 'bad playing'.

'No such thing,' said Alan, bemusing me further by casting his nymph back almost into the swirl of the departing fish, 'I did it on purpose in order to catch ... THIS ONE.' There was the rod bent double again, and this time a $14\frac{1}{2}$ lb rainbow struggling ineffectually to avoid adding to Alan's total. With an equal chance I hadn't even spotted either fish, and never would I have the confidence to shake off a five-pounder for the possibility of a larger one. A fish that size on the bank is, for me, worth any number of bigger ones swimming free. So I leave Alan to tell how to catch the big trout:

> It has not been my practice to become heavily involved in competitive trout fishing. I do enjoy fishing the drift from time to time, and adore fishing in the great Irish competitions such as the 'world cup', and the Lough Melvin international. However, I always have the sneaking feeling that this is not really a very sensible, or logical, way to set about catching good trout. There we go, putting out a team of flies, and taking the bulk of our trout on the bob fly, which we induce to skip across the wavetops, into the teeth of the wind, in a way which no natural insect could possibly emulate. Great fun, but I can scarcely regard it as anything but fun.
>
> Occasionally, I get invitations to fish other sorts of competition; events such as the Bob Church Trophy Match, where a number of us are invited to fish from the banks of a selected fishery, using whatever method takes

our fancy, and having a most enjoyable social outing. Or perhaps I will fish in the various Pro-Am competitions organized by Naughton Dunn at Patshull, but once again these are, to my mind, great social occasions.

I suppose the truth is that I am in a competition every time I venture onto the water, except that the competition is between me and the fish, rather than between me and other anglers. Since over the years I have caught a great many fish, I set myself, some years ago, a different sort of competitive task; to catch bigger and bigger trout. It very quickly became obvious to me that this could be done, provided that the fish were available for capture, and that there was a special way of approaching this business which would remove much of the element of chance.

Dr Sam Holland, of Avington fame, has done more than any other person to improve the quality and size of rainbows available for stocking fisheries. I need not labour this point, because the detail of it is well-enough known, but virtually single-handed he proved the benefits of selective breeding to produce rainbow trout which would grow quickly to sizes previously thought impossible. He also created an environment in the three lakes of his trout fishery where the thinking angler could develop a new approach to catching these big trout. Subsequently he moved into the related field of improving the genetic make-up of the American brook trout, that beautiful char which had been around the United Kingdom for very nearly as long as the rainbow trout. Here it had never seemed to produce the growth rates and ultimate size it achieves on the North American continent. Finally, he produced the hybrid between the rainbow and the brook trout, a sterile fish which is enormously fast-growing, long lived, and possibly the most exciting of all the fish that we attempt to take on the fly.

In the clear waters of Avington, I used to watch huge rainbows cruising around their selected territories. Occasionally, I would catch one by casting to it when it came close to the surface. In this way, I picked off a beautiful specimen of 13 lb 3 oz on a size 18 Buzzer Pupa to a very fine leader. Although this was the largest taken in this country at that time, I did not submit a record claim for it. Frankly, I thought much larger fish would soon be caught. As events turned out I was mistaken, and a long time elapsed before it was overshadowed by a truly lovely fish weighing 14 lb 6 oz.

Success came occasionally, but not often enough to suit a hungry angler like me. It was obvious that a new approach had to be developed. The idea of locating a feeding trout, then offering it a copy of what it was feeding upon, was the basis of successful chalk-stream trout angling. It was clear that the same tactic had to be adapted to suit these stillwater giants.

The difficulty was that whereas in chalk streams the feeding trout would rise to a floating fly presented correctly, these big rainbows declined to play that sort of game. If they were feeding at a depth of ten feet, or even deeper, there seemed no way they could be induced to move more than a few inches to take even the most tempting morsel. In other words, an additional dimension was added to the chalk-stream approach, and a way had to be found to get the offering down to the trout as quickly as possible. One suitable pattern of nymph already existed, the Richard Walker mayfly nymph, which could be tied with layers of lead foil tied on to the back of the hook-shank as an underbody, with the body dressing applied over that.

This is a magnificent imitation, quite one of the best that the incredible Walker has produced, although he rapidly followed it with a similarly excellent weighted damselfly nymph. I adapted my own Green Beast, and these three patterns proved the early armoury against the giants. Subsequently, other good patterns have emerged, of which the best two are probably Bob Church's Westward Bug, a big, brown shellback pattern, and a damselfly nymph of my own. Both patterns, needless to say, carry a good deal of lead as their underbody.

Now we had the patterns to fish deep, but we had to learn how to cast them. That is not as easy as might be thought. In fact, it is almost impossible to cast a heavily leaded fly any distance at all. So you had to restrict usage to casting within a twenty-yard limit. Careless casting results in a heavy splashing at best, a bomb-like eruption at worst, scaring any trout in the vicinity. Scared trout do not willingly accept artificial flies.

So we began to put the tactics together. First, put on a pair of Polaroids, and pull the peak of the hat forward to screen out extraneous glare, ensuring the best subsurface vision. Second, make sure to be wearing drab, inconspicuous clothes and at all costs avoid breaking the skyline when approaching the water. Third, walk as softly as possible and avoid creating vibrations that might alert the trout. Fourth, keep scanning the water until a trout reveals itself. This is particularly important. For some it is hard to understand that a trout, no matter how large, is often quite difficult to see. Not always does the whole shape loom into view: sometimes it is just a shadow on the bottom, or a fin, or a part of a tail. See something odd, that does not quite fit with the underwater scene, and study it with care. Very often, the outline of a trout appears as if by magic. A little white 'thing' that keeps moving may, on continued inspection, turn out to be the fleshy inner parts of a trout's mouth, appearing and disappearing as the mouth opens and closes. Fifth, estimate the actual size of the trout, and the depth at which it is swimming. This can be very misleading, and I have seen anglers experienced in other fields of trouting, who have assumed that a fifteen-pound rainbow swimming at twelve feet actually weighs about eight pounds and is only six feet deep. It really can be difficult making these assessments without a sound basis of historical knowledge as a guide.

Sixth, visualize the speed of the fish, and select a nymph or bug carrying a suitable amount of lead. Remember, you have to cast ahead of the moving trout, and distances and sinking speed have to be so precise that the nymph and the trout's mouth arrive virtually in the same spot at the same time. Some anglers find it easier to cast well ahead of the trout, let the nymph sink to the bottom, and then draw it up suddenly in a sort of 'induced take' retrieve, when the trout is suitably adjacent. Seventh, when you see the nymph vanish inside the mouth of the trout, and the thick lips have closed firmly, strike! Do remember that you have to strike hard enough to set the hook over the barb, which in the case of a No. 8 long-shank heavy-wire hook takes a fair amount of power.

So, following these procedures, adapted to suit every situation, big trout began to find their way into my net with some regularity, not just from Avington, but from other fisheries with fairly clear water and occasional monster inhabitants.

Richard Walker, with whom I had been developing

this approach, was also catching his share, or perhaps more than his share if you listened to less successful anglers. In 1976 he captured the largest rainbow caught up to that time in this country, and although there has been some confusion about its actual weight, I can tell you that after the required adjustment for error inherent in the scales used, it weighed exactly 18 lb 6 oz — a magnificent specimen of rainbow trout. For reasons all his own, Richard opted not to submit a record claim, but those of us who were in the know acclaimed it as the record, no matter that it had never been approved.

That fish was not bettered until April of the following year, when I took a rainbow just 1 oz heavier, as part of a total catch of two brace for $48\frac{1}{2}$ lb. (One of the four weighed $4\frac{1}{2}$ lb; the others were larger.) I made up my mind to submit a record claim, but before I could do so, Avington produced an even better specimen weighing 19 lb 2 oz. Roy Hopkins was the captor, and he then held the record until late May of the same year.

On that May day I was fishing with Melvyn Russ of *Angler's Mail*, and the well known Southern match angler, Ray Mumford. Ray had caught a marvellous trout during the morning session. If I remember correctly, it weighed 16 lb 6 oz and was the largest he had ever seen, let alone caught. I think that perhaps no more than four of us had taken larger trout at that time. I had seen little that I wanted to catch, and by early afternoon had more or less decided that it was one of those days. Then I saw a massive shape cruising slowly towards me, quite close in to the bank, which proved unusually easy to tempt into an indiscretion. That was the last easy thing that happened to me for a while.

These big trout can be really crafty, and this one was no exception. I had offered it a big Pheasant Tail Nymph, and under the buff wool of the thorax was a fair amount of lead; enough to permit the required final degree of accuracy in presentation. However, a freak ripple obscured the view just when I thought the trout might take, and when the ripple cleared, my fly was still there but the trout had moved a yard further away. I retrieved, recast, and this time there was no mistake.

On feeling the hook, that trout took off up the lake as if it was engine-powered. I applied massive sidestrain, and stopped it about thirty yards away, although the rod was groaning slightly under the pressure. So was I. I brought it back to the clear area in front of me, but again it ripped thirty yards of line through my fingers, and yet again the same sequence of events ensued.

Now a change of tactics on the part of the trout, which tried to bulldoze into a reedbed to my left. Time and again I would pressure that great head round, and time and again it would find the necessary strength to turn back. Then, so suddenly that momentarily I though I had broken, the strain came off and the trout bored down headfirst into a deeper hole. Now it started flailing that great spade of a tail, smashing it into the leader so forcefully that it felt as if some unseen power was hitting my rod with an immense club. I laid the rod over flat, parallel with the water, and heaved. That slashing tail was now missing the line, and quite soon I saw a flash of white underbelly as I turned the trout completely over. It came to the surface, lashing the water and shaking its head. I dropped the rod tip, to relieve the tearing pressure on the fly, and off went the fish again, attempting to seek refuge first in a clump of filamentous algae and then in a clump of weed. It succeeded in the latter, but the weed was very soft and sparse, and the leader sheared through it easily.

The huge fish was slowing down now, and I was in no doubt that I was getting the upper hand, until I saw that it was nosing into a patch of sandy gravel, rubbing the hook out. It was a matter of 'pull Devil, pull baker' now, because I had to get the trout up away from the danger zone. So I pulled until my arm felt as if it was coming out of its socket. And still I kept pulling, with the rod bending over until it looked as if it must break.

I jammed the butt into my groin, trapping the line with my fingers, and in desperation I tried to pump the fish up from the bottom, just as I would pump a big marlin or tuna up from the depths. I seemed to gain an inch or two, then hauling on the line with my left hand, I dropped the rod tip to take up surplus, and heaved again. There was a point when I felt that something had to break — the leader, the rod, me — but in the end, the trout conceded. It came to midwater, and hung there, still incredibly disputatious. I was in poor shape now: out of breath, saturated with sweat, and probably not of sound mind. I took a breather, just maintaining that awful strain, and then gave one final heave....

The trout hung a second longer, then rolled to the surface. As I drew it towards the net, a puff of blood came from its gills, and it never moved again. It was some time before I could do more than lie on the grass, panting for breath. I checked my watch again to know exactly how long it had taken me to beat Goliath. It felt like five hours, but the battle had lasted for just nine minutes.

An hour or so later, the weight was officially confirmed at $19\frac{1}{2}$ lb, a new British Record and, remarkably enough, a new World Record for landlocked rainbows. Fortunately, Melvyn had his camera with him, and he took what I shall always regard as the best black and white picture of a big rainbow that I have ever seen.

I have tangled with three other rainbows bigger than that, since 1977. Two of those I lost, and one I almost lost. In fact, I should have lost that, by rights, but everyone needs a trifle of luck occasionally, and I had my share that day — or maybe I did not. Judge for yourself.

I visited Avington early in September 1980, and very quickly spotted two rainbows cruising in the first lake. They were playing a slow follow-my-leader, with a trout of some 25 lb (my estimate) leading the way, and another perhaps 5 lb less in weight tagging along a yard in the rear. I spent the day stalking this magnificent pair, but without success. So I returned the following day, and the day after, with just the same level of achievement. On my fourth visit I began to feel that I might just manage to catch one — and if I could catch one, then surely I could manage both?

Shortly before lunch I found myself in a marvellous position to cast to the leading fish, the biggest of the two. My nymph drifted past its nose; it hesitated for a second or two, then swam on. The second trout swam straight up to the nymph as it lay on the sandy silt of the lake bed, upended a fraction, and picked it up. I struck very hard, set the hook, and the fight started. This was just the sort of bruising battle one expects from these dreadnoughts, and I find that it takes about three minutes before my arm goes dead, and I have to switch my rod to my left hand. Three minutes later, I have to switch back again! This went on for a while, and then for reasons best known to itself, that wretched trout elected to roll itself in my leader, until it had the whole three and a half yards wrapped round it. It is not pleasant nor easy to play a trout like that, so for the next few minutes it did pretty much as it pleased, while I hung on and prayed. But the pressure came off the hook, it came unstuck, and fell out.

So there I was, a huge trout wrapped in my leader, the hook flying free, and to make it worse, the trout had decided to unroll itself again and get rid of whatever it was entangled in. I tried pulling it to where my landing net was waiting, but only succeeded in hastening the unrolling process.

Then the hook took hold again, not in the mouth, but a fragilely insecure lodging in the operculum, the gill cover. I gave a hefty yank, hoping for the best, and set the hook very securely. By the time I inveigled it into the landing net, my arms had more or less given up on me and my legs were developing a distinct wobble.

I looked at this fantastic silvery fish, the greatest trout I have ever landed, and I was so distressed about the hook placement that I could easily have been sick. I did not want to know the weight, I did not want to take pictures, and most of all I did not want to talk to any of the 'gallery' that had been watching the fight at close quarters. I merely pointed at the hook embedded in the operculum, and explained that, according to the rules that govern such matters, I had caught that trout unfairly, which seemed to me to be very hard on a trout which deserved record status. Eventually I regained my equilibrium, and had the weight verified at 20 lb 5 oz, a potential record breaker if only the hook had remained in the mouth. A truly wonderful fish though, that fully deserves its glass case immortality which it duly received. I never saw the bigger of the two trout again.

The American brook trout, which is actually a char and not a trout at all, is to me a fascinating fish. When it is small, it rushes, like the Gadarene swine, upon its own disaster. As it grows larger, it becomes much wiser and wilier, which I think is why the British Record remained at 2 lb 7 oz for so long.

A sudden upsurge of interest in the species caused several waters in the South to arrange for some small numbers to be introduced, and over the next few years I played tag with the records. I forget how many times I actually broke the record — or rather, that I caught brook trout which themselves broke the record, but I think there must have been half a dozen such instances. Those I caught of record-beating, or record-equalling status, were at Church Hill Farm, Bossington Lake and Avington, of course. Every time I produced a record-beater, someone took another an ounce or two bigger within the week. It was great fun, and marvellous publicity for a superb species. However, when a fine specimen over 4 lb came from Scottish waters, I thought that would be the end of the contest for a very long time. I was quite wrong, and rather to my surprise I caught a hard-fighting beauty of 5 lb 6 oz, which was eventually accredited as the British Record.

That, I thought, was that. Brook trout have not revealed high growth rates in this country, not at all matching their performance in their home waters of the North American continent. All the waters which had contained stocks now appeared to be empty of everything except rainbows and brown trout.

Then, on 13 August 1981, I paid one of my irregular visits to Avington. Rumour had it that a number of cheetahs had been caught there, and I was very anxious to catch some more. In fact, I had taken quite a few there earlier, because for the previous season, and part of the current one, I had been playing tag with the record with my old friends, Peter Stone of Oxford, and John Wilshaw, Editor of *Trout Fisherman*. One of us would top the weight list, then one of the others would conjure a larger, and so it went on. On the day in question, I was in the lead with a six-pounder, having just pipped John's best by about two ounces. And we were all at Avington that day, so the contest was on again with a vengeance.

A cheetah is the hybrid produced by crossing the brook trout with the rainbow. The offspring is sterile, very handsome in its silvery bronze livery with darker irregular spots, rather like the markings of the cat after which it is named. Like the brook trout, it is something of a lurker, waiting to pounce on little items of food that go swimming by, and like the big rainbows, it responds very well to stalking and precision casting of a big nymph. At the time I write this, it does not figure on our Records list, for reasons that presumably make sense to the Records Committee, but do not ring any bells with me.

There were indeed a good number of cheetahs showing, and since they rarely show if they are not feeding, chances looked excellent. Peter Stone thought so when he speedily hooked a lovely fish and played it with his usual quiet efficiency, right into his landing net. It weighed $6\frac{1}{4}$ lb, so Peter had taken a cheetah of unofficial record status. Shortly afterwards, I hooked a beauty on a big nymph, and it proved to match that weight exactly. So now there was a draw at the head of the list. Peter then caught another, an ounce or two smaller, while I found a very lovely brown trout of exactly 5 lb. The only problem was that it managed to cause me some discomfort.

I should explain that at the end of May a careless fall had resulted in my fracturing my humerus, just below the shoulder. The fracture was not diagnosed for a fortnight, and no action was taken for yet another week, until a whole bevy of specialists had considered the problems. In the end I was instructed to keep it in a sling, without plaster, in the hope that it would mend by itself. I had been managing to fish left-handed, but my left shoulder is occasionally difficult to live with, as it was on this day, and rightly or wrongly I was using the unplastered broken arm, now hopefully mended, to fish with.

It was about noon, and I had been taking things easily for a couple of hours. So when I spotted a hugh cheetah, I did not hesitate to make the required cast. The take was immediate and savage, but the fight was not too difficult to control. Every time the cheetah tried to run, I managed to turn it, and things were going very easily. Too easily, I suppose; I should have known it could not last.

Suddenly the cheetah changed tactics, and resorted to a series of wild lunges, jerking the rod with such power that I was astounded. Apart from astonishment, I was also in considerable pain, because the jerks on the rod were jerking my arm, too. I held on for grim death, which with hindsight was undoubtedly stupid, because the pain grew steadily more unsupportable. I am not exaggerating when I say that my head was whirling, I had black spots before my eyes, and my knees buckled to such an extent that I was very lucky to have ended up on my knees on the grassy bank, instead of head first into ten feet of water. I had no option, I could not hold that violently lunging cheetah any longer, so I released the line and watched it vanish gratefully into the fastnesses of a very dense weedbed. After about ten minutes I began to feel rather better, and eventually scrambled unsteadily to my feet. The cheetah had obviously long gone.

Or had it? As I drew my line back, it tightened. Hooked in the weeds, I thought, but as I pulled more strongly I felt a distinct jolt, and then out into the open water sailed the cheetah, aggressive as ever.

I took the whole affair very steadily now, just maintaining light pressure, and easing the fish ever closer to the bank. With about five yards between fish and net, the rumpus started again. I dropped the rod, got hold of the line with my left hand, and pulled firmly. Cheetah, protesting vigorously, was obliged to follow. I stood on the line, keeping it taut, and taking a fresh grasp, pulled again. Once more, and the cheetah was over the net. Drop everything, heave left-handed, and there is a new top-of-the-table cheetah to admire. That one weighed $7\frac{3}{4}$ lb, and I really thought it had broken my arm again. I retired to The Plough in Itchen Abbas for a glass or two of painkilling medication, and failed to reappear on the fishery until nearly three o'clock in the afternoon. My arm still felt very odd, so I just strolled around, trying to spot good trout for others. Close to four o'clock, a passing angler asked me if I had tried for the very big American brook trout that was cruising the first lake. I had not seen it, and hastened to remedy my omission.

Brook trout are very easy to locate, because of their pronounced white stripe down the second ray of their pectoral fins, which seems to stand out like a beacon. Once I was on that first lake it took about two minutes to locate the brookie, and it did look to be a big one. It was maintaining a distance of a consistent twelve yards from the bank as it hunted nymphs. This is a nothing distance — except that when I tried casting, my right arm refused to cooperate, and would permit a maximum range of ten yards. That was better than left-handed casting, which might give an indication of the physical mess I was in.

It took more than half an hour of stalking before it came within my limited range, but it proved most obliging when it came to taking my Westward Bug. It also fought very reasonably, and it was merely a question of taking it easy and wearing it down. As soon as it was on the bank I knew it was *the* big one, and I took it to the official scales immediately. It registered an exact 6 lb, but unfortunately the witnesses to the weighing failed to show up for an eternity of ninety minutes, during which time body moisture had evaporated, to the tune of $2\frac{1}{2}$ oz. So the claim for a new record American brook trout has been submitted at 5 lb $13\frac{1}{2}$ oz.

It can reasonably be said of my pursuit of various species of big trout that I have not been accurate in suggesting that I am competing solely against the fish because an element of competition with other anglers does exist. Well, of course it does. When you go fishing with friends, do you not always do your best to outfish them, to catch bigger or more fish than they do? Surely that is part of the fun?

I think that is the point of the matter. Friendly competition is a facet, albeit a small one, of the social side of angling. But at the end of the day, as long as one of the 'party' has caught a good fish, or a good bag, then no one is more pleased about it than his alleged competitors.

CHAPTER 12

INTERNATIONALS FOR THE DISABLED

The competitive urge is as ingrained in man as is the instinct to fish. The disabled are as prone to the infection as the rest of us and Moc Morgan, President of the International Association for Disabled Anglers, traces how quickly in Wales friendly outings became transformed into top level competition:

> In the early seventies the Welsh Salmon and Trout Angling Association, the governing body for Game Fishing in Wales, decided to promote functions for the handicapped. Open guest-days were arranged centred on three reservoirs — Llandeyfedd in Gwent, Trawsfynydd in Gwynedd, and Brenig in Clwyd — with handicapped fishermen invited and all facilities provided.
> Advertisements in local and national papers advised the disabled to get in touch with their local angling club. Transport, tackle, boats, food, and helpers were all arranged to ensure a pleasant outing. At first these guest-days were just for fun, for mixing with other anglers and enjoying some gentle fishing. Soon the keen handicapped fly-fishers began to look on them as a chance to prove their skill and for friendly competition with each other. Prizes began to be given for the best bag and such was the enthusiasm that by 1980 the decision was taken to stage an international match for handicapped anglers on the Lake of Menteith in Scotland. The management of the Menteith Fishery generously allowed free use of the lake and its boats for the match, while the promoter, Tom Mackenzie, and his helpers worked tirelessly to make it a success. The Scots won on their home lake, but the English and Welsh had the satisfaction of many new friendships forged.

The really important fact was that a start had been made, and lessons learnt about staging such competitions. For the two visiting teams, it had been a long and tiring journey for one day's fishing, and for the future it was decided to add in a practice day. Wales had undertaken to stage the next international and our appeal for financial support raised over £4,000. This generous response allowed us to tell the Irish, Scottish, and English teams that we would meet all expenses except the travel.

The teams of six and one reserve fished the international at Llyn Brenig, and a very successful event it proved. The catches on the Friday were recorded in case adverse weather conditions made fishing impossible on the match day. But despite a keen east wind the Saturday competition went smoothly with most of the participants moving fish and enjoying their sport as they had done on the practice day. That was as important as the result. Important, too, was the social side with the extra day allowing further development of friendly contacts.

We were pleased that everyone was happy with the organization of this international, but inevitably there was room for improvement. The message we passed on to England for staging the international at Rutland at the end of June 1982 was the need for special attention to accommodation. Special requirements in this regard need to be passed to the host nation at least three months before the match as it is vital that proper arrangements are made.

After three internationals it is a good time to take stock. There have been failures and mistakes, but the greatest mistake of all would have been to do nothing to satisfy the ambitions of the disabled. The International Association for Disabled Fly-Fishers is now a much stronger and more experienced body. The anglers themselves are also more confident in their competitive ability and will soon be looking to the contests having all the trappings of full internationals. Some look forward to competitors having their own badges, ties, and the other insignia. The rules, too, will need to be more exactly drawn as the competitions become more prestigious, and arouse ever more widespread interest. No doubt they will have to include guidelines as to degree of disability, and other such matters, with tighter regulations the price of continued progress.

It has been a moving experience to be involved with this project from the outset. No doubt in a few years time our early efforts may seem very informal and amateurish. But the essential thing is that the start has been made and so many have had enjoyment from it. Without the cooperation of Water Authorities and Lake managements it would have been impossible to reach the present stage, just as the guest-days in Wales could never have started without the help of the Welsh Water Authority and the Trawsfynydd Management Committee. The willing assistance of so many helpers has been the other essential ingredient in giving the disabled anglers such a splendid outlet for their sporting and competitive instincts.

The Brenig match itself proved their considerable fishing ability as Moc recorded in these extracts of his report for *Trout Fisherman*:

> Competitors were two to a boat and had the same two boatmen for the two days. Most of the boats set off for the north and east banks, especially in the area close to the trees. The first quarter of the match was not as productive as hoped with only four fish taken by one o'clock. Then, as the weather warmed, the fish began to feed.
> The competitors had many fish move to their flies, and their major problem was in hooking them. One angler who succeeded admirably was Robert Muir from Selkirk who landed seven fish for a total weight of 6 lb 15 oz. That was close to winning the match for Scotland from his own rod, and he was unfortunate to lose four more at the net. This was no mean achievement as he has to fish virtually single-handed.
> His successful flies were a Silver Invicta, which killed a lot of fish, a Greenwell, and a Wickham's. He and his boat partner, Jack McFadyen, moved fish all day under the wood. Although the fish seemed to be moving well in the areas close to the forest, it was a difficult place to fish, as submerged trees gave the anglers no chance in playing trout unless they kept a tight line. Tommy McCallion from Sligo was one to find his fish snagged in a tree. He has only two hooks on his right arm to hold the rod, and only the small finger on his left hand to do all the intricate tasks which confront an angler. Tommy has to retrieve line through his

teeth, so his boatmen, Neil Elbourne and T.V. Jones, had some clever manoeuvring to do before the fish was worked free and netted to the general relief.

The English were unfortunate in that their best bag fell to their reserve, Brian Foster, and so did not count to their team total. Brian had four fish weighing 4 lb 3 oz, including the best fish of the match at 1 lb 10 oz. He has had a consistent international career with the second best bag at Menteith. The Welsh had an outstanding team performance with every member catching fish, and Simon Roberts as their top man. The silver salver for team performance went to Scotland with their winning 9 lb $9\frac{1}{2}$ oz beating Ireland by more than a pound. Mr Wyn Roberts, the Secretary of State for Wales, presented the prizes and complimented the organizers on giving the teams a truly Welsh welcome.

After that match the International Association for Disabled Fly-Fishers was formed and has ensured that each country in turn promotes the match with England taking over at Rutland Water in 1982.

Not only was Scotland first in staging a disabled international on the Lake of Menteith, but they have also been leaders in developing fly-fishing aids for the disabled, particularly for boat fishing. The man who organized that first international, Tom Mackenzie, was a President of the Committee for the Promotion of Angling for the Disabled and he recognizes with gratitude the assistance given by the Scottish Sports Council and by willing helpers from the Scottish National Angling Clubs Association. This is his account of how Scotland has promoted fly-fishing for the disabled up to competition level:

> As far back as the late sixties a few blind lads were taught to cast a fly towards an audible aid until competent enough to be taken out to fish. This was so successful that the committee was formed to encourage angling amongst the disabled. A unique feature of the committee was that it embraced all three types of angling — game, coarse, and sea.
> Because of Scotland's geographical formation boat fishing was judged the most suitable for the disabled since approaches to rivers and lochs are usually so rugged. One of the committee members designed a special boat-seat, as appropriate to the boat as to the disabled angler. This was a

great success and once ten had been acquired it was possible to organize a competition. The first to be held was a 'national' fly-fishing contest in 1979, arranged with the help of the Scottish Sports Council. This attracted an entry of thirty-four all of whom turned up on the day with most of them catching fish, including one blind boy from the original project.

The Lake of Menteith was chosen as the venue for several reasons. It is centrally located, the fishing is good, and the management was prepared to break with tradition and give us exclusive use of the lake on a Sunday. That made twenty boats available to us, and access to them was not too difficult. From a national competition it was a natural step to attempt an international contest the following year. Again this was held on Menteith with teams from England and Wales responding to the challenge, though Ireland unfortunately could not then get a team together.

The boats on the Lake of Menteith are small and can only seat three, limiting us to one boatman to two anglers. So teams were kept down to six with two helpers per team. Boatmen were provided by clubs and by members of the Committee for the Promotion of Angling for the Disabled. David Biggart organized the event on the day and a great job he made of it. The Scottish National Angling Clubs' Association presented a beautiful silver salver which is now the international trophy.

We had to stage the event on a shoe-string, costs being kept to a minimum. It was as much as the Scottish Committee could do to provide accommodation for two nights, pay the boat fees, and provide a dinner in the hotel after the match. We hope that in future some form of sponsorship will be forthcoming to enable Scotland to 'keep up with the Joneses' in staging the competition, and to lay on entertainment such as was enjoyed in Wales in 1981.

It was incidental that Scotland won both those first two matches. The result was of little importance compared to letting disabled people compete successfully in fly-fishing contests to their own intense pleasure and interest. Indeed once they are aboard a boat, they are no longer disabled as far as fishing is concerned.

The lead in helping disabled fishermen in England was taken

by individuals like Alan Roberts, now chairman of the English Disabled Fly-Fishers, and by Norman Woombs and Lynn Francis of the Leicester Handicapped Fly Fishers. Lynn Francis is himself an international having fished once for England and been reserve in two other matches. So he is well placed to judge competitive standards and know that this is a sport in which the disabled may hold their own with the fully fit. As this book went to press the Rutland disabled international was about to be held. This was his look at the prospects:

> 1982 is the year of the first disabled fly-fishing international in England. Leicestershire was obviously where this event had to be staged. For here in 1974 the first fly-fishing club for disabled people was formed, the Leicester Handicapped Fly Fishers, which has opened a new dimension of sporting enjoyment for many of its members. Catching your first trout is a great thrill for any angler and it's an even greater joy to a disabled person. The screaming of the reel as a good trout flies into the air — what excitement that stirs. And what pride it gives the disabled's helper to land this prize trout! This creates a close bond between them, often cemented by a good meal at the end of the day's sport.
>
> Many good anglers fish for our club. There is Brian Foster who has been second top angler in both previous internationals, and I hope will be individual champion at Rutland. There is Sandy Armstrong who always manages to hook a large one. He even hooked a Cortina when fishing for salmon in Glen Orchy! Fortunately it got off. Then we have Jason Brewer, our youngest expert, whose father is Welsh, but whose mother is English. He has divided loyalties, but it is England for whom he will hope to be top rod at Rutland.
>
> We must hope the day will be overcast with a light breeze blowing from the south-west. Then large bags of trout will deck the Rutland lawns and perhaps the first double-figure brown trout will be caught there to set someone smiling broadly. For the first time ever all the competitors will be staying in one hotel and we hope English hospitality will match that of our Celtic friends.
>
> Norman Woombs, our club secretary, always smiles when people talk about special privileges for disabled anglers: 'Treat us as equals and you may get a surprise at

how many fish we catch,' is his response. To people who are sceptical about helping disabled friends to fish I would say that we can learn a lot by teaching them, and then they in turn will help us improve our own fly-fishing!

Terry Thomas has watched the development of England's competitive fishing for the disabled, and helped publicize it as he records:

> Angling for the disabled, on a national basis, started by accident. It would have come about in any case, because fishing is an activity in which the handicapped can take part with less problems than those experienced in most other sports and games; but without the influence of fortune, the whole process would have been much slower.
>
> The man who started it all was Tommy Wadsworth, a fishing-tackle dealer from Leicester. Tommy spent some years in a Japanese prison camp; in consequence he is rather more aware of misfortune than most.
>
> At the time I was engaged in a long series of net-worked ATV half-hour programmes entitled 'Angling Today'. Tommy threw up the idea of a programme on handicapped anglers. Donald Shingler, my producer, and I discussed it. It was outside our brief. But we both agreed it was a subject which must be covered.
>
> We filmed the programme at Misterton Hall in Leicestershire, the home of Frank Craven, a man of many parts who in a very busy life finds time for all sorts of good works. On his small estate he has a lake. Here he has built a series of concrete paths whereby an angler in a wheelchair may easily find his way to the lakeside either, when reasonably mobile, on his own, or, when necessary, with help.
>
> We filmed anglers fishing from wheelchairs, and two blind men. One or two of the former had fished before they became disabled and provided they had full use of hands and arms, fished remarkably well. Some had to be coached in the necessary skills after they had become crippled. Much of the coaching by Tommy and his son Tony was carried out indoors. The most difficult cases were those in which there was only limited use of the hands. Here the Wadsworths improvised tackle. The 'push button' closed-face reel used in the American fashion on top of the rod proved a most useful tool.

The two blind men were even more interesting to watch. Their sense of touch was so acute that they had no difficulty in threading line through rings, although they did require help with terminal tackle. They could, of course, only fish with a ledger and I was amazed how accurately they cast, and always to the same place. How, I enquired, did they manage this? They counted throughout the cast and listened for the plop of lead on water. Thereafter they were able to repeat the performance nearly every time.

The three days filming proved as pleasant as it was fascinating, above all because of Frank Craven's hospitality in cooking superb barbecues and making free with his 10,000 bottle strong wine cellar. Several days after we had finished, Don Shingler phoned me. 'I've got some good news for you,' he said. 'We have had some trouble with the processing of the film.' 'How is that good news?' said I. 'Because, you fool, we have got to go back to Frank's and do it all over again.'

The programme was transmitted on the Independent network and repeated several times. Lord Grade, who rarely misses a trick, had it further networked on Christmas Eve.

The reaction from this exposure was astonishing. We found there were others besides the Wadsworths who saw the value of angling for the disabled. Peter Tombleson, the energetic Executive Director of the National Anglers' Council, organized a symposium in London attended not only by British angling bodies, but by representatives of a number of societies looking after the needs of the disabled both in Britain and on the continent. The NAC took over the interests of handicapped anglers and a permanent committee under the chairmanship of Mr A. Roberts of the Severn and Trent Water Authority in Nottingham has been set up. Very many fisheries now provide access and casting platforms for those in wheelchairs. As one disabled friend said to me, 'As long as I am sat on my bottom, either coarse fishing, or trout fishing from bank or particularly boat, I am almost as well off as a fully fit fisherman.' Competition angling in all styles is popular, and growing in popularity.

Much of the enthusiasm has come from disabled fly-fishermen in Leicester where they have in their club a number of members with considerable executive experience. They have been prime movers in organizing matches between nations.

The National Anglers' Council's *Guide to Fishing Facilities*, which also has a section on specialized equipment, is invaluable information for disabled anglers. In Scotland great strides have been made by the Committee for the Promotion of Angling for the Disabled with special boat-seats and harness based at Leven, Menteith and several other lochs. The Year of the Disabled in 1981 gave a further impetus to the development of aids and assistance for Handicapped anglers. Organizations such as the Fly-Fishers' Club made special efforts to help as did a number of private fisheries.

My own first experience of watching their remarkable versatility was in a specially arranged day for disabled fishermen at Linch Hill Farm Fishery at Stanton Harcourt near Oxford. When this fishery was built from converted gravel pits, the Amey Roadstone Corporation also took care to make it as accessible as possible for the disabled with a wealth of facilities to aid fishing, as well as toilet and other arrangements for them. There were a number of individual competitions on that day, but primarily it was for the disabled to enjoy a day's fishing with a number of helpers there to ensure even the most crippled had their sport.

Up to a hundred disabled anglers came from all over England, all with a range of serious disability from blindness to multiple-sclerosis. What an ideal sport fly-fishing can be for them was clear from their pleasure in it. Easy winner of the main competition was osteomyelitis sufferer, Brian Foster. Fishing on crutches, but needing assistance only in the netting of fish, he had eleven rainbows by noon. Standing straight, and casting long, he had an intensity of concentration and a skill any fit competition angler might envy. There was a sureness of touch to his casting and striking remarkable when you consider the balance and effort required to fish for hours on end with a crutch under either arm-pit. Much of the early advance in aiding the disabled to fish has centred on the Leicester area and it was there Brian saw an advert offering casting tuition, and had soon become a dedicated and successful trout fisherman. As he put it, 'If you are keen enough and determined enough, disability doesn't stop you learning to fish and getting a new value in your life.'

The first fish of the day went to a man who had shown to

what lengths it was possible to go with that enthusiasm and dedication. Martin James had come down from Burnley for the day. That was a nothing journey for a man who had recently realised a boyhood dream to fish the Amazon, despite being a sufferer from multiple-sclerosis: 'I caught man-eating catfish up to 70 lb, and piranhas. The Indians landed them for me. The piranhas weren't dangerous once they cut off the bottom jaw, which they were skilled in doing.' Working for the BBC, Martin had experience of facilities available for the disabled and positive views about them. 'I'm inexperienced in fly-fishing and have to rest my hands after every few casts. But I wasn't going to miss coming to a fishery which makes such intelligent provision for us.

'Access is all-important for the disabled and here they provide a track running round the lake close to the water so that you can drive anywhere on it and end near your chosen fishing spot. Then the grass verge is kept mown which is important for wheelchairs, as are the concrete casting platforms all round the lake. Not many Water Authorities concern themselves with providing facilities of this standard, and we are usually best looked after in private fisheries of this nature.'

There was, however, a warning from one angler about some of the casting platforms: 'I have to be very careful on this one, because there is a slight incline towards the water and no guard-rail. A friend of mine used to come fishing with me, but at another fishery his wheelchair ran down a platform with a sharper incline. He found himself up to his neck in water and quite helpless, and though several anglers soon came to his assistance, it put him off fishing for a time.'

There was plenty of help available to any who needed it on this day. Stephen Simmons, blind son of a policeman, was himself aided by a policeman to go out in the boat and soon caught four. 'It's a marvellous feeling for a blind person,' he told me when I motored over to talk to him, 'provided, of course, the day is as fine as this and the fish are moving.' Clive Parsons, crippled by meningitis was another who needed constant assistance, but most were able to fend for themselves. Most ingenious of these was Michael Jerrams, who drove his car onto a casting platform, unhinged the door, and fished away happily still sitting in the driver's seat. The last word, however, came from another self-sufficient fisherman, Joe Hyde: 'I've problems with my hips, heart, and a strangulated hernia. You name it, I've got it. But I still get immense pleasure from angling. Perhaps the most important thing for us is the welcome we get at any water. In general water-bailiffs and anglers are a friendly and helpful lot, who go out of their way to make us feel at home. That means a lot to us.'

Another to admire their skill and help them find that warm welcome is Steve Windsor, senior writer for *Trout Fisherman*. This is his experience of seeing them fish for pleasure or in competition:

> The modern carbon rod, weighing just a few ounces, has revolutionized fly-fishing for the disabled. Gone are the bulky leather and brass harnesses apparently designed for unfortunate victims of the First World War. Their replacement by modern tackle has brought a generation of very skilled anglers who overcome their disabilities with remarkable dexterity.
>
> When the round of fishing heavily stocked trout waters begins to pall, nothing can beat the new inspiration which comes from a day out with a group of disabled anglers. Three examples come to mind. Very different, they each illustrate the pleasure that the disabled can take in fly-fishing.
>
> The first was from a wet and dismal day at Rutland Water. Lynn Francis, a Headmaster from Ibstock and a fine angler himself, who is totally dedicated to helping the handicapped to fly-fish, had organized a day for a group of disabled youngsters from Ashfield School in Leicestershire. Along with other helpers from the oldest disabled fly-fishing club in the country, Leicester, Lynn had made sure they were well-equipped and that boats were available, though the intention was to fish from the dock where 'tame' fish often swim. It rained steadily on all the party, but that couldn't dampen the enthusiasm of the young fishermen. The vast trout that lived under the dock had gone, no longer fed and treated as pets, but the boats did yield one or two fish to two totally delighted first-time fishermen, Craig Hutchinson and Gary Hancox.
>
> They might have been inspired by the example of another youngster, Jason Brewer, who has overcome enormous problems to fish his way literally single-handed into the England Disabled Fly-Fishers team. Jason qualified at Draycote on the second day I have in mind, the 1981 England Disabled team championship. It wasn't the

high standard of the fishing that was memorable that day, nor even the smooth organization, nor the wonderful turn-out of volunteer boatmen. It was one simple two-minute incident involving just one angler.

He didn't figure in the weights and though he fished all day he caught nothing. Instead he won his personal battle right at the start. Confined as he was to a wheelchair it took six or seven pairs of determined hands to lift him into the boat. But his expression was worth all their efforts. As he lit his cigarette, settled back, and breathed deeply, his eyes told the story. For the first time for years he was going out fishing.

The England Disabled team fishes to a very high standard. Indeed their ranks contain a former full international, Brian Foster from Leicester. He was there catching plenty of fish on the third special occasion, that guest-day at Linch Hill Fishery celebrating the Year of the Disabled. It was a gathering of familiar faces, with the Leicester Disabled Anglers out in force, and really flexing their muscles on the willing Linch Hill fish. The sun shone and the Minister responsible for the Disabled, Hugh Rossi, strolled on the banks, praising the determination of the anglers. That determination was beautifully illustrated by the uncanny skills of some young anglers like Jason Brewer or the blind Steve Simmons. Fishing from a solidly built casting platform Roy Owen related how building rods and preparing tackle helped him through long painful nights. A little advice helped bring him his first fish and gave us as big a thrill as him.

If you're not involved with disabled fly-fishing you're missing out on a series of inspiring experiences. Watching these men and women overcome the myriad problems that a simple day's fishing presents for them, reminds us that all we have to do is catch fish. Fit, and with all our faculties, we can find that hard enough. The competitors in disabled internationals often overcome more problems on one trip than most of us encounter in a fishing career. They remind us how grateful we should be for our sport.

CHAPTER 13

COMPETITION LAKES AND LOCHS — AND HOW TO FISH THEM

> *Adam had a son*
> *Married Noah's daughter*
> *Nearly spoilt the flood*
> *By drinking up the water.*
>
> *This he would have done*
> *I, at least, believe it*
> *Had the mixture been*
> *Only half Glenlivet.*
>
> Anonymous — and very wisely so

Failure to introduce that Glenlivet into the Flood has fortunately left us with some magnificent loughs, lochs, and lakes whose glistening waters so often add to the joys of fly-fishing on such as Leven or Corrib. Other man-made competitive waters are not far behind, with clever landscaping giving a natural beauty to the settings of Chew or Rutland. Even a blank day's fishing can be enhanced by such scenery, but the colours seem that much richer when there are trout in the boat. That feeling was summed up by a distinguished member of an England team which had just fished an international at Llyn Alaw. Some 384 man-hours of fishing had resulted in the forty-eight team of anglers achieving a total bag of three trout so small that they did not even weigh 2 lb between them. 'In away matches recently,' was his comment, 'it's been a case of fish to the acre in Scotland, acres to the fish in Ireland, while here we've had to be content with acres and acres of pleasant water.'

Any angler approaching a new water finds his pulse beats quicker, not because of the surrounds, but at the prospect of a new fishing experience. His day is made by that first swirl in the water, that skip of a heart-beat as the line tightens. Thereafter he can relax and enjoy himself in the certain knowledge that he may catch other fish later. But how give yourself the best chance from the start of the day in an unknown water?

For Highland lochs I worked out a satisfactory method of search when fishing with my son, John, and daughter, Sarah. Faced with the twenty-mile length of Loch Shin, and no advice about the best areas, I was reminded of a Cameron Highland officer's comment when confronted by the intimidating Keren Massif in the last war: 'Mountain warfare is like fishing a strange loch. There is a daunting expanse of water, and your flies look very insignificant. But you must start somewhere if trout are to be caught, and a blend of guesswork and experience tells you where to begin.'

We tried to reduce the guesswork. Our system was to row round close to the shore (a much more promising area in such lochs, than the central deeps), side-casting with one rod, trolling with another. As soon as we moved trout, especially if it was to side-casting, we began a proper drift fishing the area intensively. Within a day we had located a number of 'hot-spots', discovered the best fishing was along peaty, rather than rocky shoreline, and found the wide-curving bays unproductive compared to the small inlets. This type of search, backed by the variety of a four-fly cast, has always proved successful for us in such waters, cutting out any waste of time before achieving large baskets by normal fishing.

Such methods are unnecessary (and trolling often illegal) in the main competition waters, which are well enough organized that some general advice is available before you start. But the competitive fly-fisherman needs a little more than that if he is to cut corners in getting to know the lake as well as he would like in order to feel confident he is fishing in the right way and the right place. This and the following chapter aim to pass on the kind of advice he might seek from those with expert knowledge of each water.

First, however, there is a lesson in the fishing of all such lakes in competition which was taught to me the hard way. Bob Church had asked me to make up the numbers in his team against the English Fly-Fishers in one Rutland match. That was not a lake I then knew well, and I was relieved when my boat rival won the toss to take charge at the start. This he was clearly glad to do, and informed me of the policy he would follow:

'There are some stock fish not far down from the lodge so we will drift down on them straight away. The start is one of the best times of the day, so we don't want to waste half-an-hour of it motoring to the top of the lake. If we start catching fish we must stay with them, and not start worrying that someone else may be catching more, or larger, in another area. So don't go motoring off somewhere else, when you take over, if we are doing well here.'

That seemed sound sense, and I was happy to agree, particularly as he was a Rutland regular. His knowledge of where to find the stock fish proved excellent, his fishing method of very long casting, and very small flies, more successful than mine. By one o'clock I had only hooked two, while he had seven in the boat. At that stage he suddenly said: 'It looks as if I'm bound to get my limit of eight shortly. Do you mind if I go in soon, and get another ticket? By then it will nearly be time for me to take over, and we can motor away up the south arm. We are only catching small ones here, and they may be getting the big browns up there.'

I willingly assented, but asked if he was wise to abandon the principles he had asked me to follow. 'Why not stay here while we continue to move fish?' He was not to be dissuaded, even though the officer issuing the new ticket made the same comment. So off we went up the south arm. We had some pleasant scenery to enjoy, and I was glad to be introduced to new areas, to which I hadn't penetrated before. But not a fish did we catch. So when it was my turn again, I motored back to where we had caught them. The journey to-and-fro alone wasted an hour. And by the time we were back at the killing spot a flat calm had descended on the lake. He didn't even get his first limit, let alone a second! How much wiser to have stuck to his original plan. Bob Church did. Having found fish moving near the aerator pumps he just went on catching them, ending with thirteen, and a victory for his side.

Bob, of course, is highly experienced in these Midland waters, and this is his advice on how to fish them:

DRAYCOTE, GRAFHAM AND RUTLAND

Our three main competition waters are Grafham, Draycote and Rutland and I assume that England will be using these, with the addition of Chew Valley Lake, in all their forthcoming home internationals.

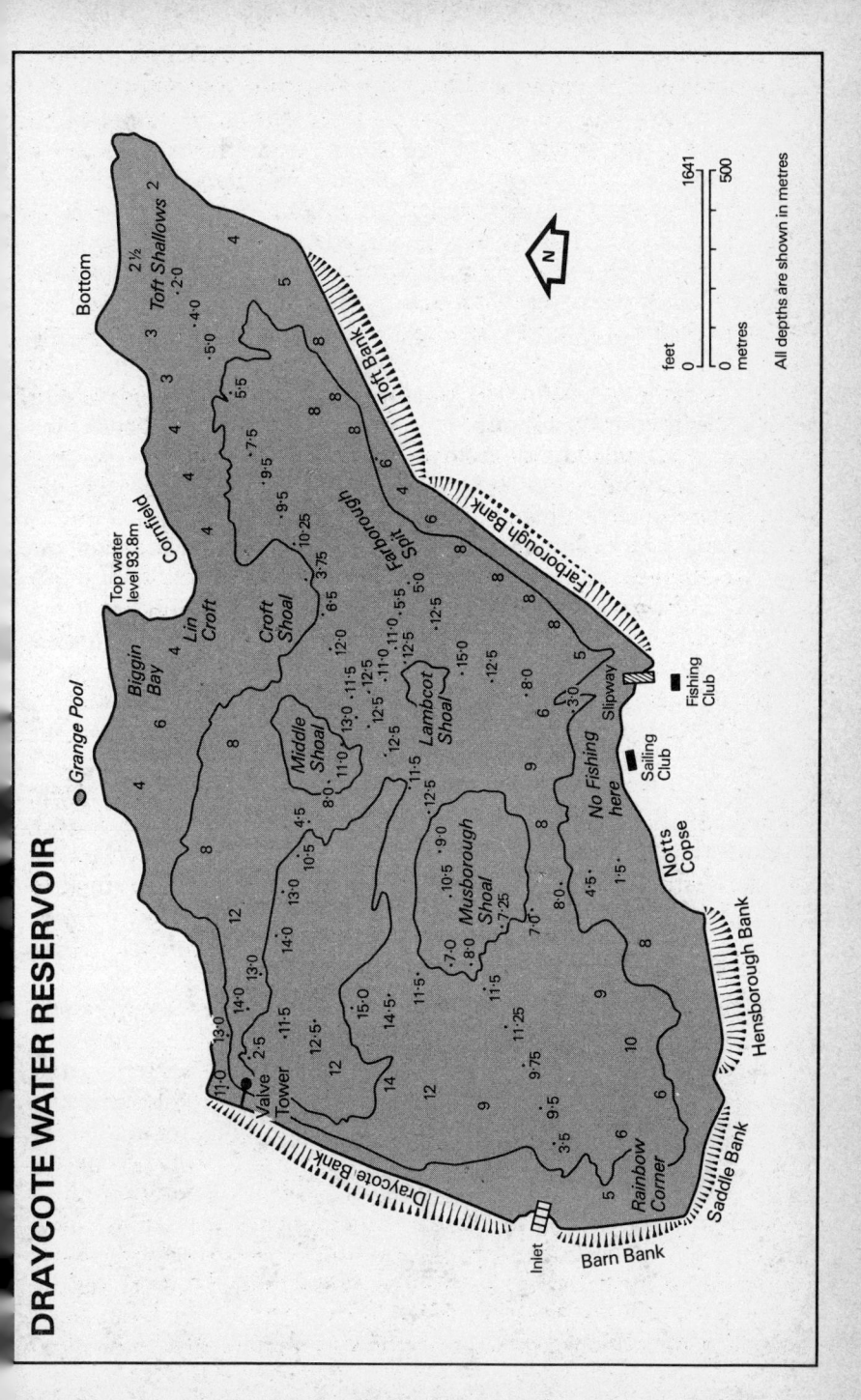

To put it bluntly, competition fishing can in most cases end up as a 'stockie bashing' session. Knowing the movements of newly introduced stock fish can therefore be of great benefit to any keen competition fly-fisher. In May of the 1981 season Draycote water was chosen for the first time to stage an international match. England of course were the hosts, ably managed and captained by that successful Northampton duo Tom Bilson and Bob Draper. There were lots of trout caught by all four countries with England winning by the narrowest of margins from the Welsh.

Ninety-nine per cent of all fish taken on the day were recently stocked fish, both rainbows and browns, and these accumulated on the down wind side of the reservoir in the area known as Toft Bank and Shallows. What usually happens is this. Fish are released from the stew ponds which are situated behind the valve tower. From this point the fish make their way down wind (usually westerly) into the area know as 'Biggin Bay' and this is a good spot for drifting into. However, the majority of the fish do not stop here, but continue round Lin Croft point and down towards Barn Bay.

If you would draw an imaginary line from the Old Barn to the end of the stone dam wall opposite, and then fish from this line in the direction towards the end of Toft Shallows by the M45 motorway, you would be fishing over the shallow rich feed area that nearly always holds the most fish. This has been my experience since the water opened in 1970. Favourite flies for Draycote are Soldier Palmer, Invicta, Mallard and Claret, Ginger Quill, Butcher, 'Mini' Black Chenille, Dunkeld and Blae and Black.

Grafham's stock fish behave with almost computer-programmed regularity of movement. After being released close to the fishing lodge they follow the westerly wind and shallower near-side bank, moving steadily past the yacht club, past the sludge pits and finishing up in the area from Gaynes Cove Bay down to the right-hand corner of the dam. As the season progresses the north shore from G marker buoy into the left-hand corner of the dam is also a very good drift. It would appear that the stronger the wind into the dam and the more overcast the day so increases the chances of a big catch. Grafham is still the best rainbow-trout water in the country. Favourite flies for Grafham for international-style fishing are, Soldier Palmer, Grenadier, Wickham's Fancy, Silver Invicta, Invicta, Mallard and Claret, Black and Peacock, 'Mini' Muddler and Greenwell's Glory.

It is the wind once again that governs the movement of the Rutland stock fish even though they are spread out well when released over the whole deep water area. When the westerly wind is on, it blows into the dam. The best drifts then are 70-80 yards out from Normanton Church drifting into the corner of the dam by the valve tower, another good drift is from the submerged bush on the Whitwell bank to the left-hand corner of the dam.

As the summer wears on and the many aerator pumps are switched on, lots of rainbow trout gather in shoals on the down wind side of this oxygenated disturbance. Drifting in the ring formed around this disturbance and then finally down wind from it usually produces plenty of fish coming to the fly on the top.

Favourite flies for Rutland are Queen-of-the-Water, Soldier Palmer, Old Nick, Wingless Wickham, Teal and Red, Invicta, 'Mini' Muddler and Goldie.

Rutland is the only one of these three which has yet to stage a full international, but it is fast becoming the most popular English competition water of them all.

RUTLAND

Brian Thomas, an English Grafham Trophy winner, and expert regular on Rutland Water, has this to add about his favourite lake:

Rutland is the pleasantest, and most productive water I've fished. It has such variety with its different depths, its sheltered bays, its sunken fences, and its ability to provide as good sport for bank anglers as for those in a boat.

Since the water opened in 1976 I have seen a number of good drifts develop. You may catch fish anywhere, but Rutland is such a big lake it pays to know the best. To start with the dam area. If in doubt, fish here. The fish stocked from Whitwell Creek all make for this part before moving up one of the arms. With the regular stocking you can catch trout near the dam throughout the season.

The most popular drift is down from Whitwell Creek to the north end of the dam. But the more productive one is along the south bank from the Three Trees down to the south-east corner of the dam, or 'fantasy island' as the locals call it. There is no fantasy, however, about the good bags this drift will produce if the wind is right.

Up the north arm there is an attractive drift between Armley wood on the Hambleton Peninsular and Barnsdale Creek. In the deep water you can usually see good fish moving, and it fishes well in any wind except a very cold north-easterly. Motoring on up this arm you come to the Tower. A lot of trout are taken here, but more by those using a sunk line and big lures. Some good browns show in this area early in the season and can be taken with loch-style fishing. The best however is saved for the last. The shallows at the top, from the entrance of Dickinson's Bay right up to the start of the bird sanctuary, usually provide splendid fishing. It is particularly attractive to traditional style anglers as fish are often to be seen moving here, and in warmer weather there is a good hatch of fly, especially in the evenings. Drifting out from or into the Burley Bank, according to the wind, can be profitable. So can the reverse drifts from the Peninsular Bank opposite. If you really start catching them here in competition don't forget it will take nearly half-an-hour to motor back in. It would be a pity to be disqualified. If you have found this area at its best, you may well have a winning bag.

'The south arm has some excellent drifts as well. Around Normanton Church is often good, particularly in the deep water out from the Sailing Club, and on down to the Church. This is at its best, however, outside competition hours. Once the boats have returned to their moorings, the fish seem to rise freely here in the evenings, as if to make up for time spent dodging the yachts. When other areas are quiet, you will often find trout moving here for the last few hours of the day. This is the ideal place to come to end the frustration of a fishless day elsewhere.

The cream of the daytime fishing in this arm is higher up. Take a line from the top of the Berrybutts Bank across to the Old Hall Bay on Peninsular Bank. Drift that and all the water up to the bird sanctuary and you have a good

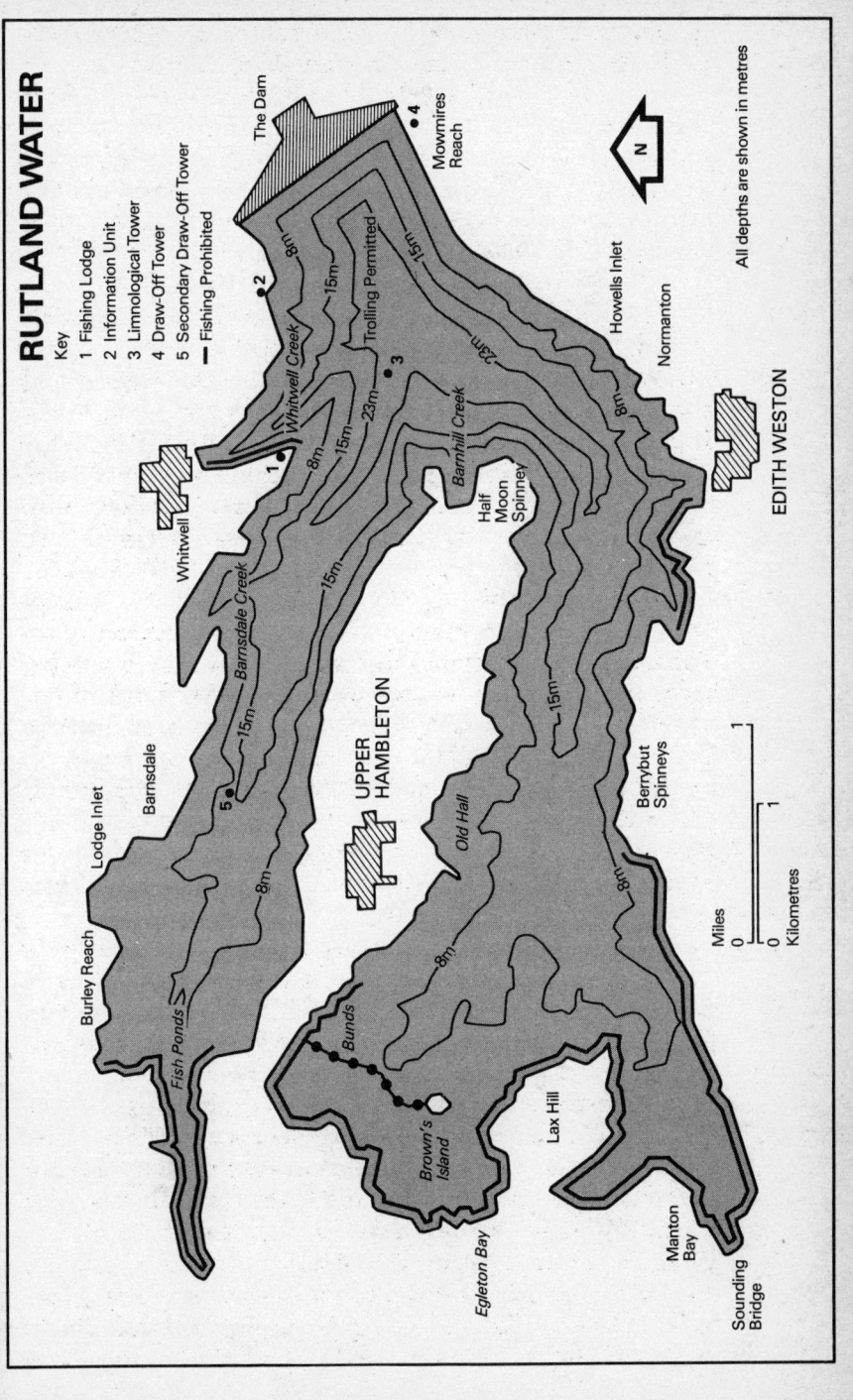

chance of a heavy basket of good fish. The bigger ones seem to home to this part, and if you have the knack you certainly have the chance of taking large browns and rainbows.

Another drift not to be missed is from the edge of Brown's Island down the point of Old Hall, and from there across Old Hall Bay down to the wood on the peninsular. It can also be productive around Lax Hill, if the wind is right. This is another relatively shallow area which can be fun to fish in loch style. But then so can many of Rutland's drifts, and to me this is an ideal competition water. Blank days are very much the exception, and at any time of the year you can hope for a really heavy catch.

There is nothing complicated either about method or flies. The traditional styles, whether short or long lining, are as productive as any. While everyone may have their own fancy about flies, just a small selection keeps me happy here throughout the season. The Soldier Palmer, both red and fluorescent red, is a *must* for me to have on the cast. So is a Grenadier tied palmer fashion. No wonder the Army won their first inter-services match here! The other flies I perm on the cast are Wickhams, winged and wingless, Invictas, silver and standard, Mallard and Claret, and the Bibio. Sometimes I also use small nymphs of my own pattern with a fluorescent green head. This selection is enough to cover all my needs at Rutland, and I fish them with confidence unconfused by wondering about alternatives. Mostly I use sizes 10 to 12, but go up or down depending on whether it is stormy or calm (and it is another advantage of Rutland that there is usually some breeze somewhere to ruffle the surface). The one constant on my cast is the Soldier Palmer on the bob. It fishes well from April to September and is first choice at the start of a normal day's drifting.

None of us are competitive fly-fishers all the time, or indeed much of the time. Some of us, however, continue to use traditional loch methods when fishing for fun. But then you are bound only by your own preference and the rules of the water you are fishing.

Many more then opt for using whatever method is legal, enjoyable, and most likely to catch fish. And why not? For fishing Rutland in these circumstances an expert on the water,

B.J. Davies, gives advice which can equally apply to other similar reservoirs:

> At the start of the season, use fast sink or hardcore line with a Black Lure dressed very fine on tandem eights long-shank hook and fish it steadily in 12–20 ft of water by day. In the evening go to a sheltered bank using the same lure, but with a slow sink line. Cover the odd rise as well and you should take some good browns. When the water warms towards the end of May, use the same tackle fished fast in mid-water. In the evening, fish with large white lures and again you will have very good chances for big browns.
>
> In June loch-style fishing is best with size 12 flies such as Soldier Palmer, or Pheasant Tail with a small Muddler on the point. On days when this doesn't work switch to a fast sink line with a size 6 long-shank Worm Fly dressed with a hot orange tail. Fish it deep. As another alternative, try anchoring the boat in 7–12 ft of water and change to a cast of three nymphs and a floating line. Fish slow with the point fly on the bottom.
>
> In July and August use a floating line and the same methods as in June, but with a Silver Invicta on the point for your loch-style fishing. If that doesn't bring fish, go to deep water and try a slow sink line and a small Black and Silver lure fished deep and slow. In a flat calm, use the same line and lure, but look for and cover rising fish, chasing round to locate them if necessary.
>
> By September trout are often hard to find on top and the best method is the Black and Silver lure fished fast in water 2–7 ft deep with weed on bottom and the lure worked just above the weed. That method holds good for rainbows in October. But if you are after big browns use a lead-core line with a large Black and Silver or White and Silver lure fished very fast in 10–40 ft of water.
>
> If you use these methods and flies you should have good bags of fish throughout the year and some memorable days or evenings with the big browns.

GRAFHAM

When I asked David Fleming-Jones, who, apart from himself,

were the experts on Grafham Water he picked out three: 'Tom Bilson can write with authority on the traditional loch method at Grafham, Bob Church and Bob Draper on the more radical approach.' So here is Tom Bilson as guide to this water:

> Grafham is approximately 1500 acres and has thirty-eight boats. It is ideal for competitive fly-fishing, with the deep water area around the dam, and the productive bays of varying depth, making for excellent fishing in any conditions.
> Stocking starts with the browns in March, and continues with rainbows from April to August. The water was first opened in 1966, a year ahead of the intended date. The 12-inch trout had grown so large so quickly that when the authorities saw 3–5 lb fish cruising round, they opened in mid-season, and the first couple of years provided remarkable sport. The strength of those early trout will never be equalled, and the fishing could not be sustained at that high level, particularly as management problems developed. The arrival of perhaps the greatest of all Fishery Managers,

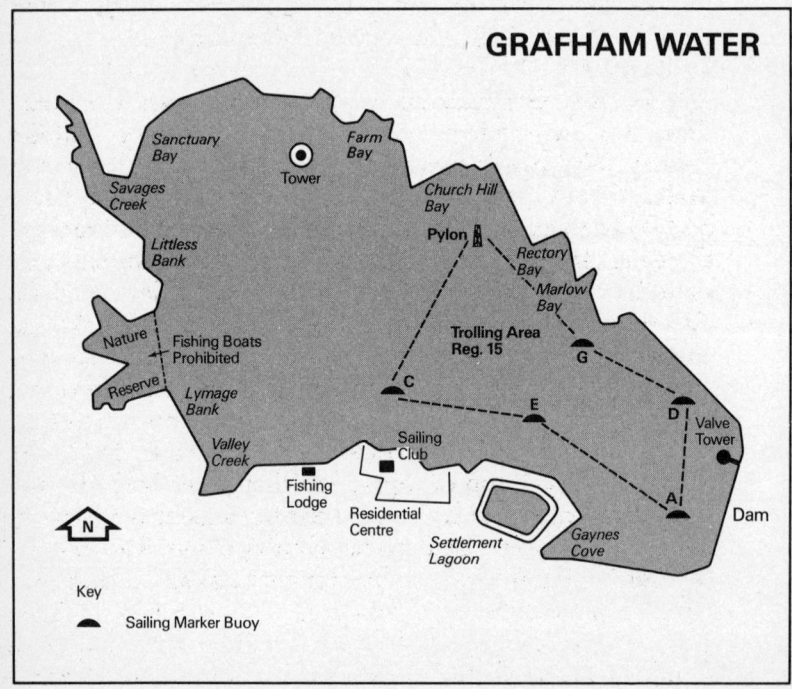

David Fleming-Jones, soon resolved that difficulty. With his wife, Pat, sharing his love of fishing, he soon made Grafham into what I regarded as the best trout water in Europe at the time. Now he has retired, we have to hope the standards can be maintained, knowing how easy it is for a fishery to slip back.

The Authority's best move was to ban Lea-boards and Rudders, which had promoted a method of fishing far removed from the traditional concept, with the boat catching the fish rather than the angler. That was no hardship for the anglers either, as fishing the drift on the surface was usually more productive at Grafham, anyway.

Though I may be biased about this, it is also my belief that proper fishing there was preserved and encouraged, as in many other areas, by the formation of the Confederation of English Fly-Fishers. In the widespread competitions with eliminators, Midlands final, and national final, tremendous encouragement was given to fish traditional loch-style with small flies tied as 10s, 12s, 14s or 16s. The East Midlands Club has members who fish almost exclusively at Grafham, and who all use the international method. The Club has the unique record of sixteen internationals, including the current England captain, Bob Draper, all in the last decade.

To fish Grafham successfully, you must use small flies. My own selection is Greenwell's Glory, Soldier Palmer, Wickham's Fancy, Invictas (Silver and Standard), Mallard and Claret and Dunkeld (standard and with silver body). The wingless Wickham can be a killer if you remove the wings from a palmer-tied Wickham. Pheasant tails and nymphs of various patterns have some good days, and we also tie mini versions of muddlers, and lure flies, like the chenilles, to conform to international fly sizes. I have also used with good effect some flies picked up in international competition. There is the Morning Glory, with which Eric Campbell won a Brown Bowl at Grafham in 1977, the Green Peter as a top dropper, and that other Irish fly, the Fiery Brown, which has accounted for a great many trout in this country, particularly at Grafham and Rutland.

At Gratham I use 7 lb breaking strain cast, taking 14 ft from the spool, and tying two droppers only. In a flat calm I go down to 5 lb, and fish Cove Pheasant Tail or a Dunkeld as a single fly on the cast. In tying a normal cast, I leave about 6 ft between the middle dropper and the tail fly, which allows me to change the point fly as often as I like. For the same reason, I tie my droppers some 9-inches long. The top dropper is the key fly. Remember that more important than any particular fly is having confidence in your patterns. So stick to those you believe in on match days, remembering that the colours black, white and orange are the most likely to take trout.

At Grafham it is rarely wise to use a drogue, and much better to drift quite quickly, in order to find fish. Once you locate them, then use a drogue if you must. My standard plan for fishing Grafham is a first drift in front of the lodge, then off to Perry Point, then to the first bay going east by the Yacht station. There you will see a seat on the bank, and you should aim your drift at this. Start your drifts about 500 yards off shore, shortening them as you find where the fish are taking. So before you start a drift mark some point which will enable you to return to the same spot if you wish. Always keep moving if you aren't taking fish, and always keep watching other boats to see if there are any taking areas.

From the seat point you go to Gaynes Cove; two drifts are enough at each of these points before moving on to the southern end of the dam. The dam has a retaining wall, and if you count eighteen slabs from the southern end this is usually a particularly good place into which to drift. Start 300 yards out, and drift in. Bank anglers know these hot spots, too, so be careful to give them plenty of room.

'The area of dam we call the Band Stand is also very good, and in 1977 John Ketley nearly won the Brown Bowl fishing this area. My next move is to the famous 'G' marker buoy. I guess more fish have been taken here than anywhere else. If you get advance information that it is fishing well, your only sensible move is to go straight there at the start, and keep there as long as you take fish.

Other good areas are Church Cove and the shore between there and 'G' marker, then from the Valve Tower fishing into Hill Farm, and what is now known as Pig Bay. Ignore the area up from there and go over to the West Bank fishing all along this, fairly close in, up to Bird Sanctuary bay, and particularly the area between the Sanctuary and Littleless bank. The central areas can also be effective between the Sailing Club and Church Hill bay from June on. It is a marvellous lake to fish, and will remain so if those in charge resist modern pressures for the introduction of coarse, and pike fishing, power boats, and the like.

CHEW VALLEY LAKE

The other great English competition lake is Chew Valley, snuggled close to the Mendips. Its brochure claims to provide 'a day's relaxation and sport amid magnificent scenery', and no Trade Descriptions Act could fault those words. With the even more beautiful Blagdon Lake close-by, West Country anglers have little incentive to travel elsewhere, as Chris Ogborne makes clear in his description of fishing Chew:

> It is a big lake, but at no time does it seem too vast, as there are always intimate bays to provide some shelter even on the worst days. With tremendous variety in depth, bankside configuration, and aquatic life, it would be hard to imagine a better venue for loch-style fishing.
> Apart from very early and late season, when water temperatures are low, surface fishing is both practical and advisable. Fly life is prolific from May onwards, and there is frequently an evening midge hatch from late April. May is the best month for buzzers, and the first sedges appear in June, as does the damselfly. At the other end of the trout's diet, of course, are the perch and other fry, which abound in the whole lake area.
> The best drifts on Chew vary with the season. In fact, to listen to half-a-dozen regulars discussing drifts, you would find it very hard to decide where to go, so great is the variety of opinion. However, to try to generalize let me take things month by month:
> In May the water-level is still high, but with the warmer weather comes higher water temperature. For many, this means the cream of Chew fishing — with the Grenadier. Indeed for the whole of May and June I tend to leave the Grenadier on the top dropper almost all the time. It is devastatingly successful, particularly when held in the surface just before lifting off, when some spectacular takes can come. If nothing obvious is hatching, a safe hedged-bet cast would include Mallard and Claret, Wet Wickhams and

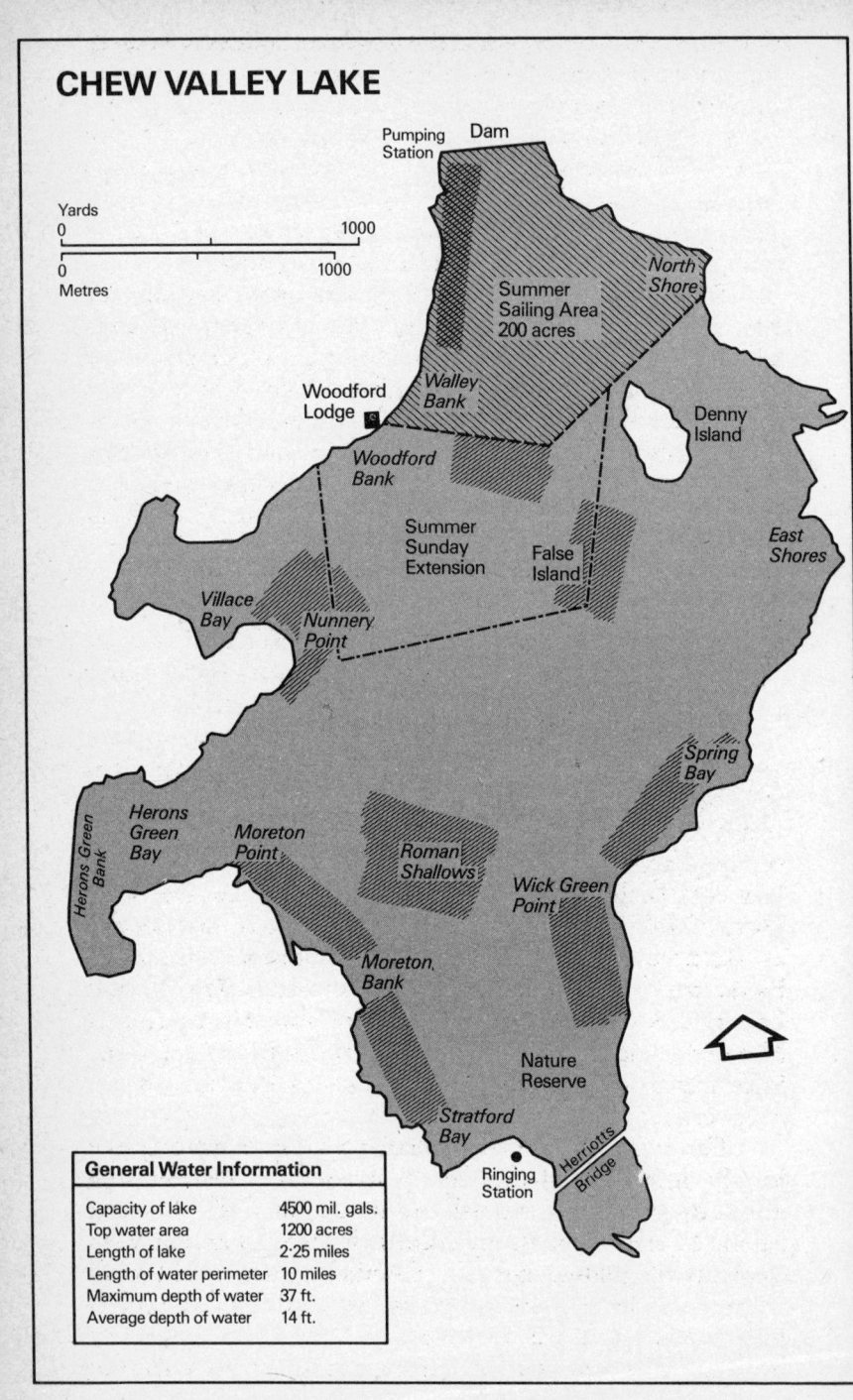

Grenadier. However, when the large red midges are hatching, I would always include Red Buzzer, and maybe even double up to two Grenadiers. On warm days in late May I have often blinkered myself and simply tied on three of them — to fish at varying levels. Depending on the wind, a drift anywhere off the False Island, or between Denny Island and Nunnery, is productive, although in early season it always pays to search for rising fish.

By June and July water-levels are dropping, and the first place to try for a morning drift is over the Roman Shallows. This has the glorious advantage of being fishable in any wind direction, and the only problem people have is finding the exact location. By July, the weed beds on the Shallows are a giveaway, but earlier on you need to be a little more scientific. Like anything else, it's easy when you know: simply line up the two bird-watching hides on Wick Green and Moreton, and you find the Roman Shallows exactly half-way across. The Grenadier still fishes well, although on cloudy days Black Pennell, Soldier Palmer, and short green nymphs can all produce. Buzzers, too, are effective, in green, red, or black — simply match the colour to the hatch.

By late July and early August, the aerators are usually working — sometimes earlier if water condition demands it. These are particularly attractive to recently stocked trout, although inevitably they become over-fished. Even so, they are situated in some of the deepest water in the lake (off Walley Bank, near the dam), and in the 'Dog Days' a sinking line may break the blank. Also productive at this time of year is a drift down Moreton or Stratford Bank, which is practical with the wind anywhere around Easterly. Alternatively, drift off Moreton Point towards Nunnery, and in Herons Green Bay itself. Add a short Stick Fly to the menu, with a Black and Peacock on top dropper.

Through September Herons Green Bay is a good place for the first drift of the day. Water-level is usually well down by now, and the fish are harder to find, although having looked through my records it seems that flies with elements of gold-orange, like Dunkeld, have fished well. By now, some fish are searching for fresher (and cooler) water, and Stratford Bank always produces some fine browns. With the weather getting colder, surface activity diminishes and on really cold days the sinking line is all but compulsory. Despite this, I will always try my favourite September drift off the shallow extension to Nunnery Point, which has given me some lovely rainbows to surface fished nymphs.

As I said at the outset, it is near impossible to generalize on a lake like Chew. The foregoing must therefore be seen as only the roughest of guides, to be taken in conjunction with the wind and the weather of the day. The best advice must be to study the depth maps in the lodge and ask one of the resident staff, who are surely the most helpful and friendly of all their kind — and arguably the best informed.

Another Chew expert with a good record for England is Jeff Loud. He has this to add about fishing the lake, and especially about taking account of wind:

> Wind lanes only appear at certain times, but when they do it's vital to fish them hard. They may be narrow and broken, or up to twenty-yards wide, and stretching for several hundred. Usually the wind is not too strong, and you can drift down them over a continuous rise of fish coming upwind. The best sport is to be had on the edge, where the ripple meets the flat oily calm. If you see a lane, fish it hard. Remember also not to spoil any for yourself, or others, by motoring back down the middle of one.
>
> At Chew the water is so shallow you can do long drifts, and pick up fish almost anywhere. Inevitably, however, those of us who fish it regularly have certain favourite drifts depending on wind direction. These are mine:
>
> *Woodford Bank*: many motor straight off to distant parts, but one of the best areas is close to the landing stage. If a north-east wind blows you can drift almost immediately about fifty yards out, continuing on to Villice Bay. With a south-west wind, simply motor to Nunnery point and reverse it. You can also fish in to the bank in a strong north or north-west wind, as it is deep water there, and a clay bottom which doesn't muddy up. But one of you will have to be quick on the motor to get you away from the bank, if it's rough.
>
> *Villice Bay*: more of the bay can be fished in an east or west wind. It is wide enough for several drifts, and can be

productive. The bottom and the Nunnery point area are shallow, and colour up easily in a strong wind. In such conditions concentrate off the point of Villice Bay to halfway across.

Nunnery Point: this can be fished as part of several longer drifts, and is always a hopeful area. In a moderate north-east wind, one of the best on the lake is into Nunnery from some 400 yards out. A south-west wind also gives a good drift out of Herons Green Bay into Nunnery, but don't go too far down the bay. If it's a dour day, go back to Nunnery, and it often comes good.

Moreton Point: this provides some of my favourite drifts in most winds, often combined with drifting to Nunnery. The best winds are north-east or south-west giving several drifts into, or out of, the Point.

The Roman Shallows: well worth several drifts in any wind, but the ideal is a south-west, which lets you drift out from Moreton Bank across the shallows.

Wick Green Point: south or north winds allow you to drift the area out of Herriot's End, across Wick Green, and on some 300 yards, drifting anything from 50–300 yards out. A west wind also gives a useful drift to Herriot's End, starting from 300 yards out and getting as close in as you comfortably can.

Spring Bay and East Shore: this is the shallowest area of all, and for that reason not much fished. It can however be very good. You want to drift fast until you find fish, then stay with them. But you can't drift the same area too often, as in these very shallow waters the trout are easily put down.

Denny Island: this area is good in south-west or north-east winds. In high water you can drift over False Island into Denny. There are many other drifts 100 yards off shore past the point even across to the new picnic area or the corner of the north shore.

North Shore: south-east or north-west are the best winds for this. They provide good long drifts from Denny Island along the north shore right up to the corner of the dam.

All the above drifts have given me memorable fishing at times.

A final word of advice on fishing Chew came from John

Ketley in his international briefings: 'It is usually worth looking around until you see some rising trout. You have a much better chance if you fish where you see them moving, as they often do throughout the day.'

The Benson and Hedges Fly-Fishing Championship will help make three other English waters into main competition centres. Most important of these is the newly available Kielder Reservoir near Newcastle upon Tyne, which was opened by the Queen on 26 May 1982, and staged the northern heat of this national club championship only a fortnight later. So short has the North of England been of lakes with the facilities for a major competition that the northern qualifiers for the English national have in the past usually been fished on Welsh lakes like Trawsfynydd, or lately down at Grafham.

KIELDER

Kielder Water was opened for fishing on 1 June 1982 providing a major lake in the North-East with excellent competition

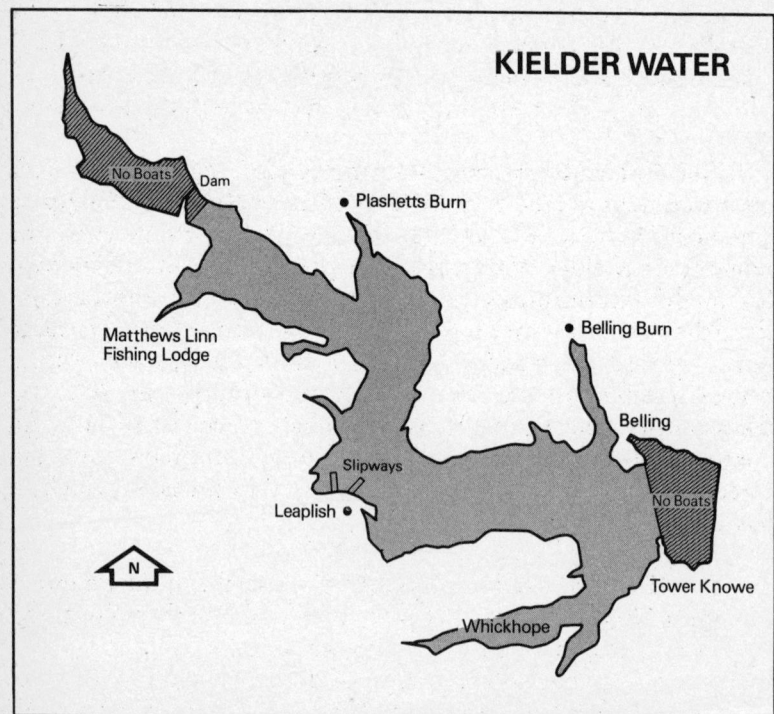

facilities. It lies only two miles from the Scottish border and is on the upper reach of the North Tyne close to Bellingham. Kielder covers 2684 acres and is Western Europe's largest man-made lake surrounded by its largest man-made forest.

How Kielder will fish is too early to say. But the first years of such reservoirs are usually productive ones for the angler and the water has been stocked with 250,000 trout which should provide good sport. At the tail of Kielder is Bakethin, a reservoir of 138 acres constructed earlier to ensure there is always a head of water rather than those unsightly mud flats when the levels fall. Bakethin was opened for fishing two years earlier and the results there give promise for the main water.

In 1981, 3650 trout were caught in Bakethin at an average of over $1\frac{1}{2}$ trout per rod day. The largest brown taken by then was 6 lb 2 oz, and the largest brook trout 3 lb. There is also a good head of native brown trout to supplement the stocked fish. Black was the best fly-colour for Bakethin and that may well apply to Kielder, too. Those who want to sample this new lake or fish in competition there can hire some of the twenty-five motor-boats from Matthews Linn. These boats must be manned by at least two people and can be reserved by writing to: The Fishing Lodge, Matthews Linn, Kielder Water, Hexham, Northumberland. Telephone enquiries about all recreational activities at Kielder should be directed to Bellingham (0660) 40398.

While England has built a strong team in recent years it is clear that their northern resource has been only partially tapped. The north-east, where lake fishing will be given a boost by the opening of Kielder Water, is not at present a region of its own for qualifying purposes, and it's a hard road for any of their fly-fishermen to take to the England team. For the large north-west region Kielder is too far distant and the lack of local waters suitable for competition has usually meant qualifying on lakes outside the region. Eliminators have been fished on main competitive waters like Trawsfynydd or Grafham, but Ian Greenwood gives these impressions of other venues on which he has qualified for the national:

> Lady Bower is a pleasant 500-acre lake in the Pennines near Sheffield, and we fished an eliminator there from the bank. Imagine what happened when forty anglers lined up close together along one shore! After half an hour all sensible fish had moved away or gone down deep to avoid

the onslaught. It was a case of waiting for your chance as others became dispirited. Patience paid off for me when in late afternoon many others began to slack off and things quietened down enough for some trout to come cruising back feeding on the surface. I only cast my dry fly, a Black Spider size 16, when I saw a rising fish moving into range. Then I would throw the fly six or seven feet in front and wait hopefully for it to be sucked in. This proved an effective method bringing me three trout in a short time.

Llyn Brenig was a much more satisfactory venue with boat-fishing facilities on an interesting lake. This windswept water is on moorland 1200 ft above sea level, but protected in part by the fir trees which march down to the shoreline and beyond. In places the trees are submerged in the water, and those are the best and most exciting areas to fish. That is where I search out the trout using a technique that has served me well in eliminators. I tie on a team of three Bibios, usually size 10, and then wax the point fly. I work these between the submerged trees where many fish shelter and feed. The wave from the waxed fly seems to attract them out, though it is usually one of the other two Bibios, drawn beneath the surface, which the trout take. On Brenig, however, you can always expect the unexpected. It can be sunny one minute, rain-lashed the next, and its trout are as unpredictable.

Some waters in the Lake District would be excellent for competition once organized for it. At present fishing one or two of them is no more peaceful than being on the MI, as speedboats towing water-skiers race by with roaring engines and foaming wake. Windermere, however, is one lake which could easily be developed to international standard. The plentiful trout there are so silvery they might be sea-trout, and they run up to ten pounds. In a day's fishing recently a friend and myself had eighteen up to $2\frac{1}{2}$ lb. What splendid sport that was in the delightful scenery of this ten-mile-long lake. The patterns I find successful are Teal and Green, Teal and Black, Teal and Brown, all size 10, and fished with floating line. All it needs is a good wave and you should be certain of good fishing. Windermere would be ideal for competition and is a lake to enjoy in any conditions.

WIMBLEBALL

For the south-west heat, Benson and Hedges centred their competition not on Chew Valley or Blagdon, but on the Wimbleball Reservoir. It lies on the edge of Exmoor, and in that wild, beautiful region it always pays to have warm waterproof clothing handy if you are to enjoy your eight hours of competition. Those wanting up to the minute information on how it is fishing can always look in at Lance Nicholson's tackle shop four miles away in Dulverton High street, since both he and his manager, Pat Veale, fish the reservoir twice a week. This is Lance Nicholson's general advice on fishing the water:

> From 1 May to mid-June it is best to fish sinking lines and flies with long-shank hooks size 6 to 8 — or, in competition with limited hook size, the largest the rules allow. The most successful patterns are Black Chenille, Viva, Sweeney Todd, Ace of Spades, Black Muddler, Black and Peacock and Grafham Snail. It is best to fish these with a slow draw. You need a strong cast with a terminal strength of 6–8 lb. Trout in Wimbleball are usually in excellent condition, fight well, and run large. A lot of the fish in this well stocked reservoir are in the 2–4 lb range, and there are some rainbows caught of around the double-figure mark.
>
> From mid-June to mid-August you should start by using the same hook sizes, but a rather different range of patterns. Best then are Whisky Fly, Worm Fly (single hook), Black Chenille, Viva, Missionary, Appetiser, Baby Dolls (white and green), Orange Muddler, Red Muddler, Black and Peacock Spider. It still pays to fish sinking line with a slow draw, waiting until late July to switch to surface flies with floating or slow sink, or sink-tip lines. In general it is best not to go below size 10 as yet and to reduce only slightly the terminal strength of the cast.
>
> Traditional wet flies also take fish from about this time. Invictas, Peter Ross, Bloody Butcher or Mallard and Claret can be productive with a quick draw just below the surface using a sink-tip line. Depending on the weather, buzzer hatches start towards the end of July. Then you can fish Green, Black, or Orange Buzzers, Pond Olive

Nymphs, Cove Pheasant Tail Nymphs, Footballers and a variety of Sedges. Hook sizes for them can come down to 14 with terminal cast strength down to 4–6 lb. They should be fished in the usual way — with an occasional twitch!

From late August to the end of the season, it's a case of reverting to the same methods as at the start. The darker lures are more successful, though they can be mixed with orange, yellow, or red ones.

While you should try and find the areas in which trout are known to be moving, some drifts usually offer a good chance. Favourite are the channel opposite the boat jetty, all of Cow Moor Bay, Bessoms Bay, and the Upton Arm Reach. Outside competition there is good opportunity for the visiting bank angler. The best shore positions are Bessoms Bay (towards the trees), Ruggs Bay, Cowling Bay, and Cow Moor (from its north bank by the hedges). For the bank angler, too, this is an attractive reservoir to fish with some very worthwhile trout to catch.

BEWL BRIDGE

The southern heat of the Benson and Hedges Championship was fished at Bewl Bridge which has also staged some qualifying matches for the English national. This is a particularly beautiful lake, so artfully landscaped that even the 1000 yd dam appears to merge into the scenery as if this was a natural water in a parkland setting. There is always a high expectancy of catching trout on this well-stocked water into which the fish are released from floating cages where they have already become well acclimatized.

The numbers caught tend to be high, the average weight low. In part, this is because the trout rise freely and the turnover rate is high. That is accentuated because Bewl's fifteen-mile bank perimeter provides a high ratio of bank fishing to water acreage and there are few places apart from the nature reserve, where trout can grow unhunted.

The flies and tactics which are effective at Grafham or Rutland will work well here. Sinking lines are, however, often more productive at times when you might expect the floater to catch more fish. Two patterns which I have found very productive are the Black Chenille on the point and a Green Peter on the bob.

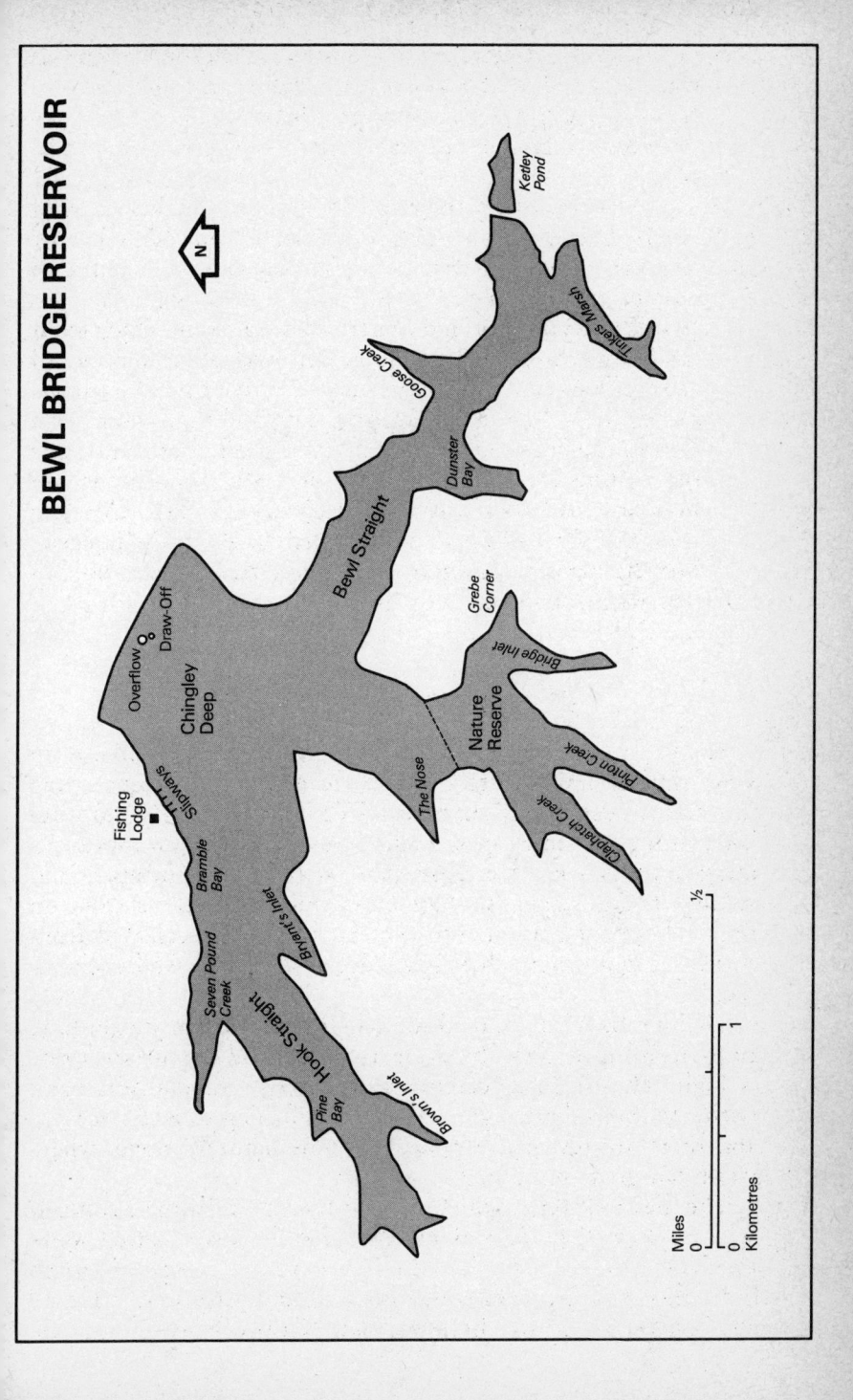

The advantage of a Green Peter is that it is likely to attract the larger browns as well as the stockie rainbows.

This is a compact lake easy to explore and with good drifts in the three main bays. When sailing is in progress the Hook Straight, much of which is reserved for fishing only, is as good a bet as any for a competitor. The Bewl Straight gives good drifts particularly if the wind allows you to keep close to either shore. Working down to the Nose or close to the opposite bank, or even down the centre of that bay leading to the no-fishing area of the nature reserve, is another favoured area. Above all keep a look-out for rising fish and if you find a shoal stay with it.

LOCH LEVEN

Much has been written earlier about Loch Leven, but it is such an intriguing lake, and so central to competitive fishing that there is more to add. Part of the fascination of Leven is its unpredictability. That is the constantly recurring theme in *The Loch Leven Angler*, first published in 1874 by Robert Begg-Burns, grand-nephew of the poet, and revised and updated sixty years later by John M. Johnstone, who took the leading part in organizing the first international.

Johnstone was mystified by the lack of success of 'many experts in really scientific fishing'. He concluded this was due to a marked, but indefinable, difference in the style required at Leven and elsewhere: 'The difference must lie in the handling of one's rod': that perhaps explains the success of the 'Harris shake' in the early internationals, but is hardly a help as practical advice.

Competitive fishermen hardly need reminding of his 'only reliable rule for successful anglers on Leven'. It ought to be embedded in them already for it is basic to all competition: 'It is that success will most often attend him who fishes most industriously, whether the trout are rising or not, and who, even in the absence of an occasional rise, will still continue to cast his flies with all his attention fixed on his pursuit.'

Having reminded his readers that Sir Walter Scott found the loch so fickle he compared its moods to those of his mischievous love, Caroline Seton, Johnstone gives more practical advice on how to fish it: 'It is immaterial whether the windward or the leeward shore is selected, as in normal weather the trout are as likely to be found on one as on the other. An easterly wind is the most favourable — Leven differing in this respect from all other

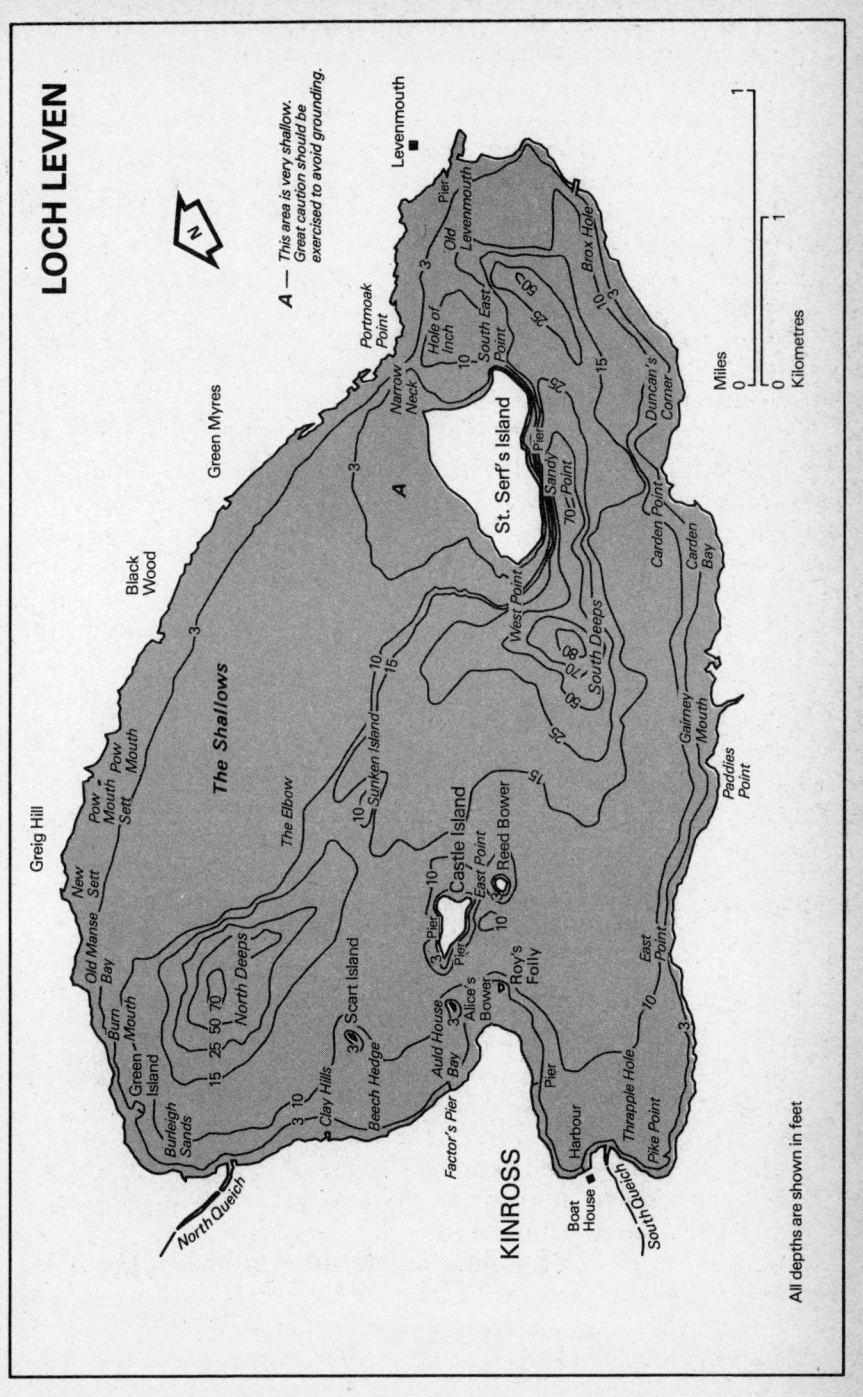

Scottish lakes; A substantial-looking wave is preferable to a mere catspaw on the surface of the water. Flies should never be drawn too rapidly through the water, nor allowed to dangle too loosely. It is the movement of the flies more than aught else which attracts the attention of the trout.'

On flies his advice is summed up as 'a bright fly for a bright day, and vice versa seems always to apply at Leven; the hook size needs to be larger in stormy weather, smaller in calm. The right size of fly is, however, a puzzle on Leven. Larger hooks which do well at the start of the season have to give place to smaller as the season advances. Since angling became so generally practised on Leven, a considerable reduction has been made in hook size. The trout have little inclination now to rise to flies approaching the size of those used a few years ago.'

The appetite of the Leven trout may well have gone full cycle now as the 'wee doubles' cease to be so effective, and big flies score as well again. Perhaps the old drifts may still be the best, too. This is Johnstone's advice in varying wind conditions:

East wind: Grahamston Avenue across the face of the bank
Form the Prap across to the Elbow Buoy
North-east wind: From the Green Isle to the North Deeps
West wind: From Paddy's point to Carden Bay
From Clayhill Bank to the Shallows
From the Strip on South Shore to the Queichie Mouth
South-west wind: Drift the Factor's pier and the Scart
South wind: From Carden Bay to St Serf's
From Brox across to the Hole of Inch and then to the Narrow Neck.
South-east wind: From the Narrow Neck, through the Shallows and over the Yellow Sands
From the Horn right along the Bank.

With that as an old-timer's guide, you would do well to purchase the little coloured map they sell so cheaply in the pier bar. This shows the depth contours, and also lists the most popular modern drifts and flies.

The reflections of the thirties are still worth studying, when you recall how successful fishermen then were compared to the present. There is also a timeless quality about some advice such as the general tendency that the more a water is hammered the more necessary it becomes to use small flies. No maxim is immutably accurate, however, not even that. As David Biggart wrote in *The First Hundred Years*. 'Angling methods have changed dramatically. No longer can one go out on Loch Leven, cast a short line and expect to catch fish. The effective method is now to fish with a fast sinking line, and when not under international rules, with large 'flies'. While catching large strong trout is exciting, many anglers think wistfully of the good old days.'

Johnstone found in his day almost as many theories as trout. It is indeed easy to become confused by the multiple choice offered, even on less complex lochs than Leven. To my mind the modern competition angler would do well to restrict his options to the methods which have brought England victory in the last three Leven internationals, or those advocated by Brian Peterson, Scotland's 1981 Loch Leven champion of champions.

The English method was summed up by Bob Draper's instruction to his team:

> Treat Leven as very similar to other large waters, and don't waste time worrying about new techniques. The long cast with floating line works well here as on English reservoirs, and so does a fairly fast retrieve. Sinking lines have also proved very useful to us at Leven, so make sure you have both types for match day.
>
> You will have heard of 'wee doubles'. They may work, but in previous years we have found flies made up on size 10 hooks to be more successful. The three most successful flies on Leven last time were Dunkeld, Greenwell with a yellow tail, and Soldier Palmer on the bob. It may be we shall discover a 'killer' fly in practice, so team members should bring fly-tying equipment with them if they have it. But this list below should be adequate for all eventualities:
>
> Soldier Palmer, Zulu, Woodcock and Mixed, King-fisher Butcher, Bloody Butcher, Teal and Green, Dunkeld, Wickham's Fancy, Blae and Black, Black Pennell, Greenwell's Glory, Cinnamon and Gold, and Hardy's Gold.

Brian Peterson has additional advice on tactics:

> When fishing Leven take your time; don't rush things. Leave your flies on the water as long as possible. That's

desirable because the most likely taking times are as soon as the flies land in the water, or when you are just about to lift them off at the end of the cast. Often the trout take right at the edge of the boat. I prefer to use a floater at Leven, but a slow sinker can be effective, especially if the fish are not showing. My favourite method is a long rod, a floating line, and flies ranging from 10 to 16, depending on the wave. The larger the wave, the larger the fly. From many hopeful drifts my own favourites are:

East Buoy to West point of St Serf's; Hole of the Inch to the Sluices; West point of St Serf's to the Sunken Island; Smiddy Hole to the Old Manse Bay; Factor's pier to Scart Island; East Buoy to Mid Buoy; the Thrapple Hole, and the Graveyard.

My selection of the best of the variety of flies I use is: Dunkeld, Kingfisher Butcher, Bloody Butcher, Wickham's, Soldier Palmer, Stoat's tail, McLeod's Olive, and Greenwell with yellow tail.

Finally, there were a few tips passed to me as a newcomer which I found useful. The first time I took a boat out on my own I soon found myself bumping over muddy shallows as I cut the first corner near Castle Isle. If you don't know the loch it pays to get advice on the shallow areas before you launch, and also to acquire that coloured map. And if you *do* get stranded don't try to force the heavy boats forward, or you will be stuck fast. Pull it out the way you came. A recommended drift which gave a couple of hours uninterrupted fishing was from East Point past Sunken Island to the Pow Mouth Shallows with a reasonable chance of fish all the way. For the evenings especially, but also in competition hours, the edge of North Deeps proved very productive on practice days, as did the drift from Scart Island to the second gap in the trees in front of the Old Manse. Around Green Isle was another area where the Welsh in particular made a killing.

For those who want to try the old Leven dodge of using something as far as possible removed from normal patterns, I have a suggestion from my own limited experience. Why not a Muddler on the tail, and a Loch Ordie on the dropper? Both raised fish for me at times when the going was hard. The Loch Ordie was particularly interesting. This is the best of all flies for trout on many of Sutherland's lochs. When I tried it on Leven I caught six trout on it in two early practice days. That was on a size 8. When I came down a size in preparation for the match day it moved nothing more.

I also tried a sunk Daddy-long-legs. That was interesting, too. Jimmy Abel told me he had never seen anyone catch a fish with it during his long career on Leven, though there are plenty of the natural fly about. I didn't either. But after a long blank period I put it on the tail one evening, and hooked three trout on the Loch Ordie dropper in the next twenty minutes. Was that coincidence, as so often in fishing? Or did the large Daddy attract the fish up, and the dropper then lure them? If desperate, it might be worth a try again.

For all its present problems Leven and its trout continue to attract hundreds of expectant anglers, eternal optimists all, thinking *this* must the day the loch comes good again. *The Loch Leven Angler* at least has a message of hope for them. Apparently Leven was for long regarded as impossibly difficult with the naturalist, James Wilson, saying in evidence before the Sheriff Court in 1840: 'No trout in Scotland, where the number is so great, are so difficult to raise with an artificial fly.'

But then comes this passage of hope: 'Angling on Loch Leven continued to be regarded in this unfavourable light until the year 1850, when a complete and utterly unaccountable change in the habits of the trout and character of the loch unexpectedly developed. Instead of the trout continuing shy and wary, they suddenly began to rise steadily to the lure.' Brian Peterson writes for all Leven anglers in hoping for another such dramatic change: 'I hope the Leven trout will be reeducated to taking fly from the surface as there are still plenty of these special fish in this very special loch.'

The Loch Leven championship goes back to the start of competition. The Lake of Menteith, however, has only recently had its own contest, currently organized by David Biggart. The basis of entry is for those clubs which regularly fish there to put in one representative. Started in 1970, this is now a regular event, with the Committee members entered under the title of Por Tanglers. Clearly that is not a fair description of their fishing talent. David Biggart won the event in gale conditions in 1973, and his son Stuart was runner-up in 1981.

LAKE OF MENTEITH

The first international to be fished at Menteith was in

September 1971. The lake fished well enough then and has been growing in reputation ever since. As Leven declines, Menteith has boomed until it is hard to say which is Scotland's premier trout lake. And a 'lake' the Lake of Menteith really is, the only one in Scotland.

With many club matches fished there the appropriate person to advise on fishing Menteith is Scotland's 1981 Leven champion of champions, Brian Peterson. This is his description of the lake and how to fish it:

> The Lake of Menteith is surrounded by beautiful countryside, a truly rural setting just fourteen miles from Stirling and thirty from Glasgow. With the Trossachs close by and an excellent hotel on its banks it is as ideal for holidaymakers as for competition fishermen.
> Fishing is from 14ft glassfibre boats wih no bank casting allowed and early booking desirable in view of the lake's popularity. No Sunday fishing is permitted, but an interesting feature is that boats can be hired for three different sessions in a day. The less common period is the 4.30–9.0 a.m. shift, which has proved both popular and very productive. We do make it hard for ourselves in international competition by fishing only in the least lively periods!
> Fishing is fly only and there are some 650 acres of water to enjoy with a nice variety of deeps and shallows, but an average depth of 19 feet. Everyone will have his favourite drifts and you can have fun experimenting to find your own as you have a reasonable chance of trout all over the lake. However, my best drifts are those in Heronry Bay, the Road Shore, the Big Buoy and Gateside Bay. Anyone who doesn't know the water well can be sure he is fishing in hopeful areas, if he keeps to these. The lake mangement are very helpful and would point them out in more detail, if required.
> The lake has a natural head of brown trout supplemented by continuous stocking with rainbows and some brook trout, though as in most places the latter seem hard to catch. The policy of putting in 1,000 or more rainbows every week keeps fish continually on the move with a good chance of catches and very few 'dead' periods throughout the season from the first week in April.

The fishery really improved under the able management of Bill Martindale with catches rising to 7,700 in 1977, passing 10,000 a year later, and expected to go on rising to 15,000 or so before long. The number of big fish has also increased. In 1978 a record was established for brownies, with a fine speciment of 4 lb 6 oz and for rainbows with the capture of one of 6 lb 12 oz. These have been left far behind now with several double-figure rainbows being taken including one of 10 lb in competition.

The fish are brought in as fry and after growing to about seven inches in the tanks they are put out into the floating cages in Gateside Bay. There they become acclimatized to the water and grow to peak condition before being released. There is no limit on catches and if you are lucky you can have a marvellous day's fishing on Menteith.

You have a fair chance of success with most well-known loch or reservoir flies with the Soldier Palmer as much a favourite as on many English waters. Black Pennell, Wickham, Invicta, particularly the silver body varieties, and Woodcock and Yellow are all killing patterns, as is the Peter Ross. All of us look for the magic fly which will ensure large catches all the time. We never find it, but at least I've had some success on Menteith with two unusual varieties. Yellow is often a popular colour with the trout there, so I tied up a pattern of my own with the inventive name of the 'Yellow One'. It is very similar to a Texas Rose Muddler, but I tie it as a size 12 rather than as a large lure. If you want one of those you can't do better at Menteith than the Honey Bear which I have found deadly on some days when fished deep as tail fly and using a sinking line.

This pattern is a particular favourite with one of our best anglers, Jim Boyd, when he fishes Menteith. In case my English and Welsh friends don't know it, I give below the dressing. It might prove equally effective on waters like Grafham or Trawsfynydd — and they can't use it against me in international competition since it needs to be fished a larger size than the rules allow! It might even be worth a try on some Irish loughs, where it might take the trout by surprise.

This is the accepted tying of a Honey Bear:

Honey Bear

Hook: 8, 10 or 12 longshank
Silk: Primrose
Body: White cotton, dubbed very lightly with yellow seal's fur, and white ostrich herl
Rib: Oval gold tinsel
Tail: Yellow goat kid hair
Hackle: Dark claret cock hackle, tied in beard fashion
Wings: Four lemon yellow cock hackles
Cheeks: Jungle cock or substitute
Head: Black silk

The lake of Menteith fishes best at the start of the season, when you may have to brave the cold for your sport, or at the back-end, with August and September often very good months. That is in line with the international experience. The first fished there was in September and the catches were excellent. Indeed, the 235 trout are second only to Draycote's 262 as the highest number caught outside Loch Leven in an international. The following matches at the lake in 1973 and 1974 were in May when the results were not so good.

In making a comparison with Leven the overall catches on Menteith have to be viewed in the light of its being fished only six days a week. The longer daily hours however mean that in relation to time on the water Menteith has the equivalent of an extra day's fishing, rather than one less. But the massive difference is in the number of rods. Leven's forty-three boats may contain up to 129 anglers, while the twenty on Menteith take out a maximum of forty a day. There can be more than three times as many anglers fishing Leven on any given day and yet the year's total on 'the' loch may be only fifty per cent up on Menteith. Unless Leven improves or Menteith deteriorates anglers from the other countries may well hope to see the choice of venue in Scotland determined soon by results, rather than reputation.

CHAPTER 14

THE LOUGH AND LLYN OF IRELAND AND WALES

All these settings said things to me.
What you get out of fishing is infinitely more than fish.
from *Going Fishing* by Negley Farson

Negley Farson might have had Ireland in mind when he wrote that. For there is much more to enjoy when fly-fishing there than the catching of trout. True, you don't need the luck of the Irish to catch big bags, but even if the trout won't rise, the wild beauty of many of the lakes should charm your cares away. The Irish lough wet-fly season is a long one with good fishing to be had from the end of March to late September. The 'competitive season' is later starting, usually ushered in by the mayfly. Pleasure fishing, however, can be as good in April as in most months. Indeed, for a fishing holiday there are advantages in coming early when prices are much cheaper than in the high season of July and August.

There are some tricks of the trade to be learnt if you want large catches, for on most Irish loughs the trout are unusually quick in taking and rejecting the fly. 'Don't strike too fast' is a good maxim for most waters with trout of a pound or more — but a fatal one for Ireland. Sharp reflexes are needed there, as well as some different flies. But the natural fly-life develops on a familiar pattern as Brian Geraghty explains:

> The very early fishing from late March on depends a lot on the water levels, the temperature, and the winds. In early April the Duck fly is often the most successful pattern. Then comes the season for traditional wet-flies, and wet-fly nymphs, until the mayfly opens the door for even more satisfying returns. It heralds also some very

fruitful fishing for the 'dappers', particularly on Lough Corrib.

Spent gnat in early to mid-June can be marvellous, especially on Lough Arrow. The July period of perch-fry feeding may be tempting to the reservoir lure anglers, but the Irish have not as yet mastered the techniques required during that activity. August is sedge time with the Peter, and the Murrough (the red sedge) leading the attack. Of course terrestrials and Daddy-long-legs all play their part then, either fished dry on the bob or dapped. In the Midland lakes in particular chironomids are prevalent for much of the season.

Among the traditional patterns of wet-fly that are good standbys for Irish waters the Black Pennell and the Connemara Black appear as the preference of many international anglers. Those going in for local competitions would do well to take the advice available. Tom Carter, fishing Conn for the first time, was delighted to find local fly-tiers selling 'the fly of the day' from the vans parked near the quay and very good patterns they were. For most of the big competitions such on the spot service is likely to be of help to anyone confused or uncertain about the best-chance team of flies. Of the atmosphere of competitions other than internationals Brian Geraghty makes this comment:

> There is big money to be won in some Irish competitions. But mainly they are fished in the true spirit of angling and good sportsmanship. Pot hunters are few, and we do not encourage them to come. We believe visitors to our competitions will find them well-organized and providing high-quality fishing. Even more they should enjoy their very special atmosphere with its ready friendship between anglers, its stimulus to the exchange of fishing stories, and perhaps a song or two to enliven the evenings.

Local knowledge is, of course, a great advantage on most waters, but international competition has shown visitors winning more frequently than the home team. Even as a newcomer, if you start with a reasonable understanding of how the lough fishes, then listen to, and assess, the advice given, you are in with a fishing chance of doing well. But the key man in your success, or failure, may well be the boatman. His knowledge should take you where you *can* catch fish. The rest is up to you. Conn is the main competition lough and the notes which follow give the general characteristics on which you can build by experience and experiment, and above all by getting help from an expert boatman.

LOUGH CONN

Lough Conn has not only been Ireland's main lake for international competition, but is also the centre for one of its largest individual fly-fishing contests. The facilities are therefore well-developed, and the fishing prospects good, particularly during the mayfly season. The trout fisherman may also have the happy experience of hooking into a salmon. During the 1975 international fished there every team, except the English, came in with a salmon on practice days.

Before that contest Bill Lamb, then Scottish Honorary President of the International Association, had this to say about the lough:

> May 31st is the chosen date, though the mayfly hatch would be better developed a week later. Then, however, the Crossmolina Club in conjunction with the local festival hold a competition which would clash with ours.
>
> We decided unanimously to fish the match from Crossmolina harbour, concentrating on the north end of the lake. That area tends to fish the better at this time, and the mayfly usually hatches there earlier than in other parts of the lake.
>
> In the event of bad weather this is also the preferable place to be. Only a gale from the south-east would prevent boats leaving Crossmolina harbour. Even in gale-force winds from any other quarter boats can quickly make the shelter of the islands on the west side to enjoy uninterrupted fishing on excellent fishing grounds as far down as Errew.
>
> If the match was fished from Cloghans, the other very suitable starting point half-way down the east side, stormy winds from any quarter could confine the boats to Cloghans bay, giving very restricted fishing.

Those international anglers caught in the great storm of 1962 could confirm the wisdom of that judgment!

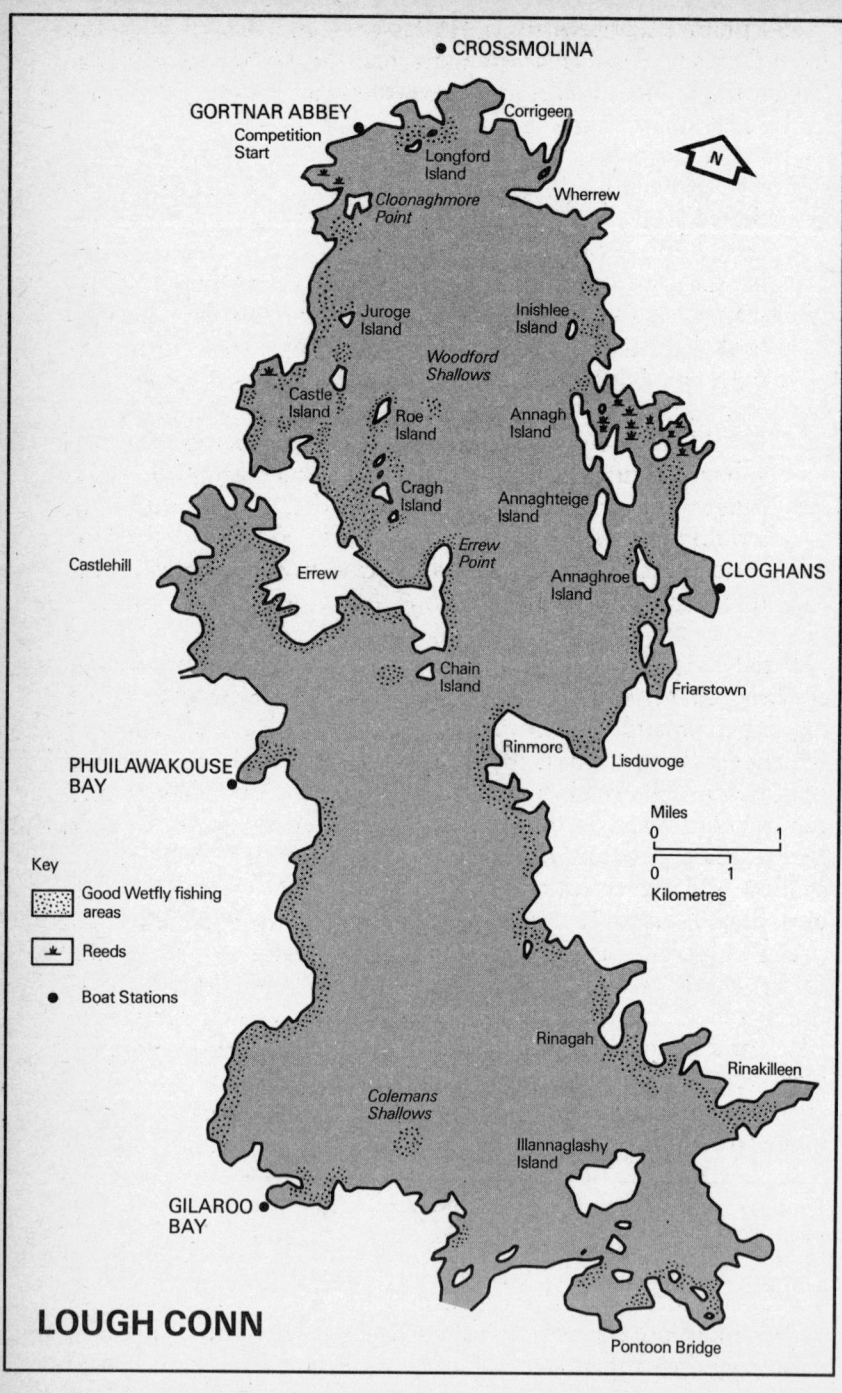

Bill Lamb's advice proved helpful to Tom Carter fishing out from Crossmolina in that international and the first time he had fished Conn. It took him time nonetheless to adjust to the lough's trout in search of the mayfly:

> The main taking places were down the wind lanes, on the edge of which flies and trout congregated. There were large numbers of rising fish of about $\frac{3}{4}$ lb, but you needed to be exceptionally fast on the strike to catch them. They seemed to spit out the artificial fly in the same instant they took it. Those of us used to tightening firmly into large trout in United Kingdom waters had to sharpen our reactions to hook into a reasonable percentage of rises.
>
> You needed to watch the birds, too. There was a local solicitor who was pointed out to us as a man who always caught a lot. He had his own motorboat, and we noticed he would roar over to any area where the sea-gulls were concentrated. At once he would take fish, then move on to the next flock of birds to find fish feeding there, too.

Patrick Langan, organizer of many matches on Conn, confirms that the best tactic is to drift along the shelving shores of the mainland, or of one of the large islands, choosing whichever the wind best suits. There are also some well-marked shallows which are always worth a try, and certain bays which can produce very good baskets. His favourites are Pratt's, Errew, Castlehill, and Pollawakouse, all of which are relatively shallow and may yield fish all over. This is his advice about the best flies to use: 'We fish mainly wet-fly and sunk line, and prefer three-fly casts. The most popular patterns are Golden Olive, Black Pennell, Mallard and Claret, Hackle Mayfly when the hatch is on, Green Peter, Cinnamon Sedge, Alder, and Black and Peacock Spider. The Invicta is another fly which has been very effective recently.' Any of these may give you the chance to practice that quick strike so essential at Conn, the main Irish lough for the internationals.

LOUGH CORRIB

The same tactic and flies can bring success at Corrib, a lough occasionally used for internationals, though more famed for its dapping. The shallows round its many islands are often happy hunting grounds. But the lough is so large it is always best to take local advice on which areas are fishing well. This is the largest of all the Republic's big lakes covering 41,617 acres, which gives the angler some 68 square miles to explore. Up-to-the-minute knowledge of where fish are moving can be vital. The Irish won the last international there in 1978 by motoring several miles up the lough to their favoured spots, the time wasted getting there more than offset by knowing where to find feeding fish. So get local advice or a good boatman, and don't trust to instinct. The lough is too big for that, and so are some of its fish for any fine tackle. Corrib is noted for its large trout with J.W. Pepper claiming to have caught one of 24 lb there in 1903, and F. Smith known to have landed one of 19 lb 2 oz in 1971, also on spoon.

Roy Purves was England's winner of the Grafham trophy in that 1978 match. He used the standard Corrib tactic of 'when you can't see the bottom, move somewhere where you can.' He was unruffled by the independent nature of the boatmen to whom the lunch-break was as sacred as any English factory's tea-break. The competition rules of eight hours uninterrupted fishing were of no consequence:

> They did their own thing, the chief aspect of which was to put ashore for lunch at the nearest island and start brewing tea in filthy, sooty kettles. No matter how long it took to get a fire going with damp wood they would not launch again until the vile-looking liquid had been boiled and drunk. On match day I caught a trout of over a pound with a lamprey stuck to its gill cover. Without a sign of interest the boatman parted the two and threw the lamprey into the bottom of the boat. So I presume this is a common phenomenon on Corrib.

LOUGH SHEELIN

While Conn has been the main centre of international fishing, Sheelin is also one which has proved productive. When I first fished for England we were all amused by the bubbling enthusiasm of the Irish captain, Canon Gargan, for this favourite lake of his, which he was always eulogizing. Only one international has been fished there, however. That was in 1976 when the catch was so heavy, the day so pleasant that the Secretary of the

Sheelin Trout Protection Association was congratulated on his water providing probably the best match in the history of the International Association.

So the Canon's addiction is understandable and Sheelin may well figure in future internationals. When he started to fish there in 1942, traditional methods worked well and there was considerable reliance on the dry fly. It was a lake for big brown trout with six- or seven-pounders quite common. In the late fifties pollution and drainage of spawning streams had an adverse effect on trout stocks, while eutrophication later altered the pattern of fly life. For the past few years Canon Gargan has been living in the border area with Melvin and Arrow as his local lakes, and rarely able to get to Sheelin.

So the up-to-date advice on the lough comes from his friend Peter O'Reilly, the Trout Angling Officer of Ireland's Central Fisheries Board, who is a Sheelin regular. In the seventies heavy stocking was necessary to maintain the excellence of the fishing, but stocks of native wild browns have so multiplied of late that in 1981 they made up eighty per cent of the trout population. That season the average catch was 2.6 trout per rod a day, the average weight almost 2 lb, making it the best trout fishing in Ireland.

Sheelin is a large alkaline lough with some 4,500 acres of relatively shallow water which supports an abundance of fly life. Once noted for its profuse mayfly and Green Peter (large Tricoptera) hatches, the onset of eutrophication in the lough has left chironomids as the main organisms of interest to the angler.

When the season opens at the beginning of March, the trout are congregated in the shallows feeding on freshwater lice and shrimp. The rise in temperature in April brings on the first duck fly hatches, which occur mainly along the northern shore from Kilnahard to Stoney Island. The best fishing is then from 11.0 a.m. to 1.30 p.m. and from 7.30 p.m. until after sunset, casting over water 12–15 feet deep.

In May there are excellent hatches of buzzers with a free rise of trout particularly in Bog Bay and Gore Port Bay. Dry Murroughs can be used from dusk until after midnight to give interesting and effective fishing. There are also hatches of mayfly, olives, stonefly, alders and *Simulium Damnosum* (the black curse), which continue into early June.

There is then a lull until trout discover perch fry. This can be an exciting time if the angler locates feeding fish which will take anything from a Dunkeld to a dry Sedge. There are also good

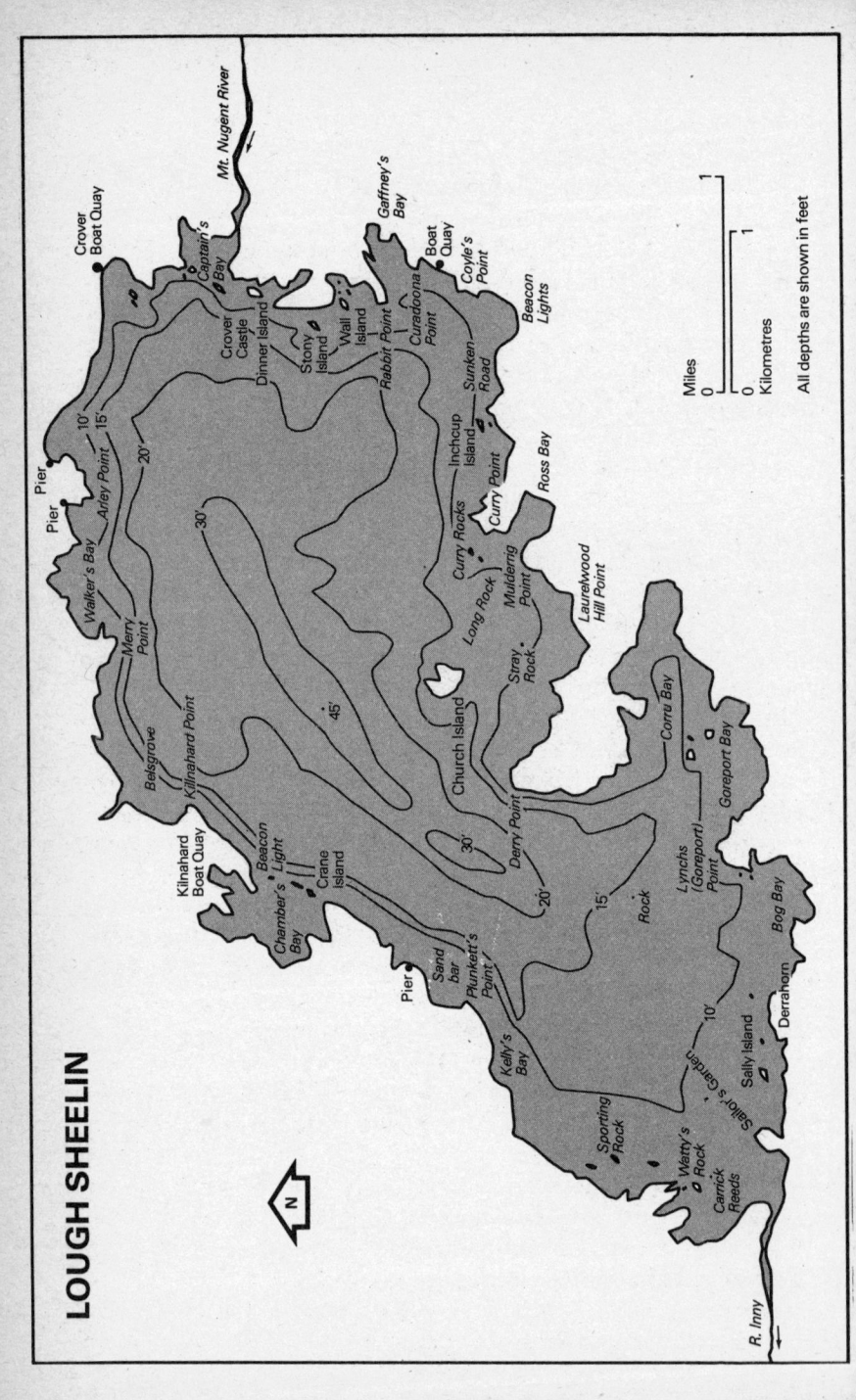

hatches of caenis making for fine sport in calm sheltered bays in early morning. On bright sunny days July fishing is very difficult, but at dusk and early morning buzzer hatches can give good catches to those fishing buzzer pupae or even dry fly.

Traditional flies will bring good bags on dull, windy August days, particularly Invictas representing a hatching sedge. Dapping a natural grasshopper or a Sedge takes some big fish, as does the Sedge fished dry in the evening. But it is in September the bigger fish really start to move. Even when there are no fly hatches and no sign of rising trout you may still catch them in shallower water with a team of wet flies such as Green Peter, Invicta, and Connemara Black up to size 8. All through the season Sheelin gives you a good chance of fish and the chance of a really good trout, too.

LLYN TRAWSFYNYDD

The main Welsh lake, Llyn Trawsfynydd, is a stocked water without any of Conn or Sheelin's wild browns, and therefore very different in character. It is not a lake easily mastered by outsiders. The mysterious influence of the hot water from the power station, and the ring of bait anglers round its banks, give it a character of its own. There are days, when stocked up for competition, it yields splendid bags of fish, though not always prizes of great beauty. It was here that the heaviest catch of any Englishman in international fishing was established by John Ketley with nine trout weighing almost 21 lb. At other times it can be implacably dour even when conditions seem reasonable.

The fly-life in the lake is limited, and rising trout rarely seen. Perhaps for that reason visiting teams tend to be uncertain about the patterns to use. The rumour goes that the Irish are catching them on the Duck fly, or the Welsh on the Green Peter, or the Scots on the Fiery Brown, and the English fall back on that fishing cliché: 'They'll take any fly if they are in the mood, and you present it to them right.'

Where to fish with the best chance can also be a problem. The bottom bay, near the competition launch point, can be very productive. With a long bridge spanning the neck, this shallow area is like a little enclosed lake of its own. It was here John Ketley made his record catch. Others favour the far end by the power station. Fish are often found here in the deep water by the dam wall. The other side also provides a hopeful drift along the wall which channels the hot water into the lake. Fishing the cool water beside the warm can be a successful tactic.

The weather is crucial to fishing prospects.

Loch Leven may be badly affected by sun, but a cloudless sky can be even more disastrous for fly-fishermen at Trawsfynydd. In other lakes you look for the 'hot spots', but here you try and avoid them. Eric Pastore, Chairman of the Macclesfield Fly-Fishers Club and five times an England international, had this experience when he went to the match there in 1976. He motored over with Stan Wood, who has qualified seven times already for internationals, and Doug Young. They arrived to find that the Scots had already spent several days practising without one of them moving a fish!

> We tried everything from bright flies to suit the sunny conditions down to the smallest nymphs. We fished fast, we fished slow, but to no more avail than the Scots. The long stone breakwater going out into the lake makes the hot water from the generators travel gradually round in the form of a 'U' to the shallow end, round to the deep water, then under some massive steel gates to the plant. By this time it is cool again. This continuous circulating system inevitably raises the temperature of the lake. When we fished in the blazing sun the temperature was 85°F. at the warmest end, 75°F. at the coolest with a 10° difference at 20 ft depth. Naturally the trout were all down there in the cooler water, since they are reputed not to surface feed in water above 70°F.
>
> The Welsh Authority boats were busy putting in stock fish, occasionally holding up a four-pounder to encourage us. But as soon as they were in the fish sank to the cooler bottom, and in the final two practice days we had not a rise between us. Panic stations. Meetings were held to decide what to do if nothing was caught on match day with fifteen trophies to be won! No decisions were reached and everyone hoped for the best. By noon not a fish had been taken. Then fortunately the wind began to freshen, clouds to appear, hope to burgeon. A storm moved past and by four o'clock there were waves beating on the shore. Still nothing. Then Don Fulcher, our captain, and the Scots' captain, Willie Nairn, were both into a fish at the same time. The tiny bay they were in should only have accommodated two boats at most, but now fish-starved anglers

appeared from everywhere, crowding into it regardless of rules about 100 yards between drifting boats. In the mad dash for fish boats were blown aground, others were so close together their casts tangled, or wrapped round nearby rods. In the chaos our engine failed, and we had to keep rowing out a little then drifting in for a few casts. I hooked a splendid trout of some 3 lb, which took against rocks, leaped ashore, flapped over the stones, shook the hook, and made the water again. My partner had two, and I soon netted one. Then I hooked another good fish which played hard and deep then got off at the net.

We were towed home in time for the finish. On the way we passed Bob Draper and his partner who signalled a big 'O' for their catch. As he waited for the final gun Bob suddenly took one of $12\frac{1}{4}$ oz, which beat mine by $\frac{1}{2}$ oz to give him fourth English place and qualification in my place for the next international.

Tom Bilson and our captain, Don Fulcher, had three trout each, Tom taking the Grafham trophy with just under 2 lb. Had my big ones stuck I might even have been a Brown Bowl winner! But that's fishing — and if you are fishing at Trawsfynydd pray for cool weather with plenty of breeze and cast close in to the bank.

The English President, Adrian Ashness, is one who has a special affection for Trawsfynydd, which the lake seems to reciprocate. This is his own successful experience of fishing there:

Horses for courses? Fishermen for waters? Do I have a special affinity for Llyn Trawsfynydd? For most members of English teams it has not been a happy hunting ground in recent years. On occasion, however, she has been very kind to me.

My first acquaintance was with the English 'select' team in September 1974, a forerunner of the return of England to the international scene. A plaque presented by the Irish for this special event hangs on the wall of my sitting room surmounted by the red plastic rose we wore for the occasion.

When boat fishing I prefer to have a boatman who takes charge and the organizers gave me the ideal gillie. We had only one practice day and he took me and my boat partner to the southern shore under the wood. Everyone else seemed to congregate on the causeway side by the water channel. 'They'll go away in time' was the gillie's comment and sure enough there was not the sport to detain them there. The wind began to freshen and by early afternoon the causeway was deserted. As it blew ever harder our boatman was superb in the way he held the boat on the oars, taking us close in to the rocks. It must have been a severe physical strain for him, but it meant my partner and I soon had five fish each, one short of the limit. Before we could get the last one the safety boat arrived shouting to us that it was going to blow too hard to stay out. That was a memorable welcome to Trawsfynydd.

The first time I fished there for England was in the September 1978 international. We knew the area by the boat station, from the bridge to the river mouth had been heavily stocked, and that fishing had not been allowed in the week prior to the international. It was said to be full of large fish and John Ketley, our captain, gave strict instructions that if we won the toss to take charge of the boat first we must all spend the whole of the first two hours in that area. Morning broke with a gale wind blowing across the lake into the river mouth, but we were cheered by winning the toss. In the crowded conditions it was very hard for the boatman who had to keep the drift steady with the boat held on the oar. I opted for fishing the far shore opposite the boat station. Unfortunately the waves there were such that the only way to control the boat was at an angle so that my opponent in the bow fished all the water first.

The boatman apologized but there was nothing he could do, and having started there we had to keep drifting it since the boats were so thick elsewhere in that area. By noon, and change-over time, I had two fish, my rival four. He then decided to head up the lake for calmer waters and for the rest of the day we caught nothing more between us. One of the English team who stayed in the bay had a harrowing time. His motor broke down, an oar then snapped, and they were at the mercy of the gale. This drove them into a fence, where they stuck fast. In such circumstances they regarded the 'drifting' rule as no longer applying and fished out the contest from there catching a few before finally being rescued at the end of the day. Very properly the captain followed his own instructions to the letter. By staying in the bay all the time John Ketley had nine splendid fish weighing almost 21 lb, a heavy enough bag to give us a second place.

In 1980 the conditions in June were the complete reverse of that earlier day with a heatwave making fishing difficult. Windless and scorched by the sun on the practice days, we were as idle as painted ships on a painted ocean. But even in hopeless conditions there is always hope if you keep fishing. On the Friday a prize had been offered for the largest fish caught. Again I had a splendid boatman who kept searching the water. Suddenly a fish swam into view quite close to the boat. At once a gentle touch of the oar straightened us and my single fly was on its way. Bull's eye! A short-tailed 4 lb rainbow was the result and the prize of a barometer, set in Welsh slate, stands in a niche at home to remind me of Trawsfynydd.

Conditions were equally bad for the international the following day. Again I was fortunate in my boatman, a local expert, and my partner, an outstanding Welsh fisherman. The boatman was an old international and a former acquaintance and I was happy to leave decisions to the two of them. They both agreed the most likely spot to catch fish and headed there. 'The first boat there is bound to get a fish,' they said. Unfortunately, we were three heavyweights and were beaten on the run-up by a lighter-loaded boat, which was already playing a good fish when we arrived second on the scene. My colleagues were confident in their knowledge. This was where the fish were so we must wait here.

Even when all went quiet and the others drifted away we still quietly searched that water. Suddenly I was into a very good fish. We guessed it at 4 lb and the guess was confirmed as it was netted. At once boats appeared everywhere as if my magic. A bending rod was quickly noticed on a day like this! My two experts kept the same counsel. 'Wait on — the others will go.' Soon they began to drift disconsolately away. Quiet again. Then bang! — into another good fish over 2 lb. The result for me was the treasured Brown Bowl for the biggest basket, the new H. Emyr Lewis Memorial Trophy for the largest trout, and the Grafham Trophy for the biggest English basket. What two days! No wonder Trawsfynydd is a favourite lake for me.

Adrian can qualify as successful at 'Traws', but the definitive guidance should come from a Welsh expert. Trevor Hirons has this to pass on from his own considerable experience of fishing it:

> Llyn Trawsfynydd covers an area of 1,275 acres in the beautiful vale of Maentwrog and lies some 600 ft above sea level. It is three miles long and varies in width from a quarter to almost two miles. A delightful water in the heart of Snowdonia, it is easily accessible with the main Dolgellau to Portmadoc road running near its east shore. The fishing on the lake is leased to the Prysor Angling club which was formed in 1930.
>
> The native trout in Traws were crossed with the Leven strain, and in 1933 rainbows were introduced growing very quickly to prove the great potential of this water. There are still many natural browns in the lake, but not many come to the weigh-in. In the spring of 1980, thirty-eight trout were taken in the international, but only two natural browns were among the stocked rainbows which provide the main sport.
>
> Trawsfynydd can be a most difficult water to fish during international hours. You start from number one mooring at the south end of the lake and it takes almost three-quarters of an hour to motor up to the dam. Once there a first drift in one of the bays can be rewarding whether you try Rainbow Bay to the east or the nameless one to the west. Stay drifting there if you find fish, move on quickly if you don't. If the wind is north-westerly drift the little bay above the inlet of the cold water channel. Continue on round the point and along the wall casting your flies into the rocks as the trout usually take a few inches out.
>
> Another good area is just below Llenyrch Leat on the west shore in the shallows there. Fish into the bank under the trees, and continue on to a point of slab rock jutting out, with dead oak trees around the corner. The deep water beyond is not very productive, but Home Bay is always worth a try and several internationals have been won by fish caught here in the final half-hour.
>
> Some boats will have preferred to start above number two mooring at the top of the shallows marked by two iron posts. Around the point, try inside and outside the islands

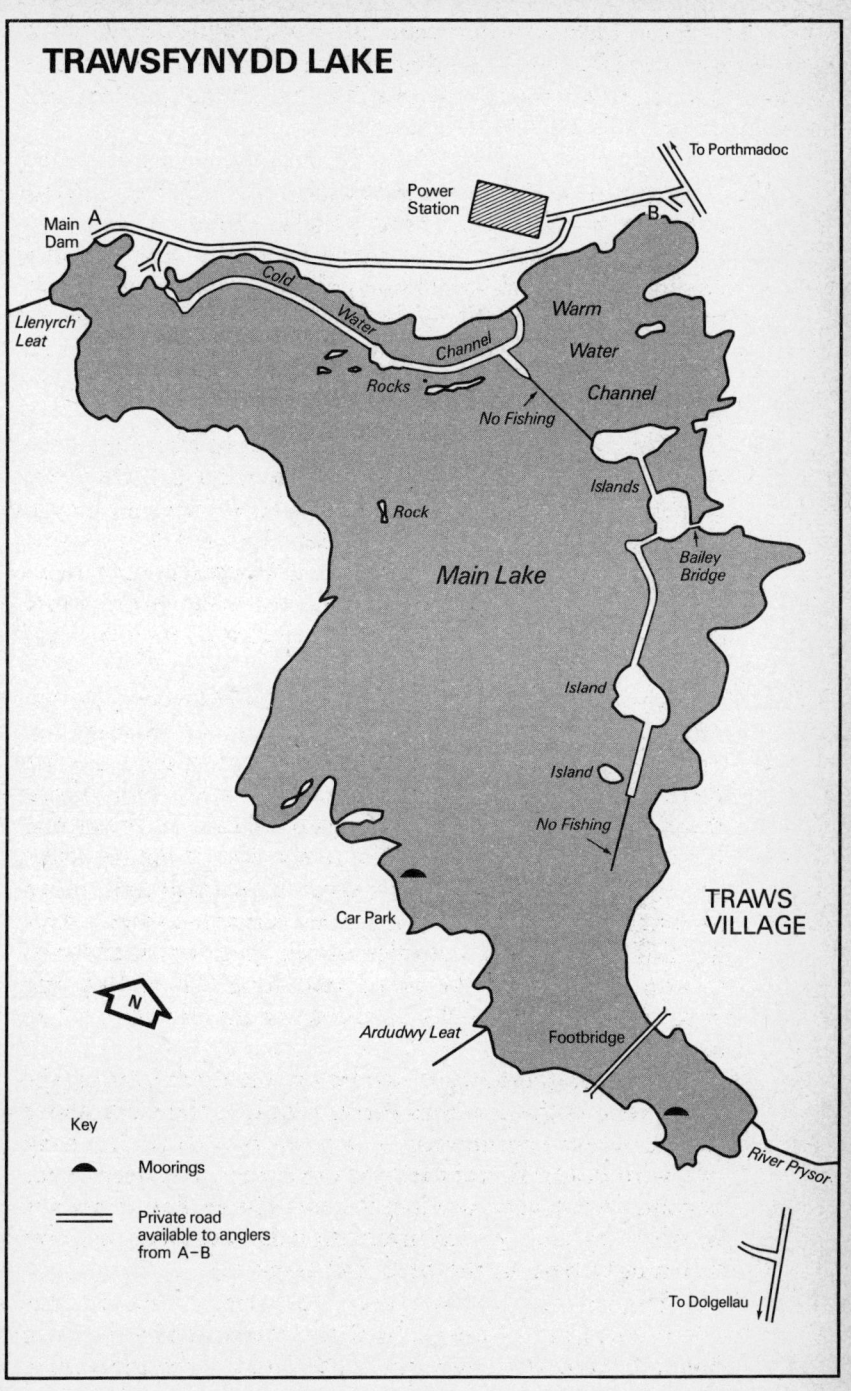

and into Pig Bay. This is an area where many are caught, so fish it thoroughly. Past the point other good spots are Tyn Twll Bay and two more small islands, though the seagulls will pester you here in May when nesting.

Below the islands towards the river watch for submerged walls from which good fish are often taken. Below the river drift the opposite bank to some islands. Go between them across the shallows to a large dead oak tree fishing close in along the point and out twenty yards or so. Sometimes it pays to fish back into the bay round the corner. Finally cut across to the east shore and try Seagull Island on your way to the Home Bay.

If you've fished hard, your legs and back will be aching as the boats at Traws are only twelve-feet long with a cover in the bow. Boatmen often have difficulty keeping you on a drift, mostly using both oars which tends to put fish down as they follow your bob fly in.

My advice to any international fisherman at Trawsfynydd for the first time is to take trouble to get to know the lake in practice. Find the best bays and shallows and note where other anglers are taking fish. Also note the times of day when the fish seem to be moving so that you don't waste these periods motoring about to other drifts. The deeps aren't popular, but try them in practice. The Irish team won the 1980 international by fishing them, while others kept to the traditional spots.

Your main catch will be stocked rainbows so the normal fly patterns for these are effective here as elsewhere using sizes 10 to 14. Sinking or sink-tip lines are usually best with nylon of 6–8 lb and a rod of 10 ft or more. The Prysor Angling Club and the Lake Management Committee run a first-class hatchery and give anglers every chance. They ensure there are plenty of fish to be caught and that boats and engines are kept in good condition.

CHAPTER 15

OF CODES, COACHING, AND COMPETITION

All power had gone from me; my limbs were trembling, and there was a looseness of the legs which made it difficult to walk. Such are the great times of sheer excitement which happen in fishing.

Lord Grey of Fallodon

That trembling of the limbs is known to many competition anglers in their moment of joy or despair as they land or lose a match winning fish. The excitement of the chase is heightened by the challenge of the contest. But their eagerness to fish well, to perform well for their team, should never blind them to the natural courtesies of the water due to other anglers and other users.

Fly-fishermen know only too surely what a maddening distraction unthinking yachtsmen can be on some waters, as they sail over the rising fish you were about to cover, or cut in dangerously close behind, threatening to slice off your drogue. That should make them all the keener to pay due respect themselves to all those they meet, all those they fish with, and to the whole environment in which they enjoy their sport. Appropriately, it is Charles Kingsley's *Water Babies* which has immortalized the 'Do as you would be done by' concept, which is particularly important for competition anglers. We are aiming at high standards of fishing, which must include high standards of behaviour to others.

National competition rules in some countries contain one which is also implied in international rules, but needs to be more explicitly stated there in these same terms: 'Anglers are reminded that there are many unwritten rules when loch-style fishing; please observe the courtesies of the boat.'

That includes of course respect for bank anglers, or those in moored boats if any are encountered in competition.

At Trawsfynydd competitors may make jokes about needing tin hats to protect them from the rain of shot as bait fishermen hurl their leads far out towards the boats. But the bank men have paid their money, and have as much right to be there as we have so respect their water space, just as we expect them to respect ours. International competition usually absorbs all the boats a lake can put out. But in national competitions at Grafham and elsewhere you may come on a 'casual' boat, anchored up and fishing deep with large lures. It is tiresome when one appears in your line of drift. But he, too, has his rights, and must be given a wide berth.

Even more important is your treatment of your partner in the boat. Rules governing this change from time to time, but in essence no competitor should fish in a way that interferes with his partner's chances. It is clearly reasonable that you be allowed to throw as long a line as you can, since good casting is the basis of good fishing. What is not acceptable, though sometimes allowed, is standing up to cast or sitting on a special chair or plank. Both raise you up high above the water level, and that may scare off fish your partner is trying to catch close to the boat. Each gives an unfair advantage both in length of casting and in working the bob fly, as against the man fishing normally. There should be no artificial aids unless some injury makes a seat imperative.

David Fleming-Jones, former Welsh international Secretary and detached observer of recent Grafham internationals, has strong feelings on one point: 'Standing up in the boat and using it as a platform for superlong casting is an unpleasant practice. Standing on the seat is even worse. I have seen some English internationals guilty of this malpractice, which the other competing countries must regard as rude, and which can be unfair to the competitor at the other end of the boat. I have heard it referred to as the "English" or "Northampton" method. That is an undesirable label for a practice which should be ended.'

The practice was in fact banned at my last international at Leven in 1981. But the rule was introduced in a way which to me was as bad as standing up itself. When we assembled for practice day the rules specifically allowed it. On the eve of the competition there was a meeting after which we were verbally informed it was now banned. The whole point of sensible practice days is to experiment with the method you will use in the match. To alter a fundamental rule *after* practice, without some overriding reason for the last minute change, seems to me quite unfair to competitors. In my other international at Chew exactly the same thing occurred, this time in relation to a late change banning any extra seats, or sophisticated bucket-type chairs, on the grounds of the delay they could cause at changeover. Both restrictions were very reasonable in themselves, and for that reason should have been written in *before* practice started. Internationals have been going for more than fifty years now, and it makes no sense to introduce some new rule after practice days and on the eve of any match, *unless* some problem has arisen in practice which demands action. No standing up, and no special seats, without proof of disability making this a necessity, should be permanent features, not last minute adjustments.

Among the unwritten rules which need to be meticulously observed is never deliberately casting within a few inches of your rival's flies. An extension from the boatman's rowlock is taken as the central dividing line beyond which you must not cast into the other person's water. But if he casts first close to that line, you should not immediately do the same, so that your flies are fishing in such proximity. When Clive Greenaway was acting as boatman in an English national he witnessed a particularly unfortunate breach of that unwritten rule.

Neither angler in his boat moved a fish for some hours, on what was clearly a dour day at Grafham, when one or two good fish would be enough to ensure qualification. Then Clive saw a rainbow making little swirls of interest as it inspected the flies cast long and close to the 'dividing line' by the stern rod. The bow rod saw them, too. At once he whipped out his own flies and cast again a few inches away from the following fish. Instantly it veered across and seized the new fly proferred, rather than the ones it was hesitating over.

Clive had to cool the argument after it was netted, but the rest of the day was fished out in hostile silence. No more trout had been caught as Clive was motoring them in. There was still eight minutes in hand as he neared the landing stage, when he noticed a good fish rise just ahead. At once he cut the motor and suggested a last try. Immediately the man who had taken the fish before hooked into this one. A large and spirited rainbow it was, too, and clearly there were going to be problems in getting back in time. 'I'll net the fish if you will start the motor,' said Clive to the other angler. 'Not a chance!' was the reply. 'I've caught nothing so I'm not bothered whether we get in in time. But I'd be delighted to see *him* disqualified.'

The fish was landed, the marker buoys entered just in time. The successful angler had broken no written rules, except 'the normal courtesies of the boat'. Fortunately, most competition fishermen would prefer not to win through at all, rather than like that. That is reflected in the attitudes of those who make it to the internationals. In their whole history there has only been one disqualification other than for coming in late. In 1950, before the present practice of pairing individuals off with a boat partner from a rival country, a Scottish pair of ex-Provost James Tennant and John Danskin were disqualified after being reported by the Welsh for allowing the boatman to fish.

This occurred while Mr Tennant stopped fishing to eat his lunch (which itself is not recommended practice for any competitor wishing to do his best for his country). It was said in defence that no fish had been caught by the boatman. But plenty had been caught by the Scottish pair who brought in eighteen trout weighing 19 lb. Their disqualification therefore had a vital effect on the match, promoting England to winners in their place, and dropping Scotland to third place. But for Mr Tennant's lunch-break England would have led by two matches only, rather than four, at the start of Jubilee year.

Perhaps, however, there was more to it than that. For when Mr Tennant was banned for life from international competition, and Mr Danskin escaped, the matter was further debated. A committee, meeting of S.N.A.C.A. decided on all the evidence then available that 'Mr Danskin's fault was the greater'. Exactly why we shall never know, but he was banned, too, and it is hinted in David Biggart's *The First Hundred Years*' that the reason was the use of illegitimate 'terror' flies, which had helped him to his large basket. To everyone's chagrin the original affair was given wide publicity in the *Sunday Express*.

Not such wide publicity, of course, is given to the sporting and friendly spirit in which all but a few fish, as has been evident in many of the accounts on previous pages. In my own case, I was particularly fortunate in both my Welsh boat partners in my two internationals. In the first, it was the highly experienced Roy Jones, manager of the Gwydyr Fisheries at Betwys-y-Coed, and I had to apologize to him when I failed to control the initial rush of a good rainbow, which surged across his line of cast. Far from being put out he responded with, 'That's all right, boyo. Pass me your rod a moment, and I'll work it behind the boat for you, where it will be easier to play.'

That kind action was matched by an equally kind thought two years later. As I stepped into my boat at Leven on match morning, both myself and the Scottish boatman were presented with the Welsh fishing badge, to start the day in friendship, and give me a memento to treasure. Sometimes, indeed, competitors can be too generous to each other at the start of a match. If you both agree, you *can* waive the rule of changing ends, and command of the boat, each two hours. If you wish, by all means select the fishing areas by joint agreement, rather than by alternating individual decision. But *don't* agree to waive changing of ends. There are days when one end of the boat consistently outscores the other, and if you waive the right at the beginning you can't later insist on it if it *is* one of those days.

B.C. Hall recalls the competition day at Leven when R.W. Beaty made his record catch of forty-two trout. His boat too started catching early. The trout were rising right on the edge of the shore, and the gillie could only hold the boat in such a way that his partner covered them first. He had fifteen before Hall had a touch. Then they started a different drift as the trout stopped rising there. This time it was Hall who reeled off the next dozen to come to the net. There also tends to be a slight natural advantage from being in the bow, which often slants forward in the drift. To be fair to yourself, and your boat partner, *don't* waive the rule about changing; but nor should you motor off to far distant parts each time you take charge, so wasting your own and your rival's fishing time.

International fishermen, indeed all competitive fishermen, ought to be experienced enough to know the unwritten laws of good fishing, of not interfering with the prospects and pleasures of others, of respecting and preserving the environment. But it is good to find these aspects being taught from the start to those who enter the new coaching schemes leading to bronze, silver, or gold awards in game, coarse, or sea fishing. In achieving the game awards the fly-fisherman is competitive only against the standards set, but like any examination beating the pass mark is competition of a kind.

The key elements of the bronze award remind that there is more to being a good fisherman than just catching fish. You have to satisfy the examiners that you understand the best practice and theory of seven aspects — water, tackle, fish and their diet, casting, tactics, water safety, and waterside code.

Water safety includes for the boat fisherman taking care not to threaten your partner or your boatman with your flies. On windy days, in the tiring conditions of eight-hour competitions, you must never relax and let a wayward cast whistle near them. Even more important you must not cast riskily across them in your eagerness to cover a rising fish at a difficult angle.

Normally, a hook in you is no more than a temporary nuisance, even if it goes over the barb. Your eyes, however, are a different matter. When teaching my children, I insisted they wear glasses, goggles, or some form of eye protection for several years until they were fully experienced casters and sensible anglers aware of possible dangers. Even experts can't afford to relax, however. My father suffered the embarrassment of a spey cast with a salmon rod which whipped a large salmon fly through the bottom of his chin, when fishing the Wye; and the pain of the Builth Wells surgery, where the angler doctor was more concerned to preserve the splendid fly than avoid hurting him! International Clive Greenaway had a convalescence of several weeks when a freak gust of wind recently blew a size-12 fly into his eye with the barb going behind the retina. That his sight is now as good as before was largely due to his foresight in arranging to be fishing at the time with a doctor as his boat partner. Accidents can happen even if you take care. Never add to the chance by being careless.

Anglers should always start by making sure of the rules of a particular fishery, and of any code of practice applying. The Code of Good Practice drawn up by the Midland Fly-Fishers for their English lakes is no bad guide for most waters:

1. Know the fishery regulations and keep to them.
2. Keep clear of anglers already fishing.
3. Know your boat and motor. If in doubt obtain advice before starting.
4. Don't concentrate all the weight in the stern.
5. Leave tackle behind which is prohibited from use.
6. Avoid cutting across another boat's drift.
7. Move your boat very slowly when near other anglers.
8. Respect the rights of other users of the water.
9. Respect wildlife. In particular, take away waste nylon.
10. Co-operate with Fishery Staff.
11. Close gates and use stiles and paths where provided.
12. After fishing leave a return of your catch.

Point 5 is especially important in competition.

OF CODES, COACHING AND COMPETITION

There are also unwritten rules for the competitive fly-fisherman to keep.

The commandment which sums up all the others is: Don't do anything which interferes with another's enjoyment of his sport, or his competitive chances, or his safety.

Don't drift close to other boats; don't motor back just in front of drifting boats; don't cast into your boat partner's water; avoid casting close to his flies; if you are making a diagonal cast warn him, or time it so as not to tangle with him on the back cast; don't distract him when he is concentrating on his fishing; if he hooks a fish which runs in front of you, get your line out of the way as soon as possible; if you hook fish try and play them in front of your half of the boat, or work them quickly round to the back; on windy days in particular take great care not to hook your flies into your gillie or your partner — so don't get slack in your casting even at the end of a tiring eight-hour stint; and finally if your boat partner needs any help, give it to him to the best of your ability.

Since it is the fish which provide us with our sport, we need to put them first in any waterside code which covers handling of fish, as well as the protection of birds and other wildlife.

While such a code was in the course of being produced by the National Anglers' Council, the need for it became more obvious.

Whether fish feel pain has long been a question to worry anglers, and a report of an R.S.P.C.A. inquiry raised it in more acute form. After considering their own 'Medway Panel' findings, the society asked fishermen 'to review their appreciation of their sport in the light of the report'. Fishermen, as represented by their National Anglers' Council, did just that, after setting up their own eminent scientific group to consider the Medway Report.

No detailed scientific study ever lends itself to a simple summary, and this has proved no exception. The Medway report however further challenged the cherished belief that fish, being low in the evolutionary scale, are not capable of feeling pain to the same degree as man. It pointed to two new discoveries. First, that the nerve-endings in the skin of fish, particularly near the mouth, are seemingly identical to those in man, which perceive tissue-damaging sensation; second, that Professor Kelly and his co-workers have recently identified two pain-related substances, substance P and enkephalin, in the brain of the trout. The final conclusion of the report has cautious reservations, but indicated, reasonably enough, that fish ought to be given the benefit of the doubt.

That is now a middle-of-the road view between the R.S.P.C.A. interpretation that fish do 'experience pain and suffering', and the anglers scientific group's view, after discussion with the main scientific contributor to the Medway Report, that the 'scientific evidence does not show that fish feel pain as commonly understood by human beings. There is nothing to indicate the Medway Panel formed any different opinion.'

The National Anglers' Council welcomed the R.S.P.C.A.'s public statements 'indicating that it is not generally opposed to the rights of anglers to practise their sport'. But, in fact, it is proper that anglers should give the fish the benefit of any doubt, and be especially careful in their treatment of those they hook. The council has implicitly accepted this on their behalf with its sensible decision to work on a code of practice to help minimize any suffering, or ill-usage, of fish.

Fishermen argue with justice that they do much more good than harm to fish life, having led the fights against pollution of waters, and the destruction of fish stocks; having countered disease, developed new strains, protected threatened species, and improved the balance of fish life in many waters. They can argue, too, that the fish themselves are cruel and voracious predators, snapping up a wide variety of life forms, including their own, and exterminating them more 'painfully' than even the most careless angler. But before complacency sets in they should recall Byron's vitriolic comment on the favoured spokesman of their idyllic sport. This was his view:

> *And angling too, that solitary vice,*
> *Whatever Izaak Walton sings or says;*
> *The quaint, old, cruel coxcomb in his gullet*
> *Should have a hook, and a small fish to pull it.*

The promised code should be rapidly available and ensure that, in general, such unsympathetic strictures remain unfair. Meanwhile, the widest publicity needs to be given to some of the recommendations of the council's own scientific group.

In their view, single hooks should be preferred to doubles or trebles, and all anglers should be equipped with disgorgers; fish which swallow hooks should be despatched as rapidly as possible and not returned; wider use of barbless hooks, particularly in competition, would be a welcome development.

Very importantly, anglers are requested not to use ultra-fine tackle out of proportion to the size of the fish to be caught. The group also endorses the national coaching scheme just launched by the Anglers' Council with the syllabus for the various awards including advice on best practice.

These awards schemes also include waterside practice, since anglers need to take care for the whole of the environment in which they have their pleasure. It is no credit to take thought for the fish, which are caught, then carelessly discard nylon, which entangles birds, or lead shot, which may have caused the death of some swans. That bird is in fact the appropriate symbol of Swan Vestas, who are sponsoring the National Coaching Scheme, which should lead to better care for swans, birds, fish, and all the life forms with which the angler comes in contact.

The rules for international fly-fishing competition have remained relatively simple, and should stay so. One of the attractions of fishing is the freedom of spirit it brings. That is a basic concept, a basic part of fly-fishing whether it be loch-style or any other style. As long as the concept of casting in front of a drifting boat with small-sized flies is protected, the other rules should be kept to a minimum. But for all anglers, in competition or not, 'do-as-you-would-be-done-by' remains an overriding rule.

CHAPTER 16
EQUIPPED FOR COMPETITION

Bring the rod, the line, the reel;
Bring, oh bring, the osier creel;
Bring me flies of fifty kinds,
Bring me showers, and clouds, and winds!
　　All things right and tight,
　　All things well and proper,
　　Trailer red and bright,
　　Dark and wily dropper —
　　Casts of midgets bring,
　　Made of plover-hackle
　　With a gaudy wing
　　And a cobweb tackle.

　　　　　　　　　　Thomas T. Stoddart

Care in the selection and use of tackle has traditionally been the mark of a good angler. Even if Thomas Tod Stoddart's list from 125 years ago might not be ideal for modern competition (the cobweb tackle would be too easily broken by a match-winning fish, the fifty flies would confuse selection), the choice and checking of tackle is still vital. The highly professional match anglers in coarse fishing may spend up to £1500 on their equipment and prepare it as carefully as did Dave Thomas in his extraordinary feat of coming first in both team and individual events of the world freshwater angling championships.

Yet any advice on equipment must start with a reminder that matches are not won by equipment alone, for this is always secondary to the skill of the angler. That, too, Stoddart knew well:

　　The art lies more in the man than his instrument. All the stores of tackle in the wide world, gossamer gut as strong as whipcord, flies the image of life, and a rod that might throw them twenty fathoms' distance, unless fitly managed, are no more likely to ensnare trout than an oak tree and a cable. Let us advise all tyros in the gentle art to be on their guard against cheap and useless materials.

The poet-angler of Teviotside might have added a warning against following every new fad or fancy and thinking that will somehow make you an expert angler. So many new flies or techniques prove better at emptying your pocket than filling your creel. As Alan Pearson once perceptively wrote about a wide-selling treatise which was to make it easy for us to catch trout: 'Everything in it that is new isn't good; and everything that is good isn't new.'

Never be too credulous about the latest panacea, for every fly-fisherman likes to imagine there is some magic fly or method which will always catch fish. If there is, it is not one bought off the peg in a shop, but learnt the hard way by constant observation and practice on the water. The best dressed fisherman, or the one with most flies in his hat, is rarely the one who comes back with the heaviest basket. A fine carbon-fibre rod, like the excellent Church Hill gold, and a super-expensive reel and line may be useful aids, but they won't suddenly convert you into a match-winner. Indeed, in competition you are likely to do better with those well tried and seasoned rods and lines with which you regularly take your trout.

Only for your casts should it be a case of no expense spared — small as is the sum involved between the best and the questionable. That great trout expert of old, Frederic M. Halford, had this to say of the casts of his time: 'When purchasing gut there is only one piece of advice to offer. Go to the best dealers, buy the very best they have and don't grumble at the price. A few shillings on the price of a hank of gut may often mean the loss of the best day of the season.' The same applies emphatically to purchasing nylon.

On my first practice for an internatinal, John Ketley made two comments to me about my cast: 'You should have "maxima" nylon. That is the best, and doesn't twist up like the one you are using. A good angler should make his cast one-and-a-half times his rod length. The best will have it double the rod length, though that is difficult to cast well.' He might have added that it can be awkward for landing, too, as you have to reel in well over the knot to net your fish; so the tying of the knot small enough to run easily through the rings is important, if you are not to be broken by a final lunge from the fish.

Maxima is indeed first-class nylon, but you may have other preferences. Brian Thomas always uses Racine Tortue and finds this at least as satisfactory. He also stresses that it is not necessary to pay out a lot of money for lines and reels in order to be well-equipped for competition.

The need to economize can be a very real one for many of us when you consider the rising price of top quality tackle. In evaluating the worth of some of the early prizes in the Scottish national, David Biggart gave this interesting comparison of a trout fly-fishing outfit in 1892 and 1979:

	1892			1979
	£	s	d	£
12ft split-cane rod	3	3	0	90.00
3½ in high quality gun-metal reel		15	0	11.00
60 yd line		6	0	10.00
Landing net with 4 ft handle		4	0	4.00
Fly-box with 60 flies		12	6	13.00
Cast box with 12 4-fly casts	1	1	0	12.00
Wicker basket plus canvas bag		18	6	16.00
	7	0	0	156.00

If you aim to have the best fly-boxes, you will want one of the Wheatley range, with a sample of which the teams were each presented at Leven in 1981. If you want a servicable one for little expense, you can simply take a large tin for sweets or whatever, and cover the bottom with that excellent Ethafoam which can be bought in various sizes for a few pence. In fact I have found the most helpful method for carrying flies in competition is to take a number of empty tins of strepsils or cough losenges, and line them with Ethafoam. You can have one in each of your four jacket pockets, each with your principal selection of a dozen or so patterns but of varying size. Replacements can then be located instantly. In your bag you can keep one large fly-box with the whole range of your other flies in case you need some desperate change from the dozen or so you had fixed on in practice, or your boat partner starts killing them on a fly not in your chosen lot.

It has always seemed to me that it is not so much the length of cast you use which marks you out as a good angler, but the strength. There are some who can use fine casts and not get broken. They tend to be both immensely skilled, and able to fish in a way which induces a slow, gentle take. Those who use nymphs or small flies and work them very slow may get away with 3 or 4 lb nylon. If you play the percentage game of the fast draw, which encourages a fierce take, or if you are an average angler, you are better off with nylon from 6–8 lb, depending on the size of fish you may expect.

That is not just because the code of behaviour advises fishing strong enough to avoid breaks. It is because you may otherwise needlessly lose a match-winning fish. In one of my last qualifiers I fished with a very competent angler so far as casting and working his flies went. With time running out after a fruitless day for him, there was suddenly a great swirl round his flies. A rainbow big enough to qualify him came and went without any bend in the rod. 'Touch him?' I asked. 'No. He missed' was an answer that made little sense when his cast made a whipcracking noise behind him. On checking his fly he found it had indeed gone, the large fish snapping it off without his feeling anything. When I asked the strength of his cast I was told it was a 4 lb leader. It was likely that was the difference between his coming in blank, or with a bag that would have qualified him for the final. Fishing an ordinary draw on a day with a good breeze, it seemed madness to me to go below 6 lb on a lake where you expect large fish.

All the danger, of course, is at the moment of take and strike. You shouldn't be broken when playing a fish on a lake free of weeds, however fine your tackle. Odd things do happen nonetheless. The final trout I caught at Draycote in a national final, which qualified me for the England team, weighed only $1\frac{1}{2}$ lb. Yet in its mouth it had an enormous and rusting lure fly, from which trailed ten feet of 12 lb nylon. How anyone contrived to be broken on that tackle by that fish I can't imagine, but in the circumstances I was very grateful for earlier incompetence.

One of those who can fish fine with success, because of his method, is former English international Ralph Williams. It brought him 320 good trout on some of the main Midland competition waters in 1981 as he relates:

> I tie my own flies, which are always different from any in shops or books. This season I started a new technique which caught me more trout than any other I had tried. I attach to my fly line three yards of 6 lb cast, then two feet of 3 lb for the point. Twenty-eight inches back from the point fly, I attach direct to the cast a large dry fly. This is

tied with blue, brown, and ginger hackle in that order down to the hook. On the point I put a nymph, tied size 12 or 14, of limegreen colour, and slow sinking. To fish these flies I grease the cast from fly line to dry fly. The 3 lb cast is allowed to sink slowly to its full depth. No retrieve is made, except for mending the line as the boat drifts down on the dry fly, by taking up the slack. If the trout take the dry fly that is easy to see. If they take the nymph, you see the dry fly move away and know it's time to tighten firmly into a fish. You may have quite a shock to find how well it works, even in calm conditions.

There is no money refunded if you are not as successful as Ralph Williams, but if you didn't catch 320 good trout last season it could be worth trying. Certainly I have used a similar method with considerable success on what Peter Malloch called 'the famous lochs at Altnacealgach' where it is still possible to catch the great baskets of which he wrote in 1910. There my son and I use on occasion a bushy dry fly on the top dropper with a team of small wet flies behind, drawn slow. The better trout take the dry fly with a spectacular eruption, while greater numbers seize the following flies.

One item of equipment which is very useful in those stormy lochs can also be valuable in competition. The parachute-like drogue is not always permitted in competition, and is unnecessary with the heavy Leven boats which ride the wave so well. If allowed, it can be very effective in slowing the drift of those fragile glassfibre boats, or other light ones, which skim before the breeze. Not only does it save fishing time, but it allows better working of the fly on days when the boat would otherwise be drifting too fast on them. The problem of the drogue can be the hazard it presents if the fish works round behind the boat. Some, who agree to the use of a drogue in competition, stipulate that it must be pulled in if a fish is being played. That may be the safest, certainly if the trout is large and lively. Another unexpected hazard surprised me the first time I used one. When I caught a large fish I was so pleased I started the motor without thought, and the drogue was wrenched off, sinking rapidly to the bottom. If you are easily distracted like me, there is a way to avoid similar misfortune. Tie an empty plastic container to the drogue just above the rope, and it will be left floating if the rope parts.

David Porter uses his drogue in an original and effective way when not in competition: 'Instead of trailing the drogue from the middle of the boat so that it drifts parallel to the waves, tie it to the bow. Then the bow will point straight down the loch, giving you three major advantages. The boat will ride the waves naturally without being continually slapped and rocked by them. That makes for more comfortable fishing. Then you can both cast out different sides, covering more water as the bow-rod casts left, the stern right. Finally, and most importantly, you will be casting across the waves rather than down them, a much more effective way of fishing.' Competition rules do not allow this, but on other occasions it is a useful tactic.

The flies can either be of no great significance on those days when trout are not selective, or vital when they are. The main importance of practice days is in finding the flies and the method in which you have confidence. It is all too easy when practising to enjoy the fishing, and forget the practising, to keep to a fly or method that starts well without trying anything else. The practice day is for sensible experiment. Two in particular were of special value to me. When we had a qualifier at Bewl Bridge in Kent, which I had never fished before, my son and I each experimented with different method and flies. It was June, and the lake looked ideal for floating line. But I fished a sinker just to check. When I had four and John none, we changed rods and still the sinker caught them, not the floater. The first fish took the Black Chenille, but we went on trying other flies and finally found that the Green Peter was equally effective. As a result, I qualified on the day and heavily outscored my boat partner, who had come equipped for a traditional assault on the lake.

On another practice day at Draycote we found from asking around one man who was very successful with a sunk Daddy-long-legs. The pattern was too large for competition use, but has proved very killing on a variety of waters from July onwards. A memorable practice day for me was at Leven 1981. Richard Webb joined me, and I hooked a couple of trout before he had a rise. Then he was into a fish. 'You'll find they fight well,' I told him. The trout of nearly 3 lb headed straight for the boat, leapt high out of the water, and into my arms. That gave Richard the confidence to do so well on match day that his catch was decisive in winning the match for England. On the day he had the sense to make full use of that most important item of all one's equipment — an experienced boatman. The rest of us had quartered the loch and decided the North Deeps was where the fish would be caught. That was where all the boats headed at the start, confident they knew the best places from Scart to Green Isle. Richard found he had one of Leven's most experienced gillie's as boatman. So instead of trusting his own limited knowledge, he and his partner simply said, 'Take us where you think best.' As a result they were eased down to St Serf's Island area, which others had written off as useless. That was where the fish were moving. The moral of that is that two days' practice may teach you a lot, but don't think it will make you more knowledgeable than a man who has fished the water year in, year out. If you are lucky enough to get an expert boatman, use him to the full. Nothing else in your equipment will be as valuable.

The boatman can take you where you have the best chance of catching fish. Then the first principle is to stick with the equipment, methods, and flies in which you believe. Confidence is the other essential item with which to equip yourself. Competition is not the time for anxious experiment.

Another to stress the importance of the boatman is Vic Williams of Wales:

> I was fortunate to fish Leven when the loch had its quota of professional gillies. In one international I drew one of the Stark brothers. It was a morning of downpour and gale with a thunderstorm centred above, and forked lightning searing down on the loch. He let all the other boats motor away only starting up as I wondered if something was wrong with the engine. All the rest turned left at Castle Island, making for the Beech Hedge and the Green Isle, from whence came the gale-force wind. We turned right for Paddy's Point and Stark was annoyed when he saw one other boat turn in that direction. He put his glasses on it and was a little mollified when he found it was gillied by his son.
>
> Drifting in to Paddy's Point I soon had my first fish. Then my boat partner, Dai Rees of Trawsfynydd, said something to distract me just as I had a take, and with my finger on the line I was broken. Hastily putting on another cast, I tied on a 16 Greenwell Spider as dropper, and was soon back in action. Still feeling hurried as we drifted fast towards the shore, I struck too soon when another fish rose in the big wave. Mr Stark made no bones about telling me, 'You're too fast, Sir.' There was no doubt now that I was under scrutiny by a knowledgeable critic.

The next five trout followed the Greenwell to within a yard of the boat and I even had to turn the cast so that the dropper tripped along parallel with the boat. Still they hesitated, not taking the Greenwell until my 10 ft Alcock rod was way behind my shoulder. Then the fly would disappear and I could flick my wrist to set the hook. All the time Mr Stark watched without comment and netted with skill.

If I've got six, I expect they are really pulling them in at the Green Isle, Mr Stark,' I said, hoping for the contradiction which came. 'And another thing', said Stark, 'if this thunderstorm moves away we will go on taking fish. But if it circles the loch, you've caught your last.' The rain ceased, but the thunderstorm went rumbling on round us and hard as we fished we moved no more. From lifelong experience he knew exactly how the trout in that loch would react and the six his knowledge had brought me were enough for me to have a winning bag. It is so important to have a good gillie, and more important still to be willing to listen to his advice.

Vic's own advice about equipment is always to be flexible and adaptable. He certainly was when he was labelled a 'lucky' fisherman by Howard Roberts, his team manager of the sixties and current chairman of the Welsh Salmon and Trout Association. Howard had developed a theory that feeding trout would always be found in a part of Leven where the shallows dipped suddenly into deep water. To test this he took out Vic and another Rhayader angler, Tom Morgan, to fish while he drifted the boat along this line. The theory seemed proven as they soon struck into trout. Vic's fourth ran under the boat and the line become caught in a gap in the iron keel. He asked Howard to beach despite warnings that this might cut his Kingfisher line on the stones. When they got to shore they all sat one side to tilt the boat and Vic then stepped out in his waders. There was a good trout lying quietly level with the keel, and it was netted as soon as the line was freed to the accompaniment of shouts of 'You lucky so and so!' Though he had the trout, Vic had gone over both waders in reaching it, and faced another six cold hours of fishing. He mystified his companions by removing his daughter's old school cardigan, which he was wearing, and snipping off both sleeves a few inches below the shoulder. He then emptied and upended his waders and put on the sleeves as dry and warming stockings. As he comments, 'You need to show initiative in dealing rapidly with emergencies — especially when there is a nice rise of trout!'

Victor Williams' six trout weighing 4 lb 13 oz won him the Brown Bowl in that 1970 international. Four years later, at the Lake of Menteith, he became the first man ever to win it twice. On that occasion, however, he departed from his gillie's advice, though emphasizing that you need a reason for doing so, and need still to respect his knowledge:

> It is difficult to decide how long to rely on that knowledge when his choice of drift is unproductive. If you do want to change, it is important to 'suggest' a move to another area. By 'suggesting' it, you retain his full cooperation, which is so important.
>
> That was the position in this Lake of Menteith match in 1974. We had been on drift for a couple of hours; there was a rumour that the water had been stocked with rainbow trout the previous evening, and we had been advised that a No. 10 Dunkeld would be irresistible. But in the bright conditions, stripping a couple of Dunkelds had become a bore. Our gillie sensed I was unhappy and asked where we would like to go? 'Take me to the weed beds in Boathouse Bay,' I suggested. The Dunkeld and other flashers come off, and on went a No. 16 Black Pennell and No. 14 Black Chironomid. After rubbing down the cast with 'a little bit of shit' as the gillie called my glycerine and Fuller's Earth, the flies were allowed to sink in a channel between two long weed beds. I waited until they were well down, then a few twitches of an inch or two at a time — and bang!
>
> A brownie of about 2 lb, covered with weed, was finally brought out from the beds and netted. Later the Black Chironomid performed and to my surprise those two trout were good enough to take the Bowl. But I still wonder when and why you should change tactics. Do you do it from boredom, or out of experience, or from an intuition which demands the change?

That Brown Bowl — donated by John Brown — was first competed for in 1956 at Leven, when H. Potter of England beat his team mate, W. Smith, by one ounce with nine trout weighing 6 lb 15 oz. By the end of 1981 the Bowl had been won thirty-seven times, but only two anglers had ever won it twice — and both were named Williams. For Mervyn Williams was also a two-times winner, his 17 lb 7 oz at Leven in 1975 proving his best catch.

Confidence in your flies is crucial for competitive fishing. Otherwise you are forever unsure of yourself, forever wondering whether to change. The expert fly-tiers are often invaluable to their team, though they may get scant reward for their labours. International Alan Whitehead always has a portable fly-tying kit in his car. That came in useful for England at Trawsfynydd in 1978, as Alan recalls: 'I had the best bag on final practice day thanks to a small brownish-orange Matuka on an ordinary No. 10 hook. Everyone then wanted one of these so I burnt the midnight oil tying Matukas for the team. On match day half our team's catch was taken on them, while I had — you've guessed it — a blank! Such are the vagaries of fly-fishing.'

Alan has found success with an interesting range of flies. At Chew, where he qualifies, apart from the usual patterns he has had good results from a Paul Jorgenssen's Hatching Pupae fished on the dropper. Another to do him well there is a variant of the Soldier Palmer using Fiery Brown seal's fur from Sue Burgess (the shade is just right). He has fished a lot in Ireland and taken fish consistently on the Bog fly, Black and Silver, Black and Fiery Brown, Bibio, Watson's Fancy JC (red or orange), Claret and Jay, Blae and Black (red Ibis tail), Mallard and Claret using a brownish Claret seal fur, and the Fiery Brown. He has found they can all be used in any of the three positions on the cast and are best fished in Irish waters with short line, and moved smoothly in the surface.

It was in Ireland, too, that he discovered a highly successful fly — the Quick Dick. In 1977 he acted as boatman in the Grafham international for Dick Willis of the Irish team. Later, when he was in County Cork with a friend, Dick took them to fish Killarney. Despite the number of rises Alan suffered from the English disease of the slow strike, and kept missing them. Willis was forever shouting 'Quicker, be quicker, you *must* be quick.' So he was christened Quick Dick and Alan tied some special flies in his honour, combining all the colours he had found successful. Willis has found the 'Quick Dick' very effective with the Irish brown trout there, and particularly with the sea-trout of Lough Currane. But that wasn't the end of the story for Alan: 'I kept one for myself, and left it in my box. It was untouched until I became desperate in a South-West eliminator on Chew. With only ninety minutes left, all I had to show for my hard fishing ws a single fish of 1¼ lb. Noticing the Quick Dick as I searched my box, I decided to give it a whirl. Quick it was, too. Within twenty-five minutes the small fly had secured me two 3 lb rainbows to put me in third place.'

Should you wish to try your luck with a Quick Dick, this is Alan's tying:

Tag.	Pale blue silk and wool
Tail	Golden Crest
Rib	Gold Wire
Body	1st half Fiery Brown Seal fur
	2nd half Black Seal fur
Hackle	Black Cock
Beard	Blue Jay
Wing	Grouse
Cheeks	Jungle Cock (with or without)

Keith Jones is one who has given his time and expertise to help competitors by acting as boatman. Indeed, international though he is, he reckons to have been even more effective as boatman than fisherman. On his home water of Draycote the boat he gillied had the best catch, and his boat was second best with twenty-one fish in the subsequent international there.

No wonder he himself is quick to praise the boatman for his own success at Conn in his first international. He owed it to him that he recovered from a sad start in which a large trout broke his hook, and he missed a couple more: 'The wind was force 8, but he rowed us right across the lough. I was petrified until he got us into the shelter of an island. Even there I had to change to a sinker from a floater because the wind was still bouncing my flies over the waves. At once I missed a fish, and he made me cover it again immediately. That brought me my first trout, and the confidence to catch more.

'Never forget your boatman. He is the key to being kept over fish. So often he never gets a mention, but in these competitions the volunteer boatmen do a really great job deserving of our thanks.' He can say that again.

On flies Keith has a couple to add to the list of those that are effective at Draycote. He has considerable success with the Treacle Parkin and Red Tag, which also work for him elsewhere.

Brian Thomas has been very successful using inexpensive tackle:

> As a personal choice I use glass-fibre rods made up from blanks. The best of these was a 'Shooting Star', costing only £7, which has lasted me eleven seasons already. Sadly, that firm went out of business, and none of the current ones seem as light. However, I use fibre tube blanks. You can get these in lengths from 6–10 ft. Normally I cut to 9 ft 6 in, fit a handle and have a reliable rod, quite cheaply.
>
> The 'Meteor' from Scientific Angler is an inexpensive line which meets my needs. From the boat I use double taper 7, but from the bank 8 or 9. I am also happy with a cheap reel, perhaps because I use it only to hold line, not play fish. In my view playing is better done by hand-lining. So for me a Rimfly Kingsize is perfectly satisfactory. Rod, reel, and line cost only £40 or so, are good enough for any type of fishing, and with care all last years.
>
> To the end of my line I tie a 2 ft length of 25 lb nylon, then one of 15 lb, then a length of 10 lb. Direct to this goes the $6\frac{1}{2}$ lb of Racine Tortue nylon, which is my personal preference. Tapering down from 25 lb gives a good roll over and better presentation.

Successful English international Peter Heddle is another advocate of Racine Tortue nylon, and one, like me, who finds the Loch Ordie a useful fly. He has three golden rules for his match-day equipment: 'If I get in a tangle, I cut off the cast immediately and replace it with another ready made up. The next rule is "Don't forget the Kendal Mint Cake, the brown sugar one". Broken up in a plastic bag in my pocket it sustains me marvellously through those final tiring two hours. Finally, it's a case of "Don't forget the seat cushion". Sitting uncomfortably can upset your concentration.'

If you are successful in the days of practice and on match day you may have problems in bringing them home. The match-day fish are often donated to a hospital or a Cheshire home, but your earlier ones may have been deep-frozen and you may have a long journey ahead.

Over the years that problem has faced me on holidays in Scotland. From Overscaig on Loch Shin or the Altnacealgach lochs it is over 700 miles to my Hampshire home by road, and if you travel by motor-rail it is a fair bet the train will be four hours or more late if you are trying to rush fish home. Since in a fortnight at either place my family expects to catch between 200 and 300 lb of trout, that is some waste if they unfreeze on the way! So we developed a system which keeps them deep frozen for up to twenty-four hours.

Take with you some of those multiply paper sacks for fertilisers and the like. Take also some old newspapers, as hotels never seem to have enough, and a liberal supply of freezer bags. Clean your fish and freeze them in the bags. When you pack them for transport fluff out the newspaper and build up from the bottom of the multiply sack, keeping the bags of fish solid in the middle with a thick layer of fluffed paper all round. Finally put the sack inside one of those large bin-liners. We used to take up the ordinary black dustbin liners until the scientists in my family pointed out that black absorbs the heat, while white reflects it. So with a white bin-liner, and perhaps an old white sheet to cover the lot, your sacks of fish should survive the journey still deep frozen. If any do start to thaw, they cannot be refrozen unless you smoke them. For that a Brooks Home smoker is preferable to an Abu. It may not be as well finished, but it is cheaper, and smokes more at one go. This method should keep you trout enough for cooking for months to come. But as Mrs Beeton would advise first catch your fish!

CHAPTER 17
FINAL REFLECTIONS

> *O the gallant Fisher's life,*
> *It is the best of any;*
> *'Tis full of pleasure, void of strife,*
> *And 'tis beloved of many:*
> *Other joys*
> *Are but toys;*
> *Only this*
> *Lawful is;*
> *For our skill,*
> *Breeds no ill,*
> *But content and pleasure.*
>
> Jo Chalkhill

That's how the fisherman sees it. But how do others regard us when we waste eight hours flogging the water, and come in empty-netted at the end? In boyhood I used to spend many happy hours reading old volumes of Punch in an aunt's house. There weren't many jokes about fishermen, until one caught my eye. The drawing showed a wild-looking man peering chad-fashion over the wall of an asylum at an angler seated below on the banks of a stream: 'Caught anything?' enquires the lunatic. 'Nothing.' 'How long have you been fishing?' 'Eight hours.' 'Come inside and join us,' calls the madman.

That theme was echoed again in two lines of a verse by R.L. Stevenson:

> *'What have you caught?' the peasant cries.*
> *'Naught as yet,' the Fool replies.*

To the casual observer anglers, and particularly competition anglers, must often seem mad or masochistic as they inflict expensive, and unrewarded, toil on themselves. As Sir Leonard Hutton once remarked to Cowdrey after the pair had battled through a morning session bruised by the thunderbolts of Miller and Lindwall: 'At least I get paid for this, Colin. I can't think why *you* put up with it.'

I had the same feeling about the sport of rowing which can look even more inane to the uninitiated. Watching the bumping races at Oxford I was amused by the coxless fours ploughing blindly on while facing back the way they had come. Beside them on the towpath coaches cycled perilously along, in danger of falling into the river as they fired blanks from pistols to indicate the imminence of a bump, the demand for a final effort. On this day, one crew soldiered on with acres of clear water behind, where the following boat had itself been bumped, and acres clear in front, where the next crew had rowed right away. Their coach, obviously displeased with his charges' performance, kept firing his blanks to urge them to frenzy as they rowed on mouths frothing, wake foaming in sightless expectation of the bump they had no hope of achieving.

Looking back on international fly-fishing competition it has needed equally dedicated men to enjoy some matches. There was the Alaw fiasco with only three trout caught; there was the Conn storm which boat-wrecked the competitors; there have been practice days with no fish caught, and many dour and dispiriting hours in vain pursuit of trout.

There can be frustration, and there can be despair. At any time the loss of a big fish is a devastating experience as Albert Cochrane recorded in these lines:

> *He girds him for his final play,*
> *And I, with victory in my heart,*
> *Summon the net to end him. Nay!*
> *My line sags emptily away —*
> *Shade of old Izaak what to say?*
> *Who christened this the 'gentle art'?*

How much greater the depression when the loss happens on a hard day in competition!

Fishermen may indeed seem fools at times to the outsider to punish themselves so. But the real fools are those who can't appreciate that the hard times serve only to make the days of plenty and success that much sweeter. The losers are those who don't understand that there is much more to fishing than fish. Even in competition you can be concentrated, yet totally relaxed and at peace, the happy state at which most other sportsmen aim, but which they never achieve.

That is the subtle difference of fishing. In other major sports like athletics, cricket, or football, man strives to impose himself on nature. His being is focused on running faster, or kicking or hitting a ball further, than nature intended, or others can match. He fights the elements as well as his rivals. He may even deliberately distort his body with steroids perverting himself into some subhuman robot, perhaps to satisfy a coach or a communist State.

In fishing, even in competitive fly-fishing, you are at one with nature, working with it, absorbed by it, and following man's natural hunting instinct. As a result, this sport really does refresh the parts other sports can't reach. Fishing has a therapeutic effect on mind and body. The exercise is gentle, the thoughts happily concentrated on wind, waves, and the reaction of the fish.

Competitive fly-fishing has the side benefit that even a blank day can end in enjoyable exchange with friendly rivals, as the wealth of stories makes up for the paucity of the catch. In Scotland's most recent champion of champions match this feeling shone through the disappointment of a day on which over one hundred of 120 champions came in both cold and 'clean'. The *Scottish Angling News* was still able to observe that the assembled company was in good voice and heart. Despite the dreary day, and deplorable fishing, the exchange of fishing tales made the correspondent 'laugh until the tears came'.

Even misfortunes may later mellow into entertaining reminiscence. The first time I heard the phrase 'You can't measure the pleasure by the catch', it was used in inconclusive argument between the old Hampshire wicket-keeper, Leo Harrison, and another angler, John Arlott. The well-rehearsed subject of debate was John Arlott's fluffed attempts at netting for Leo a vast and magnificently proportioned salmon. That was as Harrison saw it. The contrary view was that the said monster was in fact a badly played kelt, so thin and wraithlike it would only have looked respectable in a sea- angling competition where it might have been mistaken for a conger eel. The past traumas caused by that fish — whatever it was — are of no moment compared to the pleasure of the continuing discussions which will be measured in years.

Miss Ballantyne's record apart, salmon have figured here mainly in a negative sense. They don't count if caught during Lough Conn trout contests, or in sea-trout competitions. They are excluded by name from the Ellem Club river competitions. True, they might have been involved in the first of the TV Fishing Races, when Clive Gammon's partner wasted a day in fruitless pursuit of an Avon salmon. That hopeless endeavour, senseless in the terms of the competition, summed up salmon fishing. The challenge is so irresistible in itself that the contest with this majestic fish needs no other competitive spur. Can you imagine a fly-fisherman shaking off 'One of the Boys', on Lough Conn, even if landing the salmon was going to waste an important hour of competitive fishing time in an international?

There is a mythical salmon, however, which best illustrates the extra ingredient competition brings to fly-fishing. In John Buchan's *John McNab*, the story centres on elite, but world-weary, members of London's clubland, grown stale through a surfeit of life's pleasures. So to their normal sporting pursuits they add the spice of additional competitive pressures and problems. In this case the most difficult task they set themselves is to 'poach' a salmon — but by fair fishing with fly in low water conditions. The risk and the difficulty bring a new urgency to the fishing as a salmon is marked down, deceived at dusk, and landed against the clock.

While the home countries have developed international fishing, the sport is on the verge of a much wider extension of such competition. On 3 October 1981 the first international fly-fishing competition. organized by the Fédération Internationale de la Pêche Sportive *en eau douce* (F.I.P.S., the body which also organizes the World Freshwater Angling Championships for coarse fishermen), took place on Luxembourg's Lake Echternach.

This new competition was agreed at a C.I.P.S. Confederation's Congress in Bad Kreuznach the previous season with the hosting assigned to the Polish Anglers' Union. But they had as hard a time as other types of Union in that unhappy state and had to withdraw, leaving the President of F.I.P.S., Jos. Kleinbauer, to stage the inaugural competition in his own country.

F.I.P.S. naturally hope that these championships will in time attain the prestige and widespread support of the World Freshwater Coarse Fishing Championships which have grown over a quarter of a century until over twenty countries now participate with Australia the most distant entrant. Inevitably, as the organizing body is the same, some of the format of those established contests has been applied to the new fly-fishing championship. The rules differ considerably from home internationals with the result decided by points rather than solely on weight caught. Each country can enter two teams of three and the first winner at Echternach was Holland B with 38 points followed by Luxembourg A 47, Belgium A 55, Luxembourg B 60, France A 71, and Austria 82.

International fly-fishing competition will now grow apace as has been the case with coarse fishing, and these islands should play a part in the full development of what they themselves have started and of which they have greater experience than any other country.

Fortunately an unexpected opportunity came for me to participate in this exciting development. The second 'Fly Angling' World Championship was arranged for 2–6 June 1982 with the Federacion Espanola de Pesca as hosts. The venue was the Sella and Narcea rivers in the north-western Asturias region of Spain. The quarry was Salmo Salar, Salmo Trutta, and Salmo Trutta Fario 'in respective order of sport importance and weight'.

England's problem in participating was that a team could only be entered by a governing body in membership with F.I.P.S. and the one English body to qualify was the National Federation of Anglers, who only cater for coarse fishermen. In discussion with Stan Smith, the NFA's International Events Manager, it was agreed that he would register England's entry if I helped collect a strong enough team and fished with it. So as I write we have the happy prospect of being members of the country's first world cup team.

Our team includes the Chairman, David Swatland, and John Inglis, Field Secretary, of the Salmon and Trout Association. As representatives of the overall governing body of fly-fishing they can assess the importance of the competition. For at some stage in the future it is to be hoped that the representative body of this sport, perhaps in conjunction with the English Fly-Fishing Confederation, will take a more direct part in organizing our entry with a formal selection procedure.

Advance notice of the rules told us that the teams were to be quartered in Oviedo and Gijon. With Oviedo a centre for World Cup football a few days later, accommodation was likely to be a problem, though our competition was not expected to cause quite the same problems of crowd control! But all of us will be happy to camp by the river to take part in an event such as this.

To maintain the best of English fishing traditions some of us will be equipped with hand-made rods to the standard which once made such British craftsmanship the best in the world in this field. Carbon and fibre glass may have revolutionized rods for lightness and cheapness, but such rods can never match the versatility of the hexagonal split-cane models with the traditional British action. These can be designed and shaped to the exact requirement of the individual fisherman, if the craftsman is good enough. And there is none better at present than Alastair Agutter, head of Agutters of London in Hatton Garden. With his team of specialists, which includes the noted hand-engraver Michael Lawrie, he has reintroduced a quality of hand-made rods which had begun to seem a lost art. That is perhaps best expressed in a remarkable rod he has made to celebrate the Izaak Walton tercentenary in 1983. Some 200 hours of workmanship has gone into this rod of superb standard produced with the materials of Walton's day, even to the use of whipping rather than the glue which came in later. So he was asked to ensure that the team had the chance to be equipped with the finest rods so that there could be no blaming of our tools if we performed poorly.

Competition, contrived or real, does indeed add a new dimension to your fishing, but it must never be allowed to destroy the prime pleasure. In previous pages a number of international fly-fishermen have passed on their own recipes for success. You may, like me, prefer simple guides such as Brian Thomas' limited list of effective flies for Rutland. Or you may prefer bold and far-reaching experiment, testing out a variety of options offered. Or you may prefer to stick with your own proven methods, and distrust the written alternatives, echoing Sir Henry Newbold's lines:

> *Dinna trust tae the books an' their gammon —*
> *They jist try to sell ye;*

My own fishing motto is the same as the football advice I was weaned on by a famous Tottenham Hotspur coach, Arthur Rowe: 'Make it simple, make it quick.' You need to fish to an uncomplicated plan, to keep your flies always in action, and to draw them quickly as a basic tactic. Rowe's staff had one other telling phrase to pass on. As we were about to take the field at Wembley before 100,000 spectators, the last word of advice was 'Whatever you do, enjoy yourselves.' That is the best advice for competitive fly-fishing, too, and you are likely to catch more with that relaxed attitude.

The enjoyment of competition is just another facet of a sport which never palls throughout a lifetime. Andrew Lang wrote in 1890, for all us fly-fishing addicts with this remarkably perceptive comment: 'I would as soon lay down a love of books as a love of fishing. Success with pen or rod may be beyond one, but there is the pleasure of the pursuit, the delight of the impossible chase, the joys of nature. Happiness in these things is the legacy of the barbarian. Man in future will enjoy bricks, asphalt, fog, machinery, "society". We are fortunate who inherit the old, not the new spirit'.

As the bricks and asphalt spread, more and more seek release from the fog of modern life in the unchanging fascination of fishing. There are over a million active fly-fishers in Britain and Ireland, at least 100,000 of whom have now tasted competition in some form. 'An angler who reviews the pleasures of life,' wrote Lord Grey, 'will be glad he has been an angler. For he will look back on days radiant with happiness, peaks and peaks of enjoyment'. In the honeycomb cells of my own memory, competition days provide some of those peaks. No matter that far more relate to long blissful hours in the perfect freedom and solitude of lonely lochs and rivers. The same pure stream of pleasure runs through it all:

> *Water brown, water bright —*
> *Pearls and swirls that sever;*
> *Running water's my delight*
> *Always and forever.*

APPENDICES

1

INTERNATIONAL FLY FISHING ASSOCIATION

MATCH RULES

1 Matches shall be fished with artificial fly only. Lures, demons and tandem flies shall not be permitted. No flies, nymphs, casts or lines shall be artificially weighted by the angler. Not more than four flies shall be mounted on a cast and flies must be at least 20 inches apart. Sinking or floating lines may be used, but shooting head lines are debarred.
2 A fly shall comply with the following specification. The hook shall be single or double provided that in the case of a double hook the angle between the bends does not exceed 45 degrees and when viewed from the side the bends lie one behind the other. The dressing of the body excluding any 'Setae' shall not extend beyond the straight part of the shank, and any wings or hackle shall not exceed one and one half times the overall length of the metal hook. It is considered that anything other than a fly complying with this specification is a demon or lure and it is considered that the worm fly is a lure.
3 Fly irons will measure not more than $\frac{5}{8}$ in overall, that is from the eye to the centre of the bend.
4 Competitors may use any pattern of flies they please excluding lures and demons. Flies must be cast in the recognized method. The recognized method of casting is defined as casting and working flies in such a way through the water

that the speed of movement does not give the fly such speed that it may be taken as a minnow. A competitor's rod when working flies, or retrieving casts, must not point below the horizontal. Trolling of flies behind the boat is not permitted, whether the boat is drifting or being driven by motor or oars. Side casting is permitted but flies are not allowed to be trailed behind the boat.

5 One rod, not exceeding 12 feet in length, to be used by each competitor, but each competitor will be entitled to have in the boat with him a spare rod (length as before) — both rods, however, not to be mounted at the same time. A rod is considered to be mounted if any two sections are joined or if a reel or line is attached.

6 Boats and boatmen shall be allocated by ballot. Mixed pairings will apply. Competitors shall change ends every two hours. The person for the time being in the stern shall have command of the boat.

7 No boatmen shall be allowed to fish in the competition, nor to handle a mounted rod (see rule 5) during the hours of the competition.

8 There shall be no individual prizes or sweepstakes among the competitors, but boatmen's prizes may be awarded. There is no objection to a Cup or award of a similar nature being put up for competition among the team of any member country, but there shall be no individual awards other than the Brown Bowl.

9 A team member of any country shall neither accept fishing tackle gratis from any tackle maker nor allow his angling status or any success to be used for commercial purposes.

10 Subject to any direction of the Association, any match shall be fished under the rules of the governing body of the water on which the match is fished in so far as these are compatible with the rules of the Association. For every match, the Association shall fix the hours of fishing. The minimum size and species of fish which may be weighed in and the starting and finishing point will be decided by the Host organization. Such information and fly measurements (see rule 3) will be included in the match booklet.

11 When the match is fished from boats, competitors shall not fish from the bank and shall return to the finishing point in the boat in which they set out, except in the event of damage to a boat or oar, failure of motor, or being overtaken by storm, when they may return by other means, but the

circumstances shall be reported on return to the Secretary who shall deal with the report as if it was a complaint made under rule 14 below.

12 All competitors shall present their fish at the weighing point immediately after the closing hour for fishing. Nil returns are required. Any competitor not reporting to the official weigher within 15 minutes of the end of the match will be deemed to be clean.

13 During a match, no boat may encroach within a distance of one hundred yards in front of another boat from which competitors are fishing.

14 The existence of a dispute or complaint on any matter in any match shall be immediately intimated to the Secretary who shall inform the President. A Sub-Committee consisting of the Captains of the countries taking part shall be, at once, convened to investigate the matter and adjudicate thereon. The decision of the Sub-Committee shall be final.

August 1981

2

RULES FOR ENGLISH NATIONAL COMPETITION (SAMPLE)

1 The match will be fished from boats at Grafham Water on Saturday 22 September 1979 from 10.0 a.m. to 6.0 p.m. Competitors must be at the Fishing Lodge by 9.0 a.m.

2 Each competitor must have qualified through a Federation belonging to the Confederation of English Fly Fishers. A draw will be held to decide boat partners and boatmen.

3 The match will be fished to the match rules of the International Fly Fishing Association along with the English National Rules.

4 Maximum hook size $\frac{5}{8}$ in overall, dressed length of fly not to exceed $\frac{15}{16}$ in. Rule 16 of the Grafham Regulations will apply i.e. no more than three hooks permitted.

5 There must be no fishing from anchored boats and all competitors are requested to sit whilst fishing. Shooting heads are not permitted.

6 There will be no bag limit for the competition. Any angler fishing after 6.0 p.m. whether from boat or bank will be disqualified from this and any future competition.

7 Boatmen may have the use of the boats after the competition. Prizes will be awarded for the top three boatmen.
8 Winner and placings will be decided by the total weight of trout caught by each competitor.
9 Any dispute on any matter in the match must be referred to the Confederation Secretary immediately after the match. A Sub-Committee shall be convened from the Confederation Officers present (who may co-opt further members), who will investigate and adjudicate thereon, their decision being final.
10 Anglers are reminded that there are many unwritten rules when loch-style fishing: please observe the courtesies of the boat.

3

INTERNATIONAL RESULTS 1928–81

(*i*) The first four matches were fished at Leven between Scotland and England alone. Teams were twenty aside.

Winner	trout	Weight	loser	trout	weight
1928 England	137	101 lb 12 oz	Scotland	145	100 lb $12\frac{1}{2}$ oz
1929 Scotland	51	43 lb 5 oz	England	42	33 lb 2 oz
1930 England	60	43 lb 8 oz	Scotland	43	34 lb 6 oz
1931 Scotland	242	153 lb 14 oz	England	206	135 lb

(*ii*) With Wales and Ireland joining in, teams were reduced to 16 in 1932, 12 from 1950 on, but the four-country internationals continued to be fished at Leven.

	1st	2nd	3rd	4th
1932	Scotland	Ireland	England	Wales
1933	Ireland	England	Wales	Scotland
1934	Scotland*	England	Wales	Ireland
1935	England	Scotland	Wales	Ireland
1936	England	Ireland	Wales	Scotland
1937	Scotland	Ireland	England	Wales
1938	Scotland†	Wales	England	Ireland
1939	England	Scotland	Ireland	Wales

* Scotland won by $1\frac{1}{2}$ oz.
† 642 trout weighing 475 lb 11 oz.

Year	1st	2nd	3rd	4th
1950	England	Wales	Scotland	Ireland
1951	England	Scotland	Ireland	Wales
1952	Ireland	Scotland	England	Wales
1953	Scotland	Wales	England	Ireland
1954	Scotland	England	Wales	Ireland
1955	Scotland	England	Wales	Ireland
1956	England	Ireland	Wales	Scotland
1957	England	Wales	Scotland	Ireland
1958	Scotland	England	Ireland	Wales
1959	England	Scotland	Wales	Ireland
1960	England	Scotland	Wales	Ireland
1961	England	Scotland	Ireland	Wales
1962	England	Scotland	Wales	Ireland
1963	England	Scotland	Wales	Ireland
1964	England	Scotland	Ireland	Wales
1965	England	Scotland	Wales	Ireland
1966	Scotland	England	Wales	Ireland
1967	Wales	England	Scotland	Ireland
1968	Wales	Scotland	England	Ireland
1969	Scotland	England	Wales	Ireland
1970	Wales	Ireland	England	Scotland

(*iii*) Up to 1970, the only official international was the one fished each spring at Leven. 'Friendlies' were, however, fished in the autumn mainly in Ireland. Ten were held at Conn; three at Corrib; one at Lein; two in England at Grafham; two in Wales at Claerwen and Trawsfynydd. Ireland won 7 times, England 5 times, Wales and Scotland 3 times each. From 1971 two official internationals have been fished each year with the venue changing round the various waters of the four countries.

(*iv*) From 1971 two official internationals have been fished each year, one in the spring, one in the autumn with the following results:

SPRING

Year	1st	2nd	3rd	4th	Water
1971	England	Scotland	Ireland	Wales	Lein (Ire)
1972	Wales	Ireland	England	Scotland	Alaw (W)
1973	Wales	Scotland	P*	Ireland	Menteith (Scot)

1974	Scotland	Wales	Ireland	P*	Menteith (Scot)
1975	Scotland	Ireland	Wales	England	Conn (Ire)
1976	Wales	England	Ireland	Scotland	Sheelin (Ire)
1977	Scotland	Wales	England	Ireland	Grafham (Eng)
1978	Wales	Ireland	England	Scotland	Corrib (Ire)
1979	Scotland	Wales	England	Ireland	Chew (Eng)
1980	Ireland	Wales	Scotland	England	Trawsfynydd (W)
1981	England	Wales	Scotland	Ireland	Draycote (Eng)
1982	England	Wales	Scotland	Ireland	Trawsfynydd (W)

AUTUMN

1971	England	Scotland	Ireland	Wales	Menteith (Scot)
1972	Scotland	Ireland	England	Wales	Grafham (Eng)
1973	Ireland	Wales	P*	Scotland	Grafham (Eng)
1974	Scotland	Wales	Ireland	England	Trawsfynydd (W)
1975	Wales	England	Ireland	Scotland	Leven (Scot)
1976	Wales	Scotland	Ireland	England	Trawsfynydd (W)
1977	England	Wales	Scotland	Ireland	Leven (Scot)
1978	Wales	England	Ireland	Scotland	Trawsfynydd (W)
1979	Ireland	England	Scotland	Wales	Conn (Ire)
1980	England	Wales	Scotland	Ireland	Leven (Scot)
1981	England	Scotland	Wales	Ireland	Leven (Scot)

P* = The President's invited team fished in three matches after England's withdrawal.

(v) Results over fifty-two official internationals (England did not compete in three of them) up to 1982. The England v Scotland matches are excluded.

	1st	2nd	3rd	4th
England	21	12	12*	4
Scotland	16	17	10*	9
Wales	10	14	16	12
Ireland	5	9	13	25
President's team†	–	–	2	1

* England and Scotland were equal third in 1972 at Alaw.
† England was not entered on the three occasions when the President's team fished.

4

INTERNATIONAL RECORDS

(i) Individual Best Baskets

ENGLAND

	Trout	Weight lb/oz		Lake	Date
John Ketley	9	20	15	Trawsfynydd	1978
Sidney Taylor	18	18	2	Leven	1962
Harold Thomas	16	17	6	Leven	1952
Sidney Taylor	22	17	0	Leven	1966
Bob Draper	11	16	6	Leven	1976

SCOTLAND

Robert Telfer	18	20	1	Leven	1954
T. Rutherford	23	18	4	Leven	1938
William Wallace	22	17	5	Leven	1966
Brian Peterson	9	17	3	Chew	1979
R. Veitch	12	16	10	Chew	1979

WALES

Dr Rees Prytherch	17	19	8	Leven	1966
Evan Owen	21	18	15	Leven	1968
E. Bowen Hughes	21	18	12	Leven	1968
P. Medlicott	9	18	1	Trawsfynydd	1978
R.H.M. Williams	8	17	7	Leven	1975

IRELAND

D.J. Spiller	19	17	3	Leven	1966
W. Sweeny	8	14	12	Leven	1975
Christy Sleator	6	13	8	Trawsfynydd	1978
Drew Bart	15	12	13	Leven	1935
T.J. O'Connor	12	12	12	Leven	1954

(ii) Heaviest total catch
Loch Leven 1938 Teams of 16 caught 642 trout weighing 475 lb 12 oz.

(*iii*)   Heaviest total catch outside Leven
Chew Valley Lake 1979 Teams of 12 caught 278 lb 3 oz.

(*iv*)   Largest number caught outside Leven
Draycote Water 1981 Teams of 12 caught 262 trout weighing 232 lb.

(*v*)   Brown Bowl winners
The Brown Bowl for the heaviest individual catch in each international was first awarded at Leven in 1956. The initial winner was H. Potter, whose five trout weighing 6 lb 15 oz beat his team mate, W. Smith, by one ounce.

In Auguest 1981 James L. Sidey became the 37th winner with one Leven trout weighing 3 lb 5 oz. By then the winner with the heaviest weight was John Ketley of England with his 20 lb 15 oz at Trawsfynydd in 1978.

Only two anglers have ever won the Brown Bowl twice, both from Wales and both named Williams. Victor Williams was the first to do so at Leven in 1970 and Menteith in 1974. Mervyn Williams is the only man to have won it twice in succession, at Leven in 1975 and Sheelin in 1976.

(*vi*)   Best Catch by a lady angler
Mrs Wynne Kirkby caught six trout weighing 4 lb at Leven in the 1938 international.

(*vii*)   Best individual catch in any international or national final at Leven
In an English national fished at Leven in June 1966 R.W. Beaty caught forty-two trout weighing 36 lb 7 oz.

5

TEAMS IN FIRST INTERNATIONAL IN 1928

Scotland

D. Black
A.D. Cameron
D. Campbell

England Selected
(Those who fished marked*)
H.R.H. The Duke of York (capt.)
* W.R. McCreath (reserve capt.)
* Rev. Joseph Adams

J. Dawson
Dr D.E. Dickson
Charles Eason
K. Forrest
William G. France
D.A. Fraser
F. Hart
J.M. Johnston
T.S. Knox
D.T.H. McQueen
J.B. McVitea
R.T. Mitchell
J.B. Price
Geo. Scrimgeour
David Shepherd
D.S. Sloan
A. Wotherspoon

* J.W. Armstrong
* R.H. Armstrong
  Dr J.H. Blayney
* H.H. Chartress
* J.G. Crossman
* R.H. Dodds
* N.E.B. Elgar
* Sir Frederick Graham Bart.
* S.O. Hanlon
  Rev. Michael Horsfall
* P.M. Horsfall
* M.E. Meling
* Col. J.H. Openshaw
* B. Pumphrey
* C. Short
* Geo. Waddell
* Major A.W. Campbell Skinner

Stand by reserves
* S. Bury
  Major R.M. Gladstone
* J.J. Hardy
  A.E. Metcalfe-Gibson
* G. Nicholls
  J.S.E. Walker

The teams were twenty strong from 1928 to 1931. Once the four-country internationals began in 1932 teams were reduced to sixteen until 1939. After the Second World War the internationals restarted in 1950 with the present team strength of twelve.

Rod length was limited to the original 15 feet until 1939. From 1950 it has been the present limit of 12 feet.

6
INTERNATIONAL ASSOCIATIONS AND QUALIFYING METHOD

HONORARY SECRETARIES

International Association Secretary and Scottish International Secretary: Alastair S. Nicoll, P.O. Box 84, 51 Meadowside, Dundee DD1 9PQ

England: John Hedges, 52 Oldbury Road, Hartshill, Nuneaton, CVlO OTD
Ireland: George A. Timmins, 26 St Margaret's Road, Malahide, Co Dublin.
Wales: Moc Morgan, Post Office, Pontrhydfendigaid, Ystrad Meuring, Wales SY25 6EF

7

QUALIFYING METHOD FOR INTERNATIONALS

SCOTLAND

Only members of clubs affiliated to the Scottish National Angling Clubs Association may enter. Club champions fish in the three preliminary matches on Leven from which the national finalists emerge. The top ten in the final fish in the next year's internationals, plus the President and Secretary, plus the two top performers in the previous year, to make up the team and reserves.

ENGLAND

Each region arranges its own eliminating contests. From the five regions sixty qualify for the national final. The top sixteen qualify for the two internationals in the following season, the first eight in the spring match, the second eight in the autumn contest. The team is made up to twelve by the top four English performers in the previous international. The seventeenth and eighteenth in the final come in as reserves, and there is one official fishing as a reserve in each match.

IRELAND

Selection for the spring international: The team is composed of the four best available rods from the previous spring international, the five best rods taking uneven numbers from the national held in the preceding calendar year, and the five best rods taking even numbers from the interprovincial championship held in the preceding year. Where necessary the fifth best rods become the reserves.

Selection for the autumn international: The team is composed of the four best rods from the preceding autumn international, the five best rods taking even numbers from the national held in the preceding year, and the five best rods from that year's interprovincial. The fifth best rods become the reserves where necessary.

WALES

Members of any clubs affiliated to the Welsh Salmon and Trout Association may participate. Parent clubs wishing to take part arrange their own competition with the top four in that going forward to the national. These nationals are fished from the bank in a variety of large lakes or reservoirs in North, South and Mid-Wales. Traditionally there have been two nationals each year, one in the spring, one in the autumn, one on a Saturday, one on a Sunday.

The top sixty from national competition go forward to a 'final trial' always held at Trawsfynydd and fished from boats. The top six go into the following year's team in place of the six with the lowest baskets in the internationals. The next two go into the following year's team as reserves.

All such qualifying methods may be annually reviewed by each country and changed if the national body sees fit.

8

LOUGHS MASK, MELVIN AND CONN COMPETITION RULES AND ENTRY ARRANGEMENTS

LOUGH MASK: 'WORLD CUP'

Entry to: John P. Burke, Cloonkeary, Ballinrobe, County Mayo, Ireland (Tel. Ballinrobe 324). Closing date for entries normally mid-July, or 1 July for overseas entry.

Competition normally lasts five days (four heats and a final), with the final on the first Sunday in August.

RULES

1. Any competitor found trolling flies, baits or lures, spinning or dapping will be disqualified.
2. Not less than 2 and not more than 4 flies will be permitted.
3. All competitors must be ready to leave the shore at 11.00 a.m.
4. All boats must be inside the markers at 6.00 p.m.
5. All fish must measure at least 12 in. This dimension is measured from the tip of the nose to the fork of the tail.
6. Competitors must have only one rod assembled.
7. No boat may fish within 100 yards of the boat in front, or cut in on a boat adrift.
8. No boatman is allowed to fish while acting as boatman.
9. The prizes for the best Overseas rod and the best Lady Angler will be awarded on the weight of all fish taken in competition — that is in both heats and final.
10. The committee will not be responsible for accident or loss.
11. All competitors fish at their own risk.
12. Only brown trout shall weigh-in.
13. Cups are Perpetual and only held for one year.
14. The committee reserve the absolute right to postpone, alter or cancel the competition in the event of weather being inclement or for any other reason. All entries are accepted subject expressly to this condition.
15. No proxy anglers allowed.
16. Prize for Heaviest Fish confined to competitors who do not win 1st, 2nd or 3rd prize in final.
17. Each competitor must hand in his own fish to be weighed.
18. The competitor with the fewer fish will qualify for any prize when two or more anglers have equal weights of fish.
19. Any infringement of the above rules automatically disqualifies the competitors.
20. Fishing from the shore is not allowed.

— LAST MEAL ON HEAT DAYS SERVED AT 8.0 p.m. —

Note: Any angler bringing in any under-sized fish is liable to prosecution (Rule 5).

LOUGH MELVIN: WET-FLY TROUT INTERNATIONAL
Entry only on official form obtained via the Lough Melvin

Hotel, Kinlough, Co. Leitrim, Ireland (Tel. (072) 41417/or 41609).

There are two heats on the Friday and Saturday with a final on the Sunday (normally the third Sunday in June). Closing date for entries is usually 1 June or thereabouts.

RULES

1. Any competitor found trolling flies, baits, spinning or dapping will be disqualified.
2. Not less than 2 and not more than 4 Flies will be permitted.
3. All competitors must be ready to leave the shore at 11 a.m. with a shot gun start.
4. All boats must be inside the marker at 6 p.m. with shotgun finish.
5. Any competitor presenting undersized fish will have his complete catch disqualified. All fish must measure at least 10 inches. This dimension is measured from the tip of the nose to the fork of the tail.
6. Anglers must have only one rod assembled.
7. No boat may fish within 100 yards of the boat in front or cut in on a boat adrift.
8. No boatman is allowed to fish while acting as boatman.
9. The committee will not be responsible for accidents or loss.
10. All competitors fish at their own risk.
11. Only trout shall weigh-in.
12. The committee reserves the right to postpone, alter or cancel the competition in the event of weather being inclement or for any other reason. All entries are accepted subject expressly to these conditions.
13. No proxy anglers allowed.
14. Prize for the heaviest fish confined to competitors who did not win 1st, 2nd or 3rd prize in final.
15. Each competitor must hand in his own fish to be weighed.
16. The competitor with the fewer fish, will qualify for any prize when two or more anglers have equal weights of fish.
17. Any infringement of the above rules automatically disqualifies the competitor.
18. Fishing from the shore is not allowed.
19. Boatmen are responsible for measuring and returning undersized fish.

Note: Any angler bringing in any undersized fish is liable to prosecution. (Rule 5).

LOUGH CONN: TROUT FLY-FISHING COMPETITION

The Intercontinental or Crossmolina Angling Festival competition. Entries only on official form. Details obtainable from Patrick Langan, Lough Conn Anglers' Association, Mullenmore North, Crossmolina, Co Mayo. Ireland (Tel. (096) 31166).

As at Mask you can enter for a team prize, as well as the main individual prizes: 'A team may consist of four declared anglers who, submitting competition entrance fee, may form a team by including names on the team entry form.'

The competition takes place at Whit-weekend at the end of May with heats on the Saturday and Sunday, final on the Monday. Closing date for entries normally a week prior to this, but numbers are limited.

RULES

1. Any competitor found trolling flies, bait or lure, spinning or dapping, will be disqualified.
2. Not more than four flies will be permitted.
3. All competitors must be ready to leave the shore at 11.30; 10.0 a.m. on final day.
4. All boats must be inside the markers by 6.30 p.m.
5. All fish must measure at least eleven inches. The dimension is measured from the tip of the nose to the fork of the tail.
6. Competitors must have only one rod assembled.
7. No boat can fish within 100 yards of the boat in front, or cut in on a boat on a drift.
8. No boatman is allowed to fish.
9. The prizes for the Best Overseas Rod and the Best Lady Angler will be awarded on the weight of all fish taken in the competition.
10. A competitor can only enter for one team in the Team event.
11. All competitors fish at their own risk.
12. Any infringement of the rules disqualifies the competitor and boatman concerned.
13. Cups are perpetual and are only held for one year.
14. The Committee reserve the right to postpone or cancel.
15. The Committee decision on all matters relating to the competition shall be final.
16. The Committee reserve the right to refuse entries.

9

'WORLD CUP' PRELIMINARY NOTICE 1982

The Spanish Sports Fishing Federation, at the petition of and in accordance with the Chairmanship of the C.I.P.S. and the F.I.P.S.-ED assumes responsibility for the organisation of the

2nd Sports Fishing 'Fly Angling' World Championship

with the following rules for participation:

1st The championship will be held only under the modality of fly angling.
2nd One single representative team for each National Federation.
3rd The number of participant anglers will be decided once the total of registered nations is known by us.
4th Scheduled date: 2–6 June 1982.
5th Site: Narcea and Sella Rivers in Asturias (northwestern-part of Spain).
6th Species: — SALMO SALAR (weight 4,5 to 10 kg)
— SALMO TRUTTA TRUTTA (weight 0,5 kg to 3 kg)
— SALMO TRUTTA FARIO (250 gr to 800 gr)
in the respective order of sports importance.
7th Our championship will coincide with the date scheduled for the trial matches of the World Cup Finals in Spain, and therefore
WE ASK: All the Federations to send us an initial participation or non-participation reply for hotel reservations. A serious problem exists, since Oviedo and Gijon have been selected as sites of the above mentioned football matches, and Oviedo is precisely the site of our championship event.
8th We shall send a dossier to all the nations that remit to us the attached Bulletin, with their initial announcement, before 28 February.
9th The Trials Rules and Regulations will be furnished beforehand to all the registered nations.
10th Prices will be furnished in the dossier to be forwarded shortly, and these will be in full accord with the category of services.

11th As a prior guideline, we wish to inform you that fishing gear must conform to the salmon 'fly' angling technique:
Fishing Rod: — 12 ft — 14 ft — 16 ft long for salmon two-hand handling
— 9 ft long for salmon or SALMO TRUTTA TRUTTA one-hand handling.
Fishing Line: — DTF and WTF Nos. 9–12 for salmon
— DTF and WTF Nos. 6–9 for SALMO TRUTTA and FARIO
Gaff: Of the type used for salmon extraction
Landing-net: Large size, if used as replacement for hood
FOOTWEAR: waders (not indispensable) or else sea boots
RAINCOAT: Rains are frequent and it may be needed

10

CLAIMS PROCEDURE FOR RECORD FISH

Claims to: The British Record (rod-caught) Fish Committee, National Anglers' Council, II Cowgate, Peterborough PEI ILZ (Tel. 0733 54084).

CLAIMING PROCEDURE

1 (*a*) The claimant should contact the Committee Secretary.
  (*b*) Advice will then be given concerning preservation, identification, and claim.
2 Claims must be made in writing to the Secretary stating:
  (*i*) Species of fish and weight.
  (*ii*) Date and place of capture and the tackle used.
  (*iii*) Names and addresses of reliable witnesses both as to capture and the weight, who will be required to sign the forms supporting the claim.
  If no witnesses to the capture are available the claimant must sign an affidavit.
3 No claim will be accepted unless the Committee is satisfied as to species, method of capture, and the weight.
4 Identification of species:
  (*a*) To ensure correct identification, it is essential that claimants should retain the fish and immediately contact the

Secretary of the Committee, who will advise as to production of the fish for inspection.
(b) No claim is acceptable unless the fish in its natural state is available for inspection.
(c) All carriage costs incurred in production of the fish for inspection by the Committee must be borne by the claimant.

5 Method of Capture:
(a) Claims can only accepted in respect of fish which are caught by fair angling. This is defined as the fish taking the baited hook or lure into its mouth.
(b) Fish must be caught on rod and line with any legal hook or lure and hooked and played by one person only. Assistance to land the fish (i.e. gaffing, netting) is permitted provided the helper does not touch any part of the tackle other than the leader.

6 Weight:
(a) The fish must be weighed on scales which can be tested on behalf of the Committee
(b) A Weights and Measures certificate must be produced certifying the accuracy of the scales used and indicating testing at the claimed weight.
(c) The weight must be verified by two independent witnesses who, for example, should not be relations of the claimant or a member of his club or party.

7 Claims can be made for species not included in the Committee's Record Fish list.

8 No fish caught out of season or suffering from a disease by which weight might be enhanced shall be accepted as a new record.

9 Medium sized fish can be preserved by refrigeration (deep freeze) or immersion in formalin.

10 Claims for fish caught in Eire should be made to the Irish Specimen Fish Committee, Balnagowan, Mobhi Boreen, Glasnevin Dublin 9. The Welsh Record (rod-caught) Fish Committee can process Welsh claims for British records.

11

DISABLED ANGLERS

Details about facilities and any known competition can be obtained via the National Anglers' Council. Their *Guide to*

Fishing Facilities for Disabled Anglers is very comprehensive and may be obtained from the Council at 11 Cowgate, Peterborough PEI ILZ (Tel. (7033) 54084. The guide is published by the National Anglers' Council Committee for Disabled Anglers and is sponsored by the Midland Bank. Additions are made as more information becomes available.

The guide includes contact addresses for instructors for disabled coaching. The Senior Officer, for London, South & South-East Area is Mr. L.D. Warren Flat 'D', St George's Lodge, Muswell Hill, London N 10 3TE (Tel. 01 444 0719).

It includes also addresses for special manufactured products to aid the disabled angler, and a list of useful booklets and films.

Among the many addresses of helpful organizations given in the guide, the following may be of particular interest:

(*i*) *Committee for Promotion of Angling for the Disabled*
Mr T. Mackenzie, 19 Roull Road, Edinburgh EH1 27JW Tel. 031334 1373) or Mr C. Thomson, 15 Queen's Walk, The Thistle Foundation, Niddrie Mains Road Edinburgh EH16 4EA.

(*ii*) *Wales Council for the Disabled & Welsh Sports Association for the Disabled*
The Crescent, Caerphilly, Mid-Glamorgan (Tel. Caerphilly 869224).

(*iii*) *Leicester Handicapped Fly Fishers*
Mr N.T. Woombs, Secretary, 84 Roman Road, Birstall, Leicester (Tel. Leicester 673490).

(*iv*) *St John's Ambulance Association & Brigade*
1 Grosvenor Crescent, London, SWI 7EF (Tel. 01 235 5231).

The local Division address and telephone number will be in your local directory. The Brigade remind angling clubs that they may be able to provide considerable assistance to many disabled members to enable them to participate in competitions, festivals, etc.

12

USEFUL ADDRESSES

COMPETITION WATERS

National or international matches may occasionally be fished on

other lakes such as Lough Corrib or Llyn Alaw, but the nine main competition centres are:
1 Loch Leven Fisheries, The Pier, Kinross (Tel. Kinross 63407)
2 The Lake of Menteith, Port of Menteith, Nr Stirling (Tel. Port of Menteith 253)
3 Lough Conn, Conn Anglers' Association, Mullenmore North, Crossmolina, Co Mayo, Ireland (Tel. 096 31166)
4 Llyn Trawsfynydd Fishery, Kevin Lewis, Newsagent's Shop, Trawsfynydd, Gwynedd (Tel. Trawsfynydd 234)
5 Grafham Water, Anglian Water Authority, The Lodge, West Perry, Huntingdon, Cambs PE18 OBW (Tel. Office Huntingdon 810247, Lodge Huntingdon 810531)
6 Rutland Water, Empingham, Oakham, Leicestershire (Tel. Office out of season Empingham 321, Lodge, in season, Empingham 770)
7 Draycote Water, Kites Hardwick, Nr Rugby (Tel. Lodge 0788 811107 Senior Fisheries Officer 0788 810490)
8 Chew Valley Lake, Bristol Waterworks Co, Woodford Lodge, Chew Stoke, Somerset (Tel. Chew Magna 2339)
9 Lough Sheelin, Central Fisheries Board Base, Mullaghboy, Ballyhedan, or The Sheelin Shamrock Hotel, Mountnugent (Tel. Mountnugent 13)

SOUTHERN IRISH FISHING

For information about Irish game fishing: Bord Failte, Baggot Street Bridge, Dublin 2, Ireland (Tel. Dublin 765871)

NORTHERN IRISH GAME FISHING

Details are available from Northern Ireland Tourist Board, River House, 48 High Street, Belfast BT1 2DS or for direct information try The Ulster Angling Federation, Secretary Mrs P Glenn, 6 Beech Green, Doagh, Ballyclare, Co. Antrim BT 39 0QB (Tel. Ballyclare 40884). For the Fermanagh Fishery Federation the Secretary is: R.F. Bracken, Lishlake, Florencecourt, Co. Fermanagh.

For the Foyle system try: The Rod Action Committee for the Foyle system; their representative is M.J. Collins, 27 Meelmore Drive, Strathroy, Omagh, Co. Tyrone. or The Foyle Fisheries Commission 8 Victoria Road, Londonderry (Tel. Londonderry 42100).

The other statutory body for Northern Ireland's fishing is:

The Fisheries Conservancy Board for Northern Ireland, 21 Church Street, Portadown (Tel. Portadown 32276 or 34666).

IRISH FLY-DRESSING SPECIALISTS

One of those who can supply the special Irish flies: Richard Johnson, 129 Stockmans Lane, Belfast BT9 7JE, N. Ireland (Tel. 0232 667576)

MOUNTING SPECIMEN FISH

If you catch a large fish and want it mounted, those I have found good are:
   (a) England: Peter Stone, 38 Elmthorpe Road, Wolvercote, Oxford OX2 8PA (Tel. Oxford 59542); Vic Davis, 16 Wiggenhall Road, Watford WD1 8AL (Tel. Watford 25517).
   (b) Scotland: George Jamieson (Taxidermist & Wild Life Artist), 'Cramond Tower', Cramond Glebe Road, Edinburgh.

PROFICIENCY AWARDS AND COACHING

Details of the award scheme leading to bronze, silver and gold medals for game fishing can be obtained from the National Anglers' Council, 11 Cowgate, Peterborough PE1 1LZ. This national award scheme is run in conjunction with the Salmon and Trout Association, Fishmonger's Hall, London EC4R 9EL and is sponsored by Swan Vestas.

There is no upper limit on age of those who wish to take the award, but the lower age limits are 11 years at date of application for the bronze award, 13 for silver and 15 for gold. Candidates over 16 must be either an individual member of the appropriate national governing body or of a club affiliated to that body. Evidence of membership must be produced on application.

Coaching courses in England are organized through the national eduction and development officers of the National Anglers' Council. Such organizing officers are:
Jeffrey Carr, 39 Dinsdale Drive, Cheveley Park, Belmont, Durham (Tel. Durham (0385) 63899).
Rex Curtis*, 24 Woodfield Road, Peterborough, Cambs. PE3 6HD (Tel. Peterborough (0733) 63359).

* also National Coaching co-ordinator

Mark Davies, 31 Manchester Road, Knutsford, Cheshire WA16 0LY (Tel. Knutsford (0565) 51066).
Mark Downes, 49 Edgmond Close, Redditch, Worcs. B98 0JQ (Tel. Redditch (0527) 29391).
Charles Landells, 29 Looe Gardens, Barkingside, Ilford, Essex (Tel. 01 551 0477).
Michael Lloyd, 130 Deeble Road, Kettering, Northants. NN15 5HW.
Harry Lodge, 294a Horbury Road, Wakefield, West Yorks. WF2 8JL (Tel. Wakefield (0924) 77859).
Willam Rawles, 58 Sycamore Avenue, Hiltingbury, Chandlers Ford, Hants. S05 1RE (Tel. Chandlers Ford (042 15) 3877).

13

AVOIDING WEIGHT LOSS

DEHYDRATION OF FISH AFTER CAPTURE

Recent correspondence in *The Fly-fishers' Journal* confirms the importance of minimizing weight loss after capture whether in competition or claiming records. C. Ross-Munro of the Cape Piscatorial Society referred to a Paper presented to the Inland Fisheries Conference at Pietermaritzburg, Natal in 1950 by G.F. van Wyk M.Sc. Its evidence was that a trout of $1\frac{1}{4}$ lb left hanging in the sun for eight hours lost 15.4 per cent of its weight, and that a similar sized fish left hanging in shade lost nearly as much. Smaller sized fish lost an even higher percentage. The trout might also have shrunk, though they were too distorted for accurate conclusion.

Trout left in a dry jute bag, however, lost only about 3 per cent, a negligible amount by comparison. The lesson from that is clear for competitors. If you catch a 2lb trout early in the match and leave it lying on the boat bottom you can expect a loss of some 5 oz by the time it is weighed in — and teams have lost internationals by less than that. So take care to keep your fish *cool* and wet. Indeed if you keep them in cold water they might even gain in weight as Mr M.A. King-Webster indicated in these extracts from his expert contribution:

> The rate of loss of weight from fish after death is affected by so many factors that it is very difficult to

tabulate. Basically it is a matter of water loss. Rate of decomposition depends mainly on temperature, but fish which have been feeding hasten the process by digesting themselves, whereas salmon, which have ceased to feed, keep well ungutted.

Rate of water loss by evaporation depends on temperature, air flow and humidity. At the one extreme, a fish hung in a current of warm, dry air, as in a curing kiln, loses water, and hence weight, rapidly. At the other, a fish kept in cold water loses no weight at all. In fact, I suppose that a fish left in fresh water must actually gain weight, as the salts in its blood must tend to draw water into its body.

Being a salmon netsman, weight loss in storage is an important matter to me. Anyone wanting to minimize weight loss in a specimen fish should keep it cool, damp, and away from draughts. If you cannot keep it in a cool place, warm damp hastens decomposition, so it might be wisest to keep it wrapped in wet cloth or paper, but without an outer layer of plastic or other waterproof material. Evaporation would thus take place which would help cool the fish, and you could wet the wrappings from time to time.

14

INSURANCES AND DISCOUNTS

As the cost of tackle rises, and the overall cost of fishing, so does the importance of getting good value for your purchases and of being properly insured. Fortunately, the joint purchasing power of fishermen, who spend over £650,000,000 a year on their sport in Britain, has brought some attractive package offers in recent years. While there may be better ones available, two have particularly appealed to me personally:

(*i*) World Angling Club
The World Angling Club was launched in 1982 with attractive benefits for members. The initial membership fee was set at £21.60, bringing with it a wide range of discounts — up to 40 per cent on tackle, equipment and protective clothing bought from certain outlets; up to 40 per cent discount on car hire or tyre purchase; discounts on some holidays and some fishing season tickets; associate mem-

bership of over 3000 fishing clubs; an insurance policy covering not only tackle, but personal accident, and public liability; and a widening range of other services to members as set out in the Club's directory for the year.

Regular anglers, or even irregular ones who are car-users, are likely to find some economic advantages in this package, though each has to work out for himself whether the club is likely to bring him a worthwhile return if he joins. Details are available from: World Angling Club, Finland House, Haymarket, London, SW1Y 4RS. But it has yet to prove itself in practice as it has only just launched.

(*ii*) DSP Insurance Brokers Ltd
The best low-cost insurance scheme for anglers which I have encountered is that arranged by DSP Insurance Brokers Ltd with advice from the National Federation of Anglers. It provides 'All Risks' cover for fishing tackle, equipment, and personal effects on a worldwide basis and public liability cover as well. For the NFA and some other Angling organizations there is also a special reduction for their members. Details can be obtained from DSP Insurance Brokers Ltd, DSP House, 5 Wilson Street, Derby DEI IPG (Tel. (0332) 36917/8).

15

OTHER SIGNIFICANT COMPETITIONS

Of the many competitions not specifically covered in the text two may be of special interest:

(*i*) *British Open Trout Championship* — fished at Tan y Grisiau. £400 in prizes in 1982. Incorporates the Cusworth Shield competition and is organized by the Prysor Angling Association. Details from Kevin Lewis, Ffestiniog Power Station Information Centre, Blaenau Ffestiniog (Tel. 076 687 571).

(*ii*) *Ladies Only Fly-Fishing Competition* — first staged in May 1982 at Chew Valley Lake. Details from Jeanette Long, 10 Priory Road, Knowle, Bristol 4 (Tel. Bristol 776524).

INDEX

Abel, Jimmy, 43–4, 213
Agutter, Alastair, 260
Air, Sir Wilfred, 58
Alaw, Llyn, 91, 94, 184, 256
Altnacealgach, lochs 246, 253
Arlott, John, 257
Armstrong, Sandy, 177
Armstrong, T.W., 49
Arrow, Lough, 223
Ashness, Adrian, 29, 81, 82, 93, 111, 227–9
Avington, 151–4, 160, 161, 168
Avon, River, 77, 148
Awe, Loch, 155, 158

Bakethin Reservoir, 203
Ballantyne, Georgina, 156–7, 257
Ballantyne, James, 156–7
Barker, Alan, 139, 141
Barker, Neil, 140
Battisti, Vini, 128
Bayham Lake Kingfisher Club, 147
Beaty, Robert, 44, 237
Begg-Burns, Robert, 208
Bell, Billy, 72
Benson and Hedges championships, 14, 15, 130, 135, 149, 202, 205
Bevan, Tony, 103–4
Bewl Bridge Reservoir, 135, 206–8, 247
Biggart, David, 34, 44, 52, 63, 176, 211, 213, 236, 244
Biggart, Stuart, 213
Bilson, Tom, 65, 82, 106, 110, 112, 188, 194–7, 227
Blanche, Grace G., 37
Blanche, Mrs Richard, 37
Boyd, Jim, 215
Breen, J., 135
Brenig, Llyn, 172, 173, 174, 204
Brewer, Jason, 177, 182–3
Bridger, Lowther, 157
Bristol Reservoirs Fly Fishers' Association, 33

Brock, Syd, 143
Brooks, Barry, 141
Brown, Peter, 144
Buchanan, Andrew, 37
Bucknall, Geoffrey, 19
Byrne, John, 82
Byrne, Victor, 27

Calder, Sir J., 133
Campbell, Eric, 44, 86–9
Canning, John, 97
Carra, Lough, 118
Carra River, 118
Carter, Tom, 22, 30, 98-9, 115, 218, 221
Cefni Reservoir, 56
Chartress, H.H., 51
Chew Valley Lake, 21–4, 26, 68, 74, 75–6, 79, 81, 82, 103, 109–11, 184, 186, 197–202, 235, 251, 252, 280
Childs, Mike, 115
Church, Bob, 57, 136, 139, 141, 143, 185, 186
Church, Viv, 99, 107, 138
Church Hill Farm Lakes, 143, 168
Claerwen, 266
Clarke, Michael, 60
Clay, H. Hastings, 53
Clayton, Ken, 154
Cochrane, Albert, 256
Collins, Barry, 115
Committee for the Promotion of Angling for the Disabled, 175, 176, 180
Confederation of English Fly Fishers, 96–8, 136, 195, 259
Conn, Lough, 14, 15, 60, 61–3, 76, 79, 99–101, 106, 115, 117, 123–4, 218, 219–21, 252, 256, 257, 258, 266, 275, 280
Cooper, Mrs, 149
Coppal, River, 145
Corrib, Lough, 184, 221–2, 266

Cothi, River, 147
Craven, Frank, 178, 179
Cronin, John, 145–7
Crossmolina Club, 219
Currane, Lough, 144, 251
Cuthbert, James, 40, 44, 89
Cutler, Frank, 138

Dalrymple, C., 148
Daniels, Tim, 144
Danskin, John, 236
Davies, B.J., 193
Davies, Norman, 91–2
Deacy, Christy, 82
Derg, Lough, 155
Deverson, River, 157
Dickens, Charlie, 72
Dickson, Alex, 36
Dobbs, Peter, 100
Dodds, R.H. 49, 50–1
Draper, Bob, 20, 27, 28, 64, 65–8, 70, 82, 83, 84, 86, 91, 105–8, 114, 188, 195, 211, 227
Draper, Perce, 66
Draycote, 66, 81, 82–3, 84, 85, 104, 108, 110, 183, 186, 188, 216, 245, 247, 252
Drayton Water, 280
Dunn, Naughton, 140, 161
Dunn, R., 108
Dwight, S.R., 158

East Midlands Club, 195
Echternach, Lake, 14, 258
Eden, River, 157
Edwards, Gareth, 15–17, 50
Edwards, Oliver, 148
Eilt, Loch, 157
Elbourne, Neil, 175
Ellem Club, 14, 132–3, 257
English Disabled Fly-Fishers' Association, 177, 182–3
English International Fly-Fishers' Association, 44, 50, 58, 71, 72, 92, 95–7, 137–8, 185
Evans, Gwynfor, 54

Eyebrook, 141

Farmoor Reservoir, 136–7, 143
Farr, Gillie, 63
Farrell, W., 135
Fédération Internationale de la Pêche Sportive, 258–9
Ferguson, Dr, 128
Fishing Race, 15–17, 50, 257
Fleming-Jones, David, 53, 55, 139, 193–4, 195, 234
Foley, Pat, 109
Foster, Brian, 175, 177, 180, 183
France, William G., 49
Francis, Lynn, 177, 182
Fulcher, Don, 25, 65, 97, 99, 101–2, 226, 227
Furzer, Brian, 27–8

Gammon, Clive, 15–17, 257
Gargan, Canon, 112, 113, 222–3
Gathercole, Peter, 138
George VI, King, 50
Geraghty, Brian, 129, 217, 218
Glanusk, Lord, 53, 54, 148
Glanusk Park, 148
Glasslyn, 55
Glorious Tweed Festival Fishing Competition, 148
Grafham Water, 25, 26, 27, 28, 30, 53, 66, 79–80, 84, 86, 95, 96, 114, 135, 136, 186, 188–9, 193–7, 234, 235, 251, 264, 266, 280
Greenaway, Clive, 30, 79–80, 111, 112, 235, 238
Greenwood, Ian, 111, 113, 203

Halford, Frederic M., 243
Hall. B.C., 52, 55, 57–9, 61–2, 71, 94, 96, 129–30, 138, 237
Hampson, Norman, 88
Hancox, Gary, 182
Hannen, S., 108
Hardy, J.J., 50
Harms, Colin, 22–3, 97, 98
Hartley, H., 44

Hawes, Peter, 32, 33
Heddle, Peter, 113, 253
Hilliard, Robin, 62
Hinkley Club, 136
Hirons, Trevor, 45–7, 63, 76, 88, 230–2
Holland, Sam, 161
Hopkins, Roy, 164
Horseshoe Lake, 159
Hughes, Brian, 142–3
Hutchinson, Craig, 182
Hutchinson, Gordon, 90, 91
Hutton, Angus, 45
Hyde, Joe, 181–2

Inter-Services Competition, 141–2
International Association for Disabled Fly-Fishers, 172, 173, 175
International Fly Fishing Association, 262–4
Inwood, Cyril, 59, 72–3
Irish Trout Fly-Fishers' Competition Committee, 53
Ivens, Tom, 72–3

Jackson, J.A.F., 155
James, Martin, 181
Jerrams, Michael, 181
Johnson, Bob, 134–5
Johnson, Charlie, 102
Johnstone, John M., 49, 208–11
Jones, Bruce, 97
Jones, Gwynfor, 86, 104, 113
Jones, Keith, 252–4
Jones, Roy, 113, 236
Jones, T.V., 175

Keay, Peter, 44, 63
Ken, Loch, 60
Kenny, Edward, 60
Ketley, John, 65, 68–72, 108, 110–11, 112, 196, 201–2, 225, 228, 229, 243
Kielder Reservoir, 135, 202–4
King, John, 141
Kirkby, W. Wynne, 54
Kirkby, Mrs W. Wynne, 51, 54, 108
Knox, Robert, 36

Lady Bower lake, 203–4
Laerdal, River, 18–19, 150
Lamb, Bill, 219, 221
Langan, Patrick, 123–4, 221
Laver, Roy, 105
Lawrie, Michael, 260
Lees, Dr, 53
Lein, Lough, 94
Leven, Loch, 12–14, 34–48, 49, 50–1, 52, 54, 57, 61, 64, 66, 67, 72, 79, 86, 87, 88, 89, 92, 101, 102–3, 106, 107, 108, 133, 135, 136, 180, 184, 208–13, 216, 234, 237, 246, 247–8, 249, 250, 266, 280
Linch Hill Fishery, 159, 180, 183
Lindsay, Alec, 53
Llandeyfedd, 172
Llandyssul Angling Assoication, 145
Loch Leven Angling Association Ltd, 35, 36
Loud, Jeff, 200–1
Lovelace, David, 81
Lyle, Sir Alexander, 157

McCallion, Tommy, 174
McCreath, Henry G., 132
McCreath, W.R., 50–1, 132
McDonald, John, 105
McFadyen, Jack, 174
McGregor, David B., 35, 36
McIver, Gilbert, 44
Mackenzie, Andrew, 41
Mackenzie, Tom, 172, 175
McKinnell, Mike, 46–7, 89
McLeod, S., 49
Macrorie, Freda, 37
Maitland, Sir James, 36
Malloch, Gilbert, 44
Malloch, Peter, 36, 38–9, 41, 42, 43, 44, 155, 246
Malloy, Tom, 60
Marcus, Rixi, 20
Marsh-Smith, Stephen, 103
Martindale, Bill, 215
Mask, Lough, 14, 42, 117–23, 272–3
Medlicott, Peter, 103–4, 108
Meehan, James, 18
Melvin, Lough, 14, 42, 117, 124–31, 135, 160, 223, 273–4

INDEX

Menteith, Lake of, 14, 91, 92, 94, 98, 134–5, 172, 175, 176, 180, 213–16, 250, 280
Michellson, Mr, 133
Mid-Northants Trout Fishers' Association, 72
Midlands Federation of Fly-Fishers, 136, 238
Midlands Federation of Fly-Fishers (Anglia), 72
Miller, Colonel, 72
Mills, Tony, 143
Milne, Bill, 59–60, 61, 62–3, 71, 92–3, 101, 115, 137
Montgomery, Sir Basil T., 49
Montgomery, Lady Graham, 49
Moore, Arthur, 59–60
Morecambe, Eric, 141
Morgan, Moc, 54, 55–7, 73, 83, 85–6, 172, 174
Morgan, Tom, 249
Morrison, Mrs, 157
Mossop, Henry, 59, 60
Mossop, S.S., 60
Moylett, Colonel, 100
Muir, Mr, 155
Muir, Robert, 174
Mumford, Ray, 164
Mussell, David, 81

Nairn, Willie, 226
Narcea, River, 259
National Anglers' Council, 179, 180, 239, 240, 241
National Coaching Scheme, 241
National Federation of Anglers, 259
Neil, Tom, 135
Nicholls, George, 58
Nicholson, Lance, 205
Nicoll, Alastair, 52, 86, 97
Nixon, Larry, 131
Northampton Specimen Group, 136

O'Brien, Tony, 128
Ogbourne, Christopher, 30, 31–3, 81, 197–200
O'Grady, Robby, 120, 123, 127
O'Reilly, Peter, 223

O'Sullivan, Eoen, 90
Owen, Evan, 73
Owen, Roy, 183

Page, Stan, 99
Parsons, Clive, 181
Pastore, Eric, 226
Patrick, Willie, 83
Patshull Park Fishery, 14, 138–41, 161
Pawson, John, 28–9, 79, 185, 247
Pawson, Sarah, 185
Pearson, Alan, 117–23, 124–8, 139, 144, 151, 152, 155, 243
Pemberton, E., 148
Pepper, J.W., 155, 222
Peterson, Brian, 74–6, 82, 83, 103, 104, 110, 113, 135, 211–12, 213, 214–16
Pitsford, 66
Pope, Stephen, 111, 113
Porter, David, 80–1, 141–2, 246–7
Potter H., 250
Pro-Am Competition, 137–8, 139
Prytherch, Robert, 53, 55
Purves, Roy, 108–10, 222

Queen Mother Reservoir, 142–3
Quoich, Loch, 155

Ravensthorpe, 27, 66
Rees, Dai, 248
Reese, Terence, 20
Ritchie, John, 36, 39
Roberts, Alan, 177, 179
Roberts, Howard, 249
Roberts, Simon, 175
Roberts, Wyn, 175
Robertson, Jimmy, 89–90
Rone, John, 72
Rossi, Hugh, 183
Rottenberg, F.A., 39–40
Rowe, Arthur,, 260
Ruddy, Colonel, 59
Russ, Melvyn, 164
Russell, Pat, 98
Rutland Water, 14, 27, 30–3, 57, 65, 68, 79, 81, 110, 135, 136, 137, 142, 173, 175, 177, 182, 184, 185–6, 189–93, 195, 260, 280

Savours, D.S., 49
Scottish National Angling Clubs' Association, 34, 41, 49, 175, 176
Scottish Sports Council, 175, 176
Searle, Mary Radley, 108
Searle, Radley, 59, 71
Sella, River, 259
Shaw, John, 62–3
Sheelin, Lough, 84, 91, 106, 109, 112, 222–5, 280
Shin, Loch, 185
Shingler, Donald, 178, 179
Shrive, Dick, 138
Simmons, Stephen, 181, 183
Small, Bill, 46–7, 95
Smith, Arthur, 53
Smith, F., 222
Smith, Stan, 259
Smith, W., 250
Smythe, Percy, 147
Snelson, John, 84-5
Stark, Tom, 44, 89, 248–9
Stennens, Loch, 155
Stirling, John, 45, 110
Stoddart, Thomas Tod, 242
Stone, Peter, 154–5, 168, 169
Strabolgi, Lord, 52
Sundridge Lake, 19
Swatland, David, 259
Sweet, Lionel, 53, 54

Tay, River, 156–7
Taylor, Sidney, 59, 71
Teifi, River, 145
Tennant, James, 236
Test, River, 141, 156
Thames Water Authority Inter-Reservoir Charity Trout Fishing Competition, 142
Thomas, Brian, 78–9, 113, 144, 189–92, 244, 260
Thomas, Cyril, 146
Thomas, David, 77–8, 242
Thomas, P.G., 159
Thomas, Terry, 178–80
Thomson, James, 48
Thorndyke, Jack, 96
Timmins, Eileen, 108–9
Timmins, George, 53
Tolan, Michael, 86, 124
Tombleson, Peter, 97, 179
Topp, Gordon, 98
Trawsfynydd, Lake, 14, 67,

71, 81, 83, 86, 88, 97,
  98–9, 103–5, 108, 111,
  115, 135, 172, 174,
  225–32, 234, 251, 266,
  280
Trotter, George, 133
Trotter, J.P., 133
Two Lakes, Romsey, 12

Ulster Angling Federation, 130
Upcher, A.H., 158
Usk, 54–5, 56
Usk Valley Casting Club Tournament, 148

Vaughan, David, 140
Vaughan, Frankie, 132, 139, 140–1
Veale, Pat, 205
Veitch, Bob, 82

Wadsworth, Tommy, 178, 179
Wadsworth, Tony, 178, 179

Wahlstrom, Einar, 19
Waite, Terry, 109, 111
Walker, Richard, 163–4
Wallace, Jock, 157
Wallace, William, 44
Ward, Roy, 153
Webb, Richard, 114–15, 247–8
Webber, Don, 102–3
Weight, Eddie, 26
Welsh National Fly-Fishing Championship, 55
Welsh Salmon and Trout Angling Association, 55, 172
West, Peter, 87
West of Scotland Angling Club, 35, 37, 132
Wheddon, Len, 79
Whiteadder, 14
Whitehead, Alan, 251–2
Williams, Mervyn, 89–92, 103, 116, 251
Williams, Ralph, 245–6
Williams, T., 158

Williams, Victor, 54, 76, 248–50
Willis, Dick, 251
Wilshaw, John, 138, 139, 141, 152, 153–5, 159, 168
Wilson, Harry, 86
Wilson, James, 213
Wimbleball Reservoir, 135, 205–7
Windermere, Lake, 204
Windsor, Steve, 182–3
Winter's Hill Lake, 160
Wood, Stan, 83–4, 226
Wooldridge, Ian, 15, 17
Woombs, Norman, 177
World Freshwater Championships, 77, 258
World Open Wet Fly-Fishing Championship, 120–3
Wotton, Dave, 138
Wye, River, 157

Young, Douglas, 30–1, 226